The Complete Guide to
INDOOR
GARDENING

The Complete Guide to
INDOOR
GARDENING

Ann Bonar

Introduction *Caladium* hybrid. **Title page** Back row: *Ficus benjamina, Howea;* Centre: *Chlorophytum comosum variegatum, Begonia semperflorens, Dieffenbachia hybrid, Cordyline hybrid, Codiaeum variegatum pictum* variety, *Philodendron;* Front row: *Gloxinia* hybrid, *Asparagus densiflorus, Caladium* hybrid.
Contents Page Back row: *Cissus rhombifolia, Pelargonium zonale hybrid, Impatiens wallerana petersiana;* Front row: *Pteris cretica, Chlorophytum comosum variegatum*

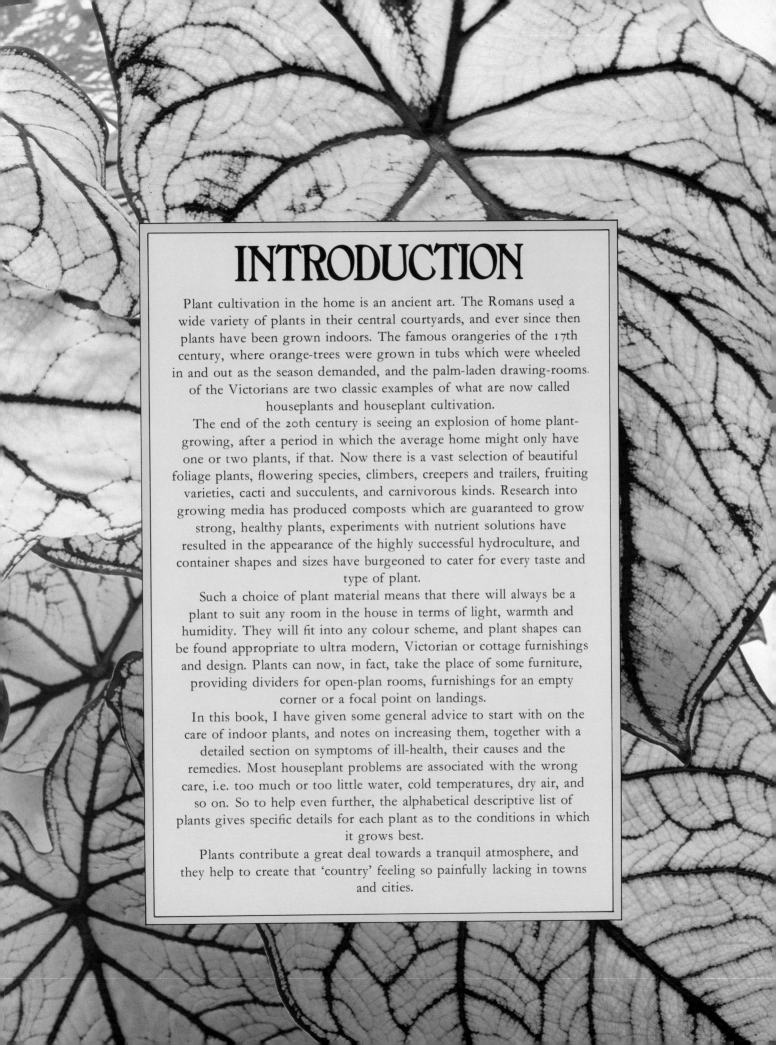

INTRODUCTION

Plant cultivation in the home is an ancient art. The Romans used a wide variety of plants in their central courtyards, and ever since then plants have been grown indoors. The famous orangeries of the 17th century, where orange-trees were grown in tubs which were wheeled in and out as the season demanded, and the palm-laden drawing-rooms of the Victorians are two classic examples of what are now called houseplants and houseplant cultivation.

The end of the 20th century is seeing an explosion of home plant-growing, after a period in which the average home might only have one or two plants, if that. Now there is a vast selection of beautiful foliage plants, flowering species, climbers, creepers and trailers, fruiting varieties, cacti and succulents, and carnivorous kinds. Research into growing media has produced composts which are guaranteed to grow strong, healthy plants, experiments with nutrient solutions have resulted in the appearance of the highly successful hydroculture, and container shapes and sizes have burgeoned to cater for every taste and type of plant.

Such a choice of plant material means that there will always be a plant to suit any room in the house in terms of light, warmth and humidity. They will fit into any colour scheme, and plant shapes can be found appropriate to ultra modern, Victorian or cottage furnishings and design. Plants can now, in fact, take the place of some furniture, providing dividers for open-plan rooms, furnishings for an empty corner or a focal point on landings.

In this book, I have given some general advice to start with on the care of indoor plants, and notes on increasing them, together with a detailed section on symptoms of ill-health, their causes and the remedies. Most houseplant problems are associated with the wrong care, i.e. too much or too little water, cold temperatures, dry air, and so on. So to help even further, the alphabetical descriptive list of plants gives specific details for each plant as to the conditions in which it grows best.

Plants contribute a great deal towards a tranquil atmosphere, and they help to create that 'country' feeling so painfully lacking in towns and cities.

CONTENTS

First published in 1977 by
Sundial Publications Limited

This edition published in 1983 by
Octopus Books Limited
59 Grosver or Street
London W1

© 1977 Hennerwood Publications Limited

Reprinted 1987

ISBN 0 7064 1943 X

Printed in Hong Kong

SELECTING
FOR YOUR HOME

Choosing and buying a houseplant

The secret of growing houseplants successfully is to choose the right plant for the right place. You will have lost the battle before you start if, for instance, you try to grow a cactus in the corner of a sitting-room that has only a north-facing window, because cacti need as much sunlight and warmth as they can possibly get in summer. Dry deserts in hot climates are the homes of very many cacti, so coolness and shade are not for them. But if you put an ivy or an aspidistra in these conditions, they will grow and thrive, almost without any help from you.

The secret of knowing how to choose the right plant for the right place is knowing where it comes from—the kind of countryside in which it grows in its homeland. Nowadays, when plants are discovered, great care is taken to record the terrain in which they were found growing. This was rarely noted by the early botanists of the seventeenth and eighteenth centuries. They simply recorded the name of the country in which they found a plant which meant that discovering its needs when trying to cultivate it was a process of trial and error, even for professional growers. Some plants that were perfectly hardy were grown in warm conditions, and succumbed, and some that were tender were put outdoors and died rapidly in their first winter.

But although much information is recorded by plant hunters and botanists, it isn't always passed on to the gardener or houseplant grower. It is also difficult to carry in your head all these details about each plant, its name, and the right growing conditions. However, plants can be very broadly grouped according to their needs and the members of these groups can be recognized by their type of growth and colouring.

For instance, most of the flowering houseplants will need sunlight (but not the hottest midday sun) or at any rate a good light. So if you want a plant of this type, think, before you buy, which way your windows face. Cacti can also be grown on hot, sunny window sills, if your fancy turns towards those prickly charmers.

The glamorous houseplants with brilliantly coloured leaves in reds and yellows and oranges, like codiaeums and coleus, will also want as good a light as possible, though direct sunlight is best filtered through a thin curtain such as net. Quite a lot of the plants whose leaves are variegated with yellow, white or cream (the spider plant and the variegated ivies for instance) also need to be in a light position, otherwise their variegation fades and their leaves change to plain green.

Plants which will grow far away from windows, in dark halls, corners of the landing, or passageways, nearly always have all-green leaves, and quite often are climbing or trailing plants, though not with flowers. You can also put bonsai in these conditions during the winter, particularly if the place is cold. These little trees need to be dormant at that time, otherwise they will not do well.

If you see a plant obviously grown for its pretty leaves, and they are thin and papery, such as maidenhair fern, and you have central heating, don't buy it unless you have plenty of time to look after it—get a plant with thick fleshy leaves instead, one of the peperomias such as *Peperomia magnoliaefolia*. The thin-leaved kind will simply wither and drop their leaves in the dry atmosphere of central heating, unless you spray them several times a day, but the ones with thick leaves can store water in them. If you haven't time to make their atmosphere humid artificially, they will survive for two or three days before they begin to turn brown at the leaf edges.

So, when you are choosing a houseplant, or something catches your eye in a shop-window, in a nursery, or on a plant stall, think before you buy it whether you have a place in the house that it will be happy in.

When you have decided that a plant will fit in, have a good look at it. Like everything else plants cost money, and because they are living, they are changing all the time and their acquisition should be given thought. A pair of shoes or a new dress can be manufactured to a set design, which will not change between factory and purchase, but your life-containing plant is likely to be quite different by the time you buy it, from the way it was in the nursery. Neglect in a shop or garden centre can result in such a damaged or weak specimen that the plant dies quite quickly after you have bought it, in spite of all your care.

Signs of trouble to look for are leaves falling or fallen, leaves brown at the edges or with brown spots on them, or yellow where they should obviously be green, and leaves which are limp and hanging down. A wilting plant with a drooping stem will have been weakened and one which is tall and straggly and rather pale is another bad buy. If you turn the container upside down and there are roots coming out of the drainage holes at the bottom, the plant should have been put into a larger pot or other container long ago. It will be what is known

Lilies, fuchsias, ferns and roses give colour and shade to this sunny patio. Previous page: *Asparagus densiflorus, Saintpaulia ionantha* hybrid, *Ampelopsis brevipedunculata* 'Elegans'

as 'pot-bound', and you would find the roots wound round and round the outside of the soil-ball if you emptied it out.

A flowering plant which is in full flower, however pretty it is, is really not worth buying either. It is likely to drop most of its flowers within two or three days of getting it home, and then won't flower again until the following year—this is a common problem when buying azaleas and African violets. Much better to buy a plant with one or two flowers out and lots of flowerbuds all ready to open.

Stems which are completely broken off or injured in any way are a sign of a battered plant. Compost which is bone dry is another bad sign and the plant should be rejected. If you see any insects on the plants, like greenfly or little white woolly creatures, or webs on the leaves, then you can be fairly certain that all the plants in that shop are infested, if not with adult insects, then with eggs waiting to hatch. Go to another shop. Grey, furry growths on the leaves or white powdery patches mean disease, so pass these by as well.

Look for a plant which fulfils the following conditions: strong and upright, glossy green, or otherwise well-coloured leaves, undamaged, moist compost, no roots coming out of the drainage holes, well-budded, with a few flowers fully open and no creepy-crawlies.

When you buy a plant, ask the assistant to wrap it up, if it has not already got a polythene sleeve around it. This will protect it from cold and draughts on the way home—very important, otherwise the leaves and/or flowers will drop. At home, put it in a warm place, out of both sun and draughts—freedom from draughts is particularly important. Make sure that it does not need water in the compost, and give it a quick overhead burst with your plant mister. Leave it alone to settle down for a few days, giving it water when needed, and you should then be able to put it in its permanent place and enjoy it for weeks, months or even years, according to which kind of plant it is.

Decorating with plants

There is no need to limit yourself to putting a single plant pot on a convenient shelf. Think how you can use the wide variety of indoor plants now available as part of your decoration scheme. You can even change your scheme every few months if you like.

For instance, hanging and climbing plants, such as ivies, rhoicissus and tradescantia, can be used as room dividers or put on bookshelves, or placed in troughs on the floor and trained to climb up canes to the ceiling. You can train cissus and philodendron as living decora-tion round mirrors or up and along window frames.

Why not try using a bottle garden where you want something decorative to fill up a difficult space? Bottle gardens will survive almost anywhere and are particularly easy to look after.

Opposite: An attractive effect can be achieved by positioning a selection of plants at different levels in a room. Below: A dish garden will brighten a dull corner. This one contains *Sansevieria*, *Dracaena*, *Philodendron* and *Chamaedorea*.

Aspidistras have come back into their own again, with their large, handsome, dark-green leaves, and their amenability to almost any sort of care and conditions. The variegated form with cream-coloured edges to the leaves is especially striking, but any aspidistra can look very attractive. Put them where they can be seen, not hidden apologetically in a dark corner.

Plants used as focal points can be placed in decorative pot hiders. Or you could look around your junk room—there is bound to be some sort of attractive container in there, not necessarily especially for pots, which could be used.

Try filling up the bathroom with plants, putting them on the tiles surrounding the bath, on shelves or window sills. Most plants take very well to bathroom conditions, provided there is some light from a window. You may find yourself spending hours in the bath, looking at the plants, deciding how to grow them and what else to get, but no matter, how relaxing!

Kitchens, too, are good places, and although gas in the atmosphere sometimes causes trouble, there are some plants which seem oblivious to it. The humidity and warmth of a kitchen are just right for many of the jungle plants like stag's-horn ferns, gynura and codiaeus, and in no time at all you will be battling your way through them to get at the herb shelf, or put a saucepan on the stove.

Groups of plants are more interesting than small, isolated specimens. Try putting them in different places in the room until you get them in the right one. Use them as you would furniture and pictures, for decoration. Hang them on the wall; stand one of the tree-like ones, such as grevillea or schefflera, by a table or standard lamp; or put a trough near a window and fill that with plants.

In other words use indoor plants lavishly, and experiment with placing them around your home. Start with easy-to-grow ones and use several of one kind to give an effect of abundance—don't worry that they are all the same—and go on from there. As you gain experience try growing the more difficult, and often more ornamental, kinds. Remember the throwaway plants—even if you don't like the idea of discarding a plant—they often produce abundant flowers for two or three months, so you will have them much longer than a bunch of cut flowers. Then, when they finish, you can replace them and change to a totally new colour scheme for another few months.

Plastic white or green tower pots are very attractive and go well with modern décor. The plants are put into small cups jutting out from the side of the tower and can

The unique 'signpost' holder, opposite, is one clever American's answer to the problem of filling a small corner of a room with a number of very different plants. *Chlorophytum* and *Cissus antarctica*, left, trail and climb from a magnificent oriental urn. Top, clockwise: *Ficus pumila* 'Variegata' in hanging basket; *F.* 'Black Prince'; *F. radicans* and *F benjamina. Kentia forsteriana* dominates the bathtub

trail or grow upwards; they can be planted in the top as well. With old beams and inglenook fireplaces try plant stands made of bamboo or wrought iron.

A miniature garden in a large dish or shallow pan can be great fun to design. You can put lawns, paths, a little pool (a mirror), a bridge, a bonsai tree, and tiny statues in it; or you could try to produce a replica of a desert scene, with sand and pebbles, small cacti and succulents and even an oasis.

If you decide to arrange a group of plants in a single large container, make sure you use plants which all like the same conditions of warmth, watering, humidity and light. For instance, it would be no good putting a pick-a-back plant with a pelargonium; one wants coolness, water and a good light, while the other needs all the sun

possible, little moisture and plenty of warmth. Later on in this book, individual plants and their special needs are described so that you can choose suitable plants to associate with one another.

A plant which proves unexpectedly easy to grow in the modern home, and has a most dramatic appearance, is the 'delicious monster', *Monstera deliciosa*, also called the Swiss cheese plant. Originally from tropical monsoon forests it has really large leaves, deeply slashed at the edges. It also has holes in the leaves. When the light shines through these and casts shadows onto a white wall, the combination of silhouette and the plant itself is extremely effective. But be warned: it is a large plant and steadily unfurls one large leaf after another—2 m (7 ft) is by no means its final height.

The right conditions

A plant which is being cared for so that it grows sturdily and healthily is automatically decorative and visually attractive. It may simply be a plain, green-leaved plant, but if its leaves are glossy, erect, bright, of a regular size and shape and its stems upright and vigorous, there will be no comparison between it and a pale, straggling plant, spotted with brown, withering, and turning yellow.

This section will tell you how to look after your plants.

Light

The first thing to think about is giving your plants the light they need. No plant containing chlorophyll—the green colouring—can live without the light provided by the sun. Even if it is only light filtered through cloud, it is still sunlight, and it must always be provided. Without it plants cannot carry on the process known as photosynthesis, by which the leaves and stems manufacture the plant's food, including the flower-inducing hormone called florigen.

The all-green-leaved plants—such as ferns, the rubber plant, the goosefoot plant and the umbrella plant—will all live away from windows, even in the shade, without coming to any harm.

Climbers and trailers like some shade and may even become a sickly yellow colour in too much light; but most variegated-leaved plants must have good light. Because parts of their leaves lack chlorophyll the green parts need particularly favourable conditions for making food. Thus the more light they get the better.

Some plants in this group are exceptions to this rule; this is noted in their entries in the A–Z section (see page 60).

Bromeliads are a peculiar group which mostly grow either perched high up in forest trees, or in the lee of

A light window free from draughts is a flattering setting: left, succulents, cacti, chlorophytum and tradescantia beautify a dull prospect. Above, *Hedera canariensis* 'Variegata' and an azalea sit prettily below a hanging basket of *Adiantum*

rocks in desert-like conditions, or on scrub vegetation. Their natural light consists of filtered sunlight so you can grow these well away from light for much of the year. Orchids also like this kind of light.

Cacti, on the other hand, cannot have enough sun, especially in temperate climates, and indeed, some of the larger ones never flower in such conditions. Put on a south-facing window sill they will revel in the heat and light of even the midday summer sun, which would quickly shrivel up many other indoor plants.

Flowering plants generally need sunlight, or at least as good a light as possible, if they are to flower well, because the production of florigen depends partly on the amount and quality of the light they receive. Pelargoniums (geraniums), especially, like sun almost as much as cacti, coming as they do from much the same conditions in South Africa.

Warmth

Once you have chosen a position which is suitably lit you should then consider what kind of temperature the plant likes. There are a great many plants which will thrive in a wide range of temperatures, and heat requirements are nothing like so crucial to their well-being as light. In general, indoor plants will not survive frost, but there are a good many that don't mind a winter temperature as low as 4–7 °C (40–45 °F), although most will be happier with a minimum of 10 °C (50 °F). The winter temperature should in any case be lower than the summer one, because plants rest during winter. Their growth processes are only just ticking over, and too much warmth may force them into full growth which would weaken them, making them susceptible to disease and pests.

In a temperate climate the temperature usually begins to rise in spring, from about 10 °C (50 °F) through to its maximum in the summer months of 21–27 °C (70–80 °F), and then gradually decreases with the arrival of autumn. There are inevitably plants which react unfavourably to these temperatures, some may prefer to be cool in summer, others like to be really hot.

The much more widespread use of central heating has certainly been responsible for much of the increase in the growing of plants indoors. In the old days, it was not uncommon for water to freeze in bathroom basins during the night, or for there to be frost on the insides of windows. No subtropical plant would survive these degrees of cold at night, however warm the room might be during the day. Although extremes of temperature still occur, they are much less common nowadays. The biggest problem is that central heating creates a very dry atmosphere which spells death to many plants. But there are ways of overcoming this, as described on page 18.

In natural conditions night is less warm than day. Nevertheless, houseplants do not like to be exposed to extreme alterations of temperature. A steady temperature is best, to avoid subjecting the plants to the unnecessary stress of constant adaptations. As the temperature increases, plants lose more water by transpiration through their leaves, and their roots must absorb more from the compost and so work harder. Energy which could be used for growing and flowering is therefore lost in dealing with this repeated strain, and you will have a less ornamental plant and a less healthy one if you subject plants to such conditions.

Draughts are especially damaging; leaf edges turn brown, leaves wither or suffer discoloured spots and blotches, flowers drop. Think how you respond to a cold wind—you can almost feel yourself curling up at the edges in an attempt to keep warm and prevent the icy air penetrating. Plants are just the same, but unlike us they cannot protect themselves from the cold. Watch out for air whistling under doors or in through minute gaps in window frames. Avoid putting a plant near an outside door that is in frequent use.

Put yourself in the plant's position. The temperature, atmosphere and light in which you feel comfortable will more than likely suit your plants as well, or at any rate the majority of them. We all have a common bond in that all life, whether it is vegetable or animal, is formed from the same chemical units of carbon, hydrogen and oxygen, and it is reasonable to assume that both kinds will grow and prosper under the same environment.

Watering

You should now have your plant in the right light and the right temperature; the next urgent need as far as the plant is concerned may well be a drink. All plants consist largely of water, perhaps as much as 90%, which is being lost steadily by day and night in the form of water vapour from most of the above-ground parts of the plant. It is replaced mainly via the roots, into which water penetrates from the soil or compost. If the growing medium is dry, obviously the plant will become dry. It will wilt and eventually die if the lack of water is sufficiently prolonged.

Exactly the same effect is produced, with the addition of yellowing of the lower leaves, if the compost is made too wet. But this time the roots suffocate—completely waterlogged they cannot get at air which contains the oxygen they must have to live. The roots stop working and die, and so no water is passed up to the leaves and stems.

There is another reason why plants must have water. The minerals plants use as food, such as phosphorus, potassium and magnesium, are dissolved in the soil water and so are absorbed by the roots, along with the water. If a plant has the wrong amounts of water it gets the wrong amounts of nutrients and therefore becomes unhealthy.

The technique for watering is simple. Each time you water, give sufficient to fill the space between the surface of the compost and the rim of the pot, pouring it on steadily until full. Allow the pot to drain off surplus water; if there is none, give another watering and repeat the process. Generally only one dose is needed, if you are watering at the right times, because the compost beneath the dry surface will still be a little damp.

What you should never do is to give the plant little dribbles of water. All that happens is that the compost surface becomes moistened while the rest of the soil gradually dries completely. Eventually the soil shrinks right away from the sides of the container, and then when you water much of it is wasted as it trickles down the space thus made and out of the drainage holes. Always give a good watering; provided the compost is correctly made up the unwanted water will drain away.

The decision on whether to water or not is more difficult. The obvious sign of water-need is a wilting plant, but it should not be allowed to get to this stage. Long before wilting occurs, compost containing soil will begin to dry on the surface. The surface compost will feel dry to the touch and will be a lighter brown than that

beneath. The pot will be less heavy than it was, and if it is a clay one will make a ringing noise when tapped with a piece of wood instead of letting out a sound like a dull thump.

Peat composts, without soil, are slightly different. They tend to stay adequately moist for longer, and then suddenly, within a day or two, they become almost completely dry. If you suspect water is beginning to run short, you have to watch very carefully so that you water just before this happens. This problem of sudden drying is particularly noticeable if the plants are in plastic containers. Peat composts get very light when dry, so the weight of the pot and plant is a good guide; the compost will also change colour a little on the surface, though not so obviously as with the soil composts.

By watering according to these methods, you will be giving the plant what it needs at the right time. The intervals between waterings will never be regular, and one of the worst things you can do is to water every Saturday morning at 10 o'clock, or in the afternoons on alternate Thursdays. The need for water will vary, depending on the temperature, the humidity, the rate at which the plant is growing, the size of pot and plant, the type of plant and the type of compost.

If your plant has got really dry, put the whole pot in a bucket of water so that the compost surface is covered, and leave it there until bubbles of air stop coming up from the surface. This is the only way to make sure that the centre of the root-ball has been thoroughly wetted.

In summer, plants will need to be watered more often, because they transpire more water at higher temperatures. In winter, sufficient water should be given to keep the soil-ball moist. Depending on the temperature, this may mean watering only once a fortnight, whereas in summer liquid refreshment may be required every two or three days.

Use water at room temperature, preferably rain-water, or water which has been boiled or softened, so that it is slightly acid. No plant minds acidity, but some plants don't like alkaline or chalky (hard) water, so it is better to be on the safe side and use lime-free water whenever possible.

Humidity

I have mentioned humidity once or twice and you may be wondering why it is so important and how to get it right.

As I said in the previous section, plants, even desert plants, consist largely of water. The water circulates through the plant carrying mineral foods and other substances and helping the plant to maintain its structured rigidity. What causes the water to move through the plant is that the leaves constantly let water out in the form of vapour (this process is called transpiration). When water goes from the leaves it creates a kind of vacuum which has to be filled by water from lower down the plant. In this way the leaves constantly 'pull' water up the plant. If the atmosphere is dry, the roots cannot absorb water as quickly as the leaves lose it. So the leaves become dry, may wilt and turn brown at the edges. If the air is humid—that is, already full of water vapour—it won't take much more from the plant which therefore transpires slowly so that the water inside moves slowly and the cells remain turgid and the leaves stay healthy. The drier the air the faster water moves and the more likely is it the leaves will suffer.

Remember, every plant is adapted to live in a particular environment. If a plant (e.g. a cactus) grows naturally in a dry atmosphere then it adapts by having fewer outlets for water vapour. To get your indoor plants to grow successfully you have to provide them with the humidity conditions that they like best.

If you put several plants in a group, they will make their own local humidity, and you will find they flourish in such conditions.

Specimen plants, grown alone, can be misted or sprayed with clear water every day, or more often if necessary. Shallow containers of water put close to them will provide a large surface from which water can evaporate. Dishes of water, with shingle in the centre for the pot to stand on, will serve the same purpose. A larger container, surrounding the one which the plant is in, can be packed with moist material to fill the space between the two. Peat, scrunched-up newspaper, oasis or polystyrene granules will do—in fact anything which absorbs water.

Whatever you do, the plants must not be stood on a shelf over a radiator. The roots get lovely and warm, but the compost dries up visibly, and the atmosphere is so dry that the plant is likely to shrivel up before your eyes. It is, actually, one of the quickest ways of killing a plant.

Feeding

Any living organism which uses energy needs fuel, in the form of food, to replace the energy expended in growing, working and/or playing. Plants need energy for growing, which they do all the time, and the fuel, or food, for them is partly absorbed from the soil, or compost, by the roots and partly made by the leaves during photosynthesis. Beyond supplying exactly the right amount of light and warmth, there is not a great deal more that can be done as far as the leaves are concerned, but you can help the roots considerably by supplying the necessary elements.

The ones considered to be most important are nitrogen (N), phosphorus (P) and potassium (K). Broadly speaking, nitrogen is essential for healthy growth of leaves and shoots—all the vegetative parts. However, plants have no way of absorbing pure nitrogen gas, which is in the air around them: they have to get their nitrogen from compounds containing the element— mainly from nitrates. Phosphorus is used throughout the plant, but is especially needed by the young roots and root tips. Potassium is associated with the plant's

maturity, and is used to produce flowers, viable seeds and fruits, and to ripen the plant's vegetative buds so that they flower the following season.

Many more elements are used by the plant, for instance magnesium, which is used to make chlorophyll, calcium used in cell walls, iron, sulphur, boron, molybdenum, copper and so on. However, these are 'trace' elements, meaning that the plant only needs them in minute quantities, or traces. It can be safely assumed that the necessary quantities will always be contained in a good compost.

The elements you will probably have to help the plant with are N, P and K, because they are used quickly and in appreciable quantities. In particular, nitrates have to be given because they are very soluble and are easily washed through the compost by watering. There are many proprietary brands of mixtures of these nutrients in liquid form (liquid fertilizers), each with different quantities of N, P and K. They are, in fact, tailored to the particular needs of various plants. For example, one which contains a relatively high percentage of K and little N should be chosen for flowering plants. Similarly, one with plenty of N is the best for plants grown for their foliage.

The proportions of nutrients in a fertilizer will be shown on its container as percentages, thus N 6%, P_2O_5 5%, K_2O 8% (those particular proportions would be useful for flowering plants). Instructions for rates of dilution and frequency of application will also be given but as you get to know your plants' needs, you can adapt the instructions slightly to fit each plant.

For most plants you should start liquid feeding about halfway through the summer, if the plant was freshly potted in spring, and cease in autumn. Once every two weeks is an average application frequency. Compost must always be damp when the solution is given, and feeding can take the place of the ordinary watering which would otherwise be done.

As with humans, the needs of individual plants vary: some are greedy and will use all the food in the compost long before mid summer, others, especially bulbs, may need feeding at quite different times, as they have different life cycles. Some, such as bromeliads and cacti, hardly need any food; others, like the Christmas cherry, need not be fed until their fruits have set and begun to swell. Plants in soil-less composts will need feeding almost from the time of potting.

Plants change their appearance when they are short of nutrients. Usually the leaf colouring alters. The symptoms vary according to the deficiency and can be very marked; they are described in detail on page 28.

Grooming and pruning

As your plants grow, their shapes will change. Leaves will mature until they are no longer useful, flowers will fade, and shoots, especially those of the climbers, may become too long and spoil the outline of the plant. This is when grooming makes the difference between an ordinary plant and a first-class one.

Old yellowing, damaged or brown leaves should all be taken off—they are no longer any use to the plant. Broken or injured stems should be cut off cleanly below the damaged part, just above the junction of a leaf or another shoot with the stem. Dead flowers need removing, especially if they have fallen onto a leaf below. Plants with large leaves look better for, and relish, being wiped gently with a soft moist cloth, to clean off dust and grit and the white spots left after spraying with hard water. Dust and grit on the leaf block the stomata, and cut down the amount of light reaching the leaf. As well as being ugly, dust can be chemically damaging if you live in an urban area. However, hairy leaves will be damaged by wiping and prickly cacti cannot be sponged; such plants should be gently brushed.

If you want a foliage plant with glossy, mirror-like leaves, there are proprietary plant polishes available which will supply this effect without harm. However, many plants in good health will be naturally shiny and this extra gloss can make a plant look rather like an artificial one.

Keep trailing plants shapely by pinching back straggly stems. Climbing plants may occasionally need cutting right back (below right).

Besides removing damaged material, some plants need regular pruning every year to flower well and maintain their bushiness. In general this is done in very late winter, just before repotting, and usually consists of cutting the previous year's *new* growth back by half. This spurs the plant on to produce plenty of new shoots, on which there will be flowers.

Climbing plants may need cutting down almost to the base, or by about half, in spring, or may even need cutting back during summer to keep them within the space available, or to thin them. The shoots to remove are the smallest and weakest ones, those that are not flowering well, and finally, any that are still causing crowding.

One form of pruning is known as 'pinching back'. This is carried out in late spring and the technique is to nip out the tip of a shoot, just above a leaf or pair of leaves, sometimes back to the second or even third pair. More shoots grow in the axils of leaves lower down the stem, and the result is a bushier plant, or one with more flowers.

Trailing plants can become straggly, with yards of bare stem and a few leaves at the tip; pruning them back will induce 'breaks' higher up the main stem.

Always supply supports for climbing plants and for tall, delicate plants. Put the supports in position in good time before the plants become misshapen. Tie the stems loosely to the supports so that the stems are not strangled.

Containers and Composts

At some stage in the not-too-distant future your plants will need more room for their roots and also fresh compost. Nowadays most plants are sold in plastic pots, though clay pots can still be bought. The plastic ones are made in various colours besides terracotta, such as green, black or mottled; they are light to carry and more or less unbreakable, though the smaller ones tend to crack easily around the rim. Clay pots are heavier and cost more, but last indefinitely, provided you do not drop them, and many people still prefer them.

Troughs and window-boxes can be made of wood, of expanded polystyrene which feels, and is, warmer than the surrounding temperature, of mixed stone and concrete, or of fibreglass moulded and coloured to look like the old Italian lead containers. Wooden tubs, parsley pots, strawberry barrels, tower pots and urns provide variation of container shapes and sizes.

Whether your plant is strong and healthy or whether it languishes and eventually fades away depends on the compost you put it in. You will have seen from the watering section that the roots must have oxygen and, from the advice on feeding, that various minerals are essential, so it is no good filling the pot with earth dug out of the nearest flower-bed in the garden, if you are lucky enough to have one, because it will not have the right structure or food balance for a pot plant.

The roots of container plants live in a highly artificial world, and the plant relies on you to give it what it needs just as a domesticated animal does, but a plant's reliance is even greater because it cannot attract your attention.

A good standard compost contains sieved loam, coarse river sand, granulated peat, fertilizer and chalk. These ingredients are used in proportions which have been experimentally determined as the best for the majority of container-grown plants. Variations can be bought or made to suit groups of plants which have special needs, but in general a standard compost will ensure good drainage of water, aeration of the compost, a supply of food for three months or more, and a quantity of water in the compost sufficient for the roots, without drowning them. Being fairly heavy, such a compost also enables the roots to anchor the plant firmly in its pot.

Good loam or soil-containing compost, however, is becoming scarce, expensive and costly to transport. A modern substitute is soil-less compost, which consists of peat and sand, usually in the proportion of 3:1, with some fertilizer added. Soil-less compost is proving to be quite satisfactory, and even better for some plants than the previously used loam compost. It is light to carry, but a plant with a lot of top growth which is grown in soil-less compost in a plastic pot may become top-heavy and fall over, so such composts need to be used with caution. Large plants are still best grown in soil-based composts. Either type can be obtained in various pack sizes at chain stores, garden shops and garden centres, or you can make up your own mixtures as you become more experienced.

Repotting

The time for repotting plants is when the roots have just filled the pot, although the time of year should also be taken into account. You can repot during the growing season, up to about the beginning of late summer, but the best time is usually early spring.

In autumn the plant gradually ceases to produce new

The technique of repotting, (1) to (5). When repotting a prickly cactus use a cardboard holder to avoid scratching the hand or damage to the plant

growth, and in winter will be resting so that the roots do not take very much water and food out of the compost. If you put the plant into a larger pot (called potting-on), with new compost, in early autumn then the roots would not absorb either the extra water present in the larger pot or the fertilizer. The compost would become 'sour' because the unused, stagnant water encourages the increase of bacteria which produce substances harmful to plant roots.

When you are potting-on—into a larger pot—use one which allows 1.5–2.5 cm (½–1 in) (depending on pot size) all round between the side of the root-ball and the inside of the pot. If the pot is clay, put a few pieces of broken clay pot at the bottom to help with drainage and aeration, and put a little compost on top.

Turn the plant out of its old pot, gently loosen the soil-ball a little with your fingers, and cut off any straggling roots or any which are brown all the way through. White roots are young, though remember that a plant which is only just coming out of its winter rest will not have any.

Put the plant centrally in the new pot, and make sure that the level of the surface of the soil is 1.5–4 cm (½–1½ in) from the top of the pot to allow enough space for watering. Fill the sides in with compost, firming it with your fingers only—your thumbs will put too much pres-

sure on the compost and compact it—tap the pot base on the working surface to level the compost, and water at once. Then put the plant somewhere warm and slightly shaded.

Soil-less composts should be filled in and lightly firmed only.

If you are repotting without changing the size of the pot, because the plant has reached its full size but has used all the goodness in the old compost, tease out what remains of the old compost, spread the roots out as naturally as possible, and crumble the new compost in over them until the pot is full, firming as you go.

Prickly cacti can be difficult to deal with but you can use a pair of tongs or a paper collar round the base of the plant, or a very tough pair of leather gloves.

Plants which grow fast may need potting-on once or twice more during the growing season, but generally the spring repotting is sufficient, and some only need this every two years. Once more, be guided by what the plant needs rather than 'because it is spring it must be repotted'. A very frequent need for water, a rather pale plant, roots wound round the soil-ball or coming out of the drainage holes, are all signs of an urgent need for a larger pot and/or fresh compost.

One final point: break up the compost surface occasionally with a household fork, to prevent the formation of a crust that will encourage the growth of moss and prevent fresh air percolating into the growing medium.

Holidays

Summer holidays mean leaving plants without watering, feeding or misting for two, three or more weeks. If there are no friends or neighbours who can help, perhaps the best thing to do is to stand the pots on water-absorbent plastic matting and then allow water to drip onto the matting through a tube from a water container placed higher than the plants.

You can stand a group of plants together, with moist peat or newspaper packed between them and polythene sheeting over the moist material, or you can push fibreglass wicks into the pot base, with one end teased out into separate strands and placed in water. Or you can put each plant in a clear polythene bag, so that the pot as well as plant is contained, fastening the open end with a rubber band.

Whatever you do, water the plants well first and put them out of the sun, but in a good light.

In winter, most plants are resting, and cold is more likely to be the problem than lack of water. Put plants well away from windows, give sufficient water to just moisten the soil, but only just, and hope that the temperature does not fall too low.

Every plant has a time when it rests from growing and flowering, and with northern-hemisphere plants this is between mid autumn and very early spring. You can rest at this time, too, since watering will be occasional only, and feeding will not be needed, though misting is still as important, especially with the central heating turned on. However, a few plants grow during this time and this is noted under the individual descriptions in the A–Z section.

Increasing Plants

Growing new plants of your own is ridiculously easy, sometimes embarrassingly easy, because certain plants need no encouragement to reproduce, and grow miniatures of themselves with great enthusiasm. All you have to do is to cut the new growths off the parent and pot them; they will already be growing roots and in very little time they will be proper plants. For instance, mother of thousands, *Saxifraga stolonifera*, spins out long dangling thread-like stalks, on the ends of which

are miniature replicas of the parent. The spider plant, *Chlorophytum comosum variegatum*, does the same, except that the runners arch up into the air, and bend over with the weight of the growing plantlets. Tiny plants like this will need only 5 cm (2 in) diameter pots to start with.

Some plants can be divided into several separate pieces, with roots on each, and potted singly into small containers. The cactus called *Chamaecereus silvestrii* grows lots of 'branches' from the crown. Take one off and put it *onto* compost, rather than into it, so that the base has sufficient soil round it to support it. It will put out roots very quickly. Early summer is the best time for this, though in general division should be done in spring. Plants like *Billbergia nutans*, mother-in-law's

Propagation by (1) Offsets
(2) Soft tip cuttings (3) Leaf cutting
(4) Leaf incision *(Begonia rex)*

tongue (*Sansevieria trifasciata* 'Laurentii') and *Cyperus alternifolius* are among those which can be increased by this method.

The commonest way to increase houseplants is by taking cuttings, that is, pieces cut off the plant. The commonest type of cutting is a stem-cutting—that is, a section of a young stem produced earlier in the season. A stem-cutting is, therefore, always less than a year, and sometimes only a few months or even weeks old.

Putting the cut end of the stem in compost encourages it to produce roots, provided the cut was made immediately below the point at which a leaf or pair of leaves grew from the stem. This is the part which produces roots most readily. A stem-cutting should not have flowerbuds on it, otherwise it may not root.

Many plants can be increased from soft tip cuttings, that is, stem tips about 5–7.5 cm (2–3 in) long. Remove the lowest leaves. Put the cutting into compost up to about half its own length, water it in and then cover with a polythene bag. Keep it in a warm, shady place and roots will appear within a few weeks, and the cutting will begin to lengthen. It can then be potted separately. The best time to make these soft cuttings is in summer. Some plants, such as ivy, tradescantia and busy Lizzie, whose soft cuttings root very easily, can

Propagation by air layering. Make an incision near top of main stem and dust with hormone rooting powder. Attach polythene sleeve below cut, fill with sphagnum moss and close up sleeve. Sever from main stem when roots are visible and pot on.

be rooted in ordinary water. With some plants, the stem tips which you nip out to make them bushier can be used for cuttings.

Some plants can be increased by using their leaves. African violets can be increased by removing a leaf with a stem attached and putting it singly into a soil-less compost to about half its length. Plantlets will appear from the base of the leaf stem, with their own roots. Begonia leaves can be laid flat on a compost surface, cut across the main veins, and covered with polythene. Kept in a warm place, plantlets will appear at the cuts.

Air layering is a special method used mostly for the rubber plant, for which it is very successful. Monstera and dieffenbachia can also be treated in this way, see *Ficus*, page 97.

Hydroculture

A method of growing plants which has recently been introduced to Britain, although it has been in use for some years in Europe, is a form of hydroponics—that is, growing plants in water instead of compost, with liquid fertilizer supplied regularly. Although initially more expensive to buy, the plants are more likely to grow well, and are less troublesome to look after.

Two containers are required: one in which clay granules are placed—through which the roots penetrate and which help to support the plant, taking the place of the compost—and a lower one in which the nutrient-containing water is placed. The roots grow down to this solution, and feed and drink from it. It has to be topped up occasionally, and replaced completely every few months. There is an indicator to show the need for more solution.

Plants can be bought already growing in these containers, or you can buy the containers on their own, with instructions on how to convert your own plants to them. Not all plants are suitable, though fortunately many houseplants seem to be, especially the aroid family, which includes such plants as philodendrons and monstera.

Plant health

Many plants grown in containers are tough and long-suffering, others are delicate and easily upset, but all will show signs of distress sooner or later if they are not looked after as they need to be. Most of these signs appear as a result of a 'physiological disorder'. In other words an upset in the plant's system because it hasn't had enough water, or has had too much, or the light is too harsh, or something similar.

So you must alter your care of an ailing plant to correct its deficiencies. For instance, a plant whose leaves are yellowing can be revived by giving it more warmth, different water or extra nitrogen. There are small differences in the kind of yellowing, according to the cause, which you will gradually learn to notice as you acquire more experience of plant care and become more observant of plant reactions.

The wrong kind of care leads to a weakened plant, which may be attacked by and infested with insect pests and fungus diseases, possibly so badly that it is killed. If you notice either pests or diseases on a plant, more often than not it means that you have not been growing the plant correctly. The most common faults are not enough light or warmth, too dry an atmosphere or too much water. On the other hand, many plants will not be infested with pests or diseases at all during their lives. The list given below details all possibilities, so that you know how to cope in any situation.

The leaves of indoor plants are the parts which generally reflect ill-health, and have the widest range of symptoms. An extensive list of these signals of distress and their causes is given on pp. 28–9.

Pests and diseases

If you find from the list of symptoms that your plant's troubles are mainly due to insect pests or fungus disease, rather than your ill-treatment of it, then the detailed descriptions which follow will help you to identify what is attacking your plant and how best to deal with it.

Fungus diseases are rarely troublesome. Mildew and grey mould, *Botrytis cinerea*, are the two most likely to infect plants, but sometimes rust is seen, and fungal gall invades azaleas occasionally.

Although there are many pesticides available for treating plant pests and diseases—often the same chemical with different trade names—there is really no need to keep more than the two or three mentioned on the following pages. Even these should only be used in an emergency. If you keep your eyes open and cultivate the ability to observe the small changes that take place in your plants as they grow, you will be able to spot an infestation as soon as it starts. Cutting off the affected parts is then all that will be necessary at such an early stage, and you will save time, money and possibly a plant, since death would follow a build-up of bad infection.

Always, always, read the directions for use and dilution on the container of a pest killer. If you don't, you may damage the plant, or not eradicate the trouble. Always keep the containers out of the reach of pets and children.

Pests

Caterpillars
Comparatively large, up to 2.5 cm (1 in) long, these are generally the young or larval stage of moths or butterflies. Often green, sometimes brown, sometimes spotted or striped in these and other colours, they eat irregular holes in leaves, soft stems and flower petals, during the spring and summer. They are not often seen on indoor plants, though plants in hanging baskets and on window sills may provide a feast for them, and it pays to keep a particular eye on such plants. There is no need to use chemicals on caterpillars—just remove them by hand.

Greenfly (Aphids)
These insect pests are a very successful species. They reproduce extremely rapidly, and are now becoming resistant to the various chemical insecticides with which

Far left: Aphids feed on the young growth of plants. They are the most troublesome pests, unsightly in themselves and in the damage they do. Inspect plants frequently and take immediate action if you detect this pest, as they breed rapidly. Left: Root mealy bug are difficult to detect until the plant has already suffered some damage. A strong plant will be less damaged by their attacks.

control has been attempted. Also called plant lice, they are tiny green creatures up to 2 mm ($\frac{1}{8}$ in) long, sometimes with wings. They feed by sucking the sap from a leaf through needle-like mouthparts which are stabbed into the leaf tissue. They move very little, and can be seen clustered at the tips of new shoots, and on the underside of leaves. Plant growth becomes distorted and stunted. Leaves curl and sometimes turn yellow. New shoots stop growing until the greenfly have gone. Infested plants become weakened. The insects secrete honeydew, a sticky liquid which falls onto leaves, and on which sooty mould can grow.

Thumb-and-finger squashing will get rid of most of them, and sometimes complete removal of a shoot tip is the best solution. Spraying with water under pressure will wash off the rest, or you can spray with derris, resmethrin or malathion.

Leaf-miner

The adult leaf-miner is a minute fly but it is the tiny maggot which does the damage. Eggs are laid on the leaves of plants, and the maggot which hatches eats its way into the leaf tissue, just below the skin, and stays there, moving about as it feeds. Very pale brown or light-green wavy lines and blisters appear on the upper surface of the leaf, and can cover it. Chrysanthemums and cinerarias suffer badly, but almost any plant may be attacked. Remove affected leaves and spray the rest with malathion.

Mealy-bug

The mealy-bug is an almost stationary dark-grey insect which covers itself with a small blob of white fluff and feeds as greenfly do, mainly at stem joints or on bark, or tucked into crevices such as the necks of hippeastrum bulbs. Mealy-bugs are often not noticed until there is a big infestation which has done a good deal of damage. Scraping them off with the back of a knife is a good way of dealing with them, and the point can be inserted into awkward parts of the plant where the bugs may be lurking. The young have no protective fluff, but are flattish blobs of pale brown, red or yellow on the stems, easy to miss. A hand lens or magnifier will help you to see them clearly. Spray the plant afterwards with malathion, or use methylated spirits on individual bugs if the plant is sensitive to malathion. Treat root mealy-bug on cacti as you would root aphis, using resmethrin for the insecticide.

Red spider mite

One of the most frequent and troublesome pests on indoor plants, as the hot dry atmosphere of central heating suits them perfectly. A hand lens is needed to see them on the underside of the leaf. They are pale yellow or pale red, tiny round pests which suck the sap, and moult their skins as they grow, leaving a white ghost-like replica of themselves behind. They also produce webbing, which can be seen festooning stems. They take only a month to become adult and lay eggs and increase rapidly during the summer. Prevent them appearing by always keeping the atmosphere humid and ensuring that the plants never run short of water. Plants which are infested should be thoroughly sprayed with malathion solution, repeating twice more at about ten-day intervals.

Root aphis

Root aphis lives in the soil and, like greenfly above ground, it sucks the sap from the plant, but through the roots not the leaves. Root aphis is whitish-grey in colour and will be found on the roots and in the compost. Treat the plant by washing away from the roots all the compost and root aphis you can see. Then repot in uncontaminated compost. Water with a solution of malathion, and repeat the process about ten days later. For plants sensitive to malathion, use bioresmethrin instead.

Scale insects

Like mealy-bug, scale insects are immobile, feeding in the same place throughout their lives, protected by a hard horny case, brown, grey or black in colour. The adults lay eggs under the scales and the resultant young move out to their own feeding grounds and grow their own protective shells, which gradually enlarge and darken in colour from pale green as time goes on. Their feeding results in the production of large quantities of sticky honeydew, on which sooty mould grows. This and the feeding may weaken a plant considerably. The scales will be found on the stems and bark as well as on the leaves, close to the main veins on the underside. Scrape off gently with the back of a knife onto a sheet of paper beneath, and then spray thoroughly with malathion, repeating twice more at ten-day intervals.

Slugs and snails

Most likely to be a problem with window-sill and hanging-basket plants, but if you see large holes in leaves and lumps missing from stems on any plant, for no apparent reason, suspect slugs and snails. They hide during the day and feed at night, so are seldom seen. Look for them in the base of pots, just inside the drainage hole, tucked into the undergrowth of a group of plants, or any kind of crack or crevice near to the damaged plant. Remove and destroy.

Whitefly

Minute, white-winged, fly-like creatures, found on the underside of leaves. The damage is done by the larvae which are also minute, and look like round, transparent, green scales adhering to the leaf. They suck out their food and produce honeydew in large quantities. Leaves turn greyish and become very messy and curled in bad attacks, and the plants cease to grow and may die. Remove badly infested parts and spray the remainder several times at intervals of three to four days with bio-resmethrin, which destroys the larvae—the adults eventually die naturally.

Diseases

Mildew

A white powder in patches on the surface of leaves and stems, sometimes also on flowers, is the main symptom of mildew, to which begonias and chrysanthemums are especially prone. It is seen mainly in summer, when plants are dry at the roots, rather enclosed and very warm. Remove affected parts as far as possible, and spray plants with dinocap or benomyl, or dust with flowers of sulphur.

Grey mould, Botrytis cinerea

Grey mould starts with brown patches on leaves or stems from which grey fur grows and rotting quickly spreads. It is most likely to break out in cool, damp conditions and following an injury to a plant caused by insect attack, mechanical damage and so on. Cut off the infected part and spray with benomyl.

Sooty mould

Sooty mould is a fungus disease which lives and feeds on the honeydew that is produced by the insect pests that suck sap. Sooty mould does not live on plants and does no harm to them. But the mould and the honeydew block the stomata, collect dust and prevent transpiration, so they should be wiped off with a moist cloth.

Rust and azalea gall

Rust takes the form of raised reddish-brown powdery spots underneath leaves. Azalea gall results in thickened and blistered leaves, grey-white in colour, and sometimes also discoloured flowers. Hand removal of diseased leaves and flowers is usually sufficient to keep either disease under control.

Left to right: Pests—Mealy bugs; scale insects, and white fly. Diseases—Botrytis (grey mould); the fungal spots shown on the ivy are unattractive, but not often seen and not seriously damaging. Remove affected leaves if necessary, and spray weekly with Benomyl three times

Symptoms of trouble on leaves

Lower leaves turning slowly yellow and eventually falling.	Too much water in the compost. Remove from the container for a day to dry, and do not water for several days.
Lower leaves turning yellow and falling quickly.	Sudden cold, or drop from normal temperature.
Leaves turning yellow, but not dropping.	Lime in the compost, or the use of limey or hard water; use rain-water or soft water, or boiled tap-water.
Gradual appearance of yellow mottling, rings or streaks, stunting of plant and slow growth.	Virus disease, spread by greenfly or other sucking insect pests.
Minute yellow speckling, possibly with webbing on leaf or leaf stems.	Red spider mite; see page 26.
Leaves pale green, gradually turning yellow; plant straggly and with poor new growth.	Lack of nitrogen: give extra liquid fertilizer with higher nitrogen content, or pot into fresh compost, or give more light.
Naturally variegated leaves change to plain green.	Not enough light, if all leaves do it. If those on one branch only become plain, then reversion is occurring: cut off such shoots.
Coloured leaves fading, or becoming all-green.	Quantity and quality of light insufficient. Also keep compost slightly on dry side, to give best and most intense colours.
Pale green or white speckling in patches, increasing very slowly.	Leaf-hopper, worst with plants on a window sill or in a hanging basket in hot weather.
Brown edges and tips to leaves.	Atmosphere dry, or draughts, or lime in the compost or water; occasionally, a lack of potash in the compost.
Brown spots on leaves.	Cold, especially if a succulent; dry fertilizer on leaves; feeding too heavily; sun shining through drops on the leaves; gas; poorly structured compost.
Raised brown or pale-yellow spots on leaf under-surface.	Scale insects, see page 27.

Symptoms of trouble on leaves cont'd

Large pale-brown patches on leaves, which may become papery.

Beige coloured, wavy lines and blisters on leaf.

White markings on leaves, especially furry ones, sometimes looking like marbling.

White powdery patches on leaves (also stems and flowers).

Fluffy white spots on leaves and at stem joints.

Patches of grey fur on leaves, with brown and yellow marking.

Greyish appearance to green leaves, lack of new growth, leaves withering and falling.

Thickened leaves with a grey covering, on azaleas.

Leaves hanging down, limp and whole plant wilting.

Leaves curling and distorted, also yellowing sometimes.

Black sooty patches on leaves.

Sticky patches on leaves.

Large holes in leaves.

Fleshy leaves which turn brown at soil level.

Leaves falling without discolouring.

Sun scald, especially with African violets.

Leaf-miner, see page 26.

Cold water on the leaves, or watering with water that is cold instead of at room temperature—often affects African violets and gloxinias.

Powdery mildew, see page 27.

Mealy-bug, see page 26.

Grey mould, see page 27.

Red spider mite, see page 26 (has different effects on different plants).

Azalea gall fungus disease, see page 27.

Too dry a compost, or too much water if wet. Remove from pot for a day. Do not water for several days.

Greenfly, sometimes also scale insect, see page 27.

Sooty mould, due indirectly to scale insect, whitefly or greenfly, see pages 25–7.

Scale insect, whitefly or greenfly, see pages 25–7.

Slugs, especially if lower leaves are affected, or caterpillars, see page 27.

Too much water and/or too low a temperature. Cease watering for a few days.

Draughts or sudden drop in temperature. Change position.

Flowers falling prematurely, or flowerbuds dropping without opening.

Draughts; dry atmosphere; infestation by red spider mite (see page 26); cold, insufficient or excessive water; moving the plant; turning it away from the sun. Be particularly careful with watering, humidity and temperature at start of flowering.

No flowers at all on a plant normally grown for its flowers.

Insufficient nourishment and light; too much nitrogen, especially if plant very lush and leafy; not enough warmth; give high-potash feed and increase humidity.

Hyacinth florets brown or flower spike wholly discoloured or stunted.

Not enough water when the bulbs were in the dark developing their roots.

Flowers not setting fruit.

A dry atmosphere; insufficient food, especially potash; compost too dry.

Fruit badly shaped.

A dry atmosphere at pollination.

Fruit shrivelling or falling.

Shortage of water at roots, high temperature and dry atmosphere.

Raised brown, grey or black spots, round, oval or mussel shaped, on bark of trunk and branches; plant growing slowly or not at all.

Scale insects, see page 27.

Fluffy white spots on stems and inside neck of bulbs, especially hippeastrum.

Mealy-bug, see page 26.

Brown rotting of stems at soil level, also crowns of complete plants, grey fur may follow on brown areas.

Cold combined with overwatering, often happens in winter; grey mould then infects. See page 27.

Complete plant looks 'tired', rather greyish, not growing, has a rather dry appearance.

Possibly root aphis or root mealy-bug, see page 26. Turn plant out of pot and examine root-ball to confirm. Or, too much water, roots then brown, stunted and easily broken off. Healthy roots are white and strong. Remove from pot for a day, and do not water for several days.

PHYSICAL & GROWING CHARACTERISTICS

Foliage plants

When plant-growing in the home was first attempted, the plants used were the ones grown for the beauty of their leaves—the aspidistra, the tradescantias and the ferns. For a long time, the image conjured up by the word houseplant was of a green, leafy plant. Then, houseplants came to include those that flowered—short-term plants that could be kept for a few weeks only and then died—climbing plants, cacti and many others. In fact, it became apparent that a great many plants which had been thought to thrive only in the well-lit conditions of a greenhouse were quite happy in the home, provided their needs were reasonably well met.

If you live in a home which is on the dark side, perhaps a basement flat or an old house with tiny windows, or a house getting little sun because of trees, don't think you will not be able to grow indoor plants. You can, very successfully, but you will do best to concentrate on foliage plants, and you will find that they can be extremely ornamental, and can be grown in practically any situation. They have the great advantage of being much hardier and more able to put up with conditions not tolerated by other plant groups. If neglected, they will just tick over until you remember them again, and rarely do they turn up their toes and die. Many will grow much

Opposite below: Brilliantly coloured leaves of *Codiaeum variegatum pictum*. Below: Three foliage plants of contrasting form, colour and texture disguise an unused fireplace: *Sansevieria* behind a glossy *Asplenium nidus* and *Maranta leuconeura* 'Tricolor'. Right: The shapely leaf form of *Philodendron laciniatum*, which should be trained up a stake clothed with sphagnum moss

Previous page: *Aechmea rhodocyanea*

better and be a deeper green if kept slightly shaded.

Since light is one of the two major limiting factors (the other being warmth) to growing plants in the home, as opposed to a greenhouse, your choice of foliage plants will be far greater than that of other groups more dependent on these factors. There is a wide variety of form. Some may be bushy and spreading like the *Fatsia*, *Aspidistra*, *Pilea* or *Maranta*, while others are tall and sometimes narrow, such as *Grevillea*, the rubber plant, *Dizygotheca*, or *Cyperus* and the umbrella plant. The climbing and twining kinds are good plants for dark places. Their habit of growth has been developed to make them grow upwards, either to reach light from a dark beginning, or because there is no room for them

at ground level. They can only survive by getting out of the way of the crowd, and growing up and round tree trunks. The ivies, the sweetheart vine, the grape ivy and the kangaroo vine are all climbers, and are easy to grow.

Finally, there are the trailers—wandering Jew (*Tradescantia* and *Zebrina*), mother of thousands (*Saxifraga stolonifera*), ivy, which looks just as pretty cascading down as growing up, hearts-entangled (*Ceropegia woodii*) and × *Fatshedera lizei*, to mention just a few.

The foliage plants offer a great variety of leaf shapes. Take *Dizygotheca*, with its extraordinary toothed, narrow leaves, elegantly poised in mid air on delicate stems; the Swiss cheese plant (*Monstera deliciosa*), whose enormous cut and holed leaves make the most dramatic of shadows

Above: The multi-coloured leaves of the begonia can reach stately proportions; left, *Begonia rex*, right, *Begonia masoniana*. Below left, a flourishing example of *Dieffenbachia*. Opposite: the pretty leaves of *Fittonia argyroneura* grow closely together

and silhouettes, and the ubiquitous ivy, whose leaf shape has been used in design since the times of the Greeks and Romans, the green leaves of which hanging down a white wall have a classic simplicity of unique beauty.

An illusion which the newcomer to houseplant growing will soon have shattered is that leaves are always green. There must be just as many plants grown for their different coloured leaves as for their green ones, to say nothing of the variegated-leaved kinds.

The coloured-leaved plants now available for growing indoors are exotic and rainbow-like. They outdo the flowering plants in their dazzle and brilliance—plants like the codiaeums (croton) and dracaenas, the lovely purple-furred *Gynura*, *Begonia rex* in all its variations of rose-pink, wine-red, silvery-grey, pale green and cream, and the flame nettle (*Coleus*), with its really fantastic range of brilliant colours and, in the most recently produced varieties, exciting shapes.

For those who still like green in their leaves but think all-over-green a bit dull, there are many, many, foliage houseplants whose colouring is relieved with cream, white or yellow variegation—in the form of spots, blotches, edgings or centre colouring—outlining the veins, or taking up most of the leaf. Mother-in-law's tongue (*Sansevieria trifasciata* 'Laurentii'), the goosefoot plant (*Syngonium podophyllum*), *Aglaonema*, *Peperomia magnoliaefolia* and the spider plant (*Chlorophytum comosum variegatum*) all have variegations of one kind or another.

There are some general rules that can be applied to the care of foliage plants, as distinct from the other groups. For instance, nitrogen has priority as a plant food over all the others. This is the nutrient plants need most for strong, well-coloured leaves and stems, so make sure that it is always contained in the compost, and use liquid fertilizers which have a high or higher percentage of nitrogen (N) than of the other foods.

The foliage plants with plain green leaves will grow in places distant from the light, in some shade, and in rather dark corners. The variegated and coloured-leaved varieties need a good light, such as a window sill facing north, or one facing the sun which has a net curtain over it. They can be put on a table near an un-

shaded sunny window sill but not in the direct sunlight.

Leafy plants need more grooming than the others. Grit and dust must be regularly wiped or sponged off the leaf surface with tepid water, or brushed off in the case of hairy leaves. Occasional polishing with a proprietary leafshine will give them a larger-than-life look for special occasions.

Slightly more water is needed in the compost than for other groups, and a humid atmosphere is especially important for those with thin papery leaves, such as *Caladium* (if you have the courage to attempt to grow it), *Maranta* and *Dieffenbachia*.

There are other groups of plants grown entirely or mostly for their leaves; these include the bromeliads, the cacti and succulents, and the palms and ferns, but these are rather special groups, with special needs and are described later in sections of their own.

Flowering plants

Everyone wants to have flowers in the home, but unless you have a garden, cut flowers need to be bought fresh every week. A flowering plant, on the other hand, will bloom for several weeks at the very least, and often for several months. Some will flower all the year round, if allowed to. Don't forget you can have pot plants in flower in winter, too, a time when the garden may be bereft, or when flowers from a florist are at a premium.

There is something peculiarly satisfying about having a plant of your own which flowers, especially if you have grown it to that stage yourself. Flowering plants are not as easy to care for as leafy ones, and the successful cultivation of these, and especially of fruiting plants, says a lot for your horticultural skill.

Above: Delicate flowers of *Jasminum officinale*. Left: *Cineraria cruenta*, an annual flowering plant. Opposite: The exotic *Gloxinia* with its velvety leaves is becoming increasingly popular

Flowering pot plants are an extremely good way of adding colour, fragrance and a great deal of beauty to the home. As with leafy plants, there are different shapes; the trailing ones with their hanging stems festooned with blooms, such as the Italian bellflower (*Campanula isophylla*), or the climbers, such as the passion-flower (*Passiflora caerulea*), *Hoya carnosa* (the wax flower) or *Jasminum grandiflorum*, white-flowered and strongly scented. You can have great fun training these in all sorts of ways—circular, triangular, upright—on moss sticks and trellises, or to surround window-frames.

Most of the flowering plants have a rounded or bushy shape; some, like the African violet, are very small, some really large—the hydrangea and the African lime (*Sparmannia africana*)—and many are in the medium-size range, such as the cyclamen, gloxinia, primulas and pelargoniums. But there are tall-growing ones to choose from as well, if that is the kind of shape you want, for instance fuchsias, clivia and anthuriums.

Whatever the season, there will always be an indoor plant to flower during it and, although the winter might be thought a bad time for such plants, there are almost more at that time than in the summer. Aphelandras, azaleas, Cape heaths, poinsettias or *Pachystachys lutea* are a few winter-flowering plants whose blooms will last, with care, for several weeks or months.

Above: A very old favourite, *Calendula officinalis* or the common marigold, will thrive indoors or in a window box. Below: *Erica carnea* an easily grown winter-flowering plant

In summer, you can go in for gloxinias, streptocarpus, the double-flowered begonias, achimenes and calceolarias, to say nothing of the legions of cactus species which can so easily be brought to flower. You can welcome the spring with cinerarias, astilbe, genista, and later, epiphyllums; all kinds of bulbs which flower outdoors in spring can be brought on indoors to flower in late winter and very early spring. As the summer ends and autumn arrives, the nerines, hibiscus and autumn crocus will begin to bloom, epiphyllums will have their second season, and many other summer plants will still be in flower.

Some flowering plants have the endearing habit of blooming the whole year round if you let them. It is not, actually, a good idea for a plant to flower non-stop; it gets exhausted and dies sooner than it need, but you can let it flower for most of the year, with the right feeding. Busy Lizzie (*Impatiens*), and the shrimp plant (*Beloperone guttata*) are two that bloom continuously as do small-flowering begonias, both the kinds used for bedding and the winter-flowering ones. Others which flower for many months are *Exacum affine*, with a mass of deep-purple flowers, African violet, chrysanthemum, *Streptocarpus*, the crown of thorns (*Euphorbia milii*) and *Dipladenia*.

If you have a special affection for fragrant flowers, you will find that some of the indoor plants can have an overpowering perfume. Fragrant plants include jasmine, *Stephanotis floribunda*, *Exacum*, *Iris reticulata*, hyacinth, narcissi, miniature roses, calamondin, and some of the epiphyllums and cyclamen.

Flowering plants often have highly ornamental evergreen leaves, so that they are doubly worthwhile, but there are some with a third bonus, the fruiting plants. The calamondin probably tops all these for value for money, because it can easily be in flower and fruit at the same time, as well as having glossy, deep-green, evergreen leaves. Others are the Christmas cherry (*Solanum capsicastrum*) with white flowers in summer and marble-sized red berries in autumn and winter, and the ornamental pepper, *Capsicum frutescens*.

In the same way that foliage plants have special needs, so flowering indoor plants have basic requirements which should be met if they are to enjoy first-class health and provide you with the pleasure of a superbly ornamental plant.

Light is the most important ingredient in the recipe for success. Without a good light—preferably direct sunlight—very few plants can ripen their growth so that they produce flowers, and later fruits. So put your flowering plants close to windows and glass doors.

However, if the summer sun is very hot and bright, as can happen at midday, move them away temporarily, or provide light shading. If you have any skylights, make the most of them, because the biggest problem with bringing indoor plants into flower is the lack of overhead light. Greenhouses and lean-to garden rooms are successful because they have this built-in advantage, as well as being extra warm.

Even if you cannot give flowering plants a window sill, try to put them on a plant stand or table (or a Victorian whatnot), as near to a source of light as possible, so that they at least have a good light even if they are not directly in the sun.

If you are totally bereft of any good natural light, you can supply it artificially, in the form of a light cabinet, which has strip neon lighting, and often thermostatically controlled supplementary heating as well. Light cabinets are not cheap, but are very pretty when filled with plants, and are of course permanent once bought.

To some extent, you can also overcome a lack of intense light by giving the plant a high-potash fertilizer,

Above: Site pots of *Begonia hybrida* 'Pendula' where their hanging blooms can be best appreciated. Left: *Kalanchoe blossfeldiana*

because potassium is the nutrient associated with flowering and fruiting. Like light, potash helps in the maturing of plant growth and, as well as making sure it is present in the compost, you can use a liquid feed which has a higher percentage of potash in it than the other two major plant foods, nitrogen and phosphorus.

The duration of light, or day-length, is important to quite a lot of plants, since it affects whether they actually flower or not. Some are 'short-day' plants, that is, they will only flower when the daylight hours are less than the night-time or dark ones. Because of this, they can be made to flower at any time of the year, by giving them short or long days as required, to bring them on or hold them back. This is why you can now get chrysanthemums in flower at any time of the year, not just autumn. Poinsettias are also short-day plants and they will not form coloured bracts in winter unless given short days in autumn.

Humidity is vital. A dry atmosphere can ruin all your care at the last minute because the buds will drop off without opening, or if they do unfold, the flowers will drop almost at once. Be doubly careful to spray or mist regularly just before flowering time, although afterwards, when in full flower, it is better to use trays of evaporating water close to the plants so that the petals

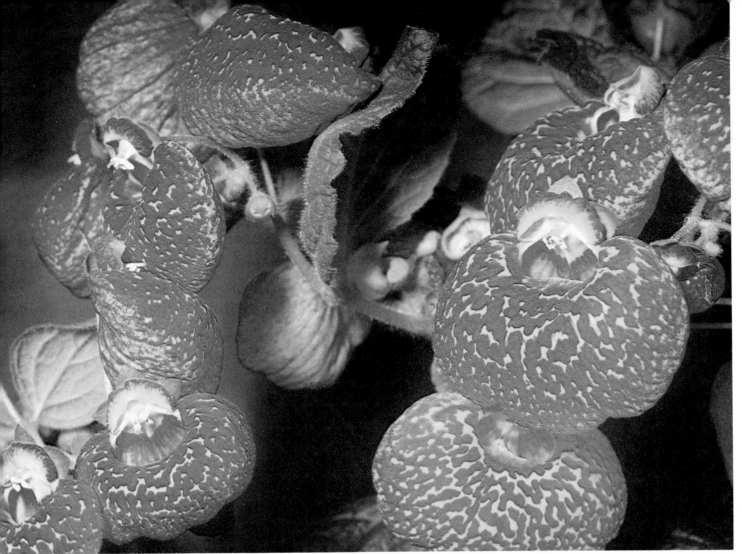

Above: The speckled blooms of *Calceolaria* are distinctively pouch-shaped. Below: Azaleas well repay the little extra care they demand. Opposite: The gorgeous bloom of an *Hibiscus rosa-sinensis*

are not marked by drops of falling water.

When flowering is near, do not move plants if you can avoid it as this also encourages buds to drop; so does dryness at the roots, and draughts. Once the flowers are dead, take them off so that they neither rot the leaves onto which they have fallen, nor provide a place for grey mould to get a hold.

The shrubby and climbing or trailing flowering plants will need careful pruning if you are not to remove all potential flowering. In general, it is the practice to prune container plants in late winter, shortly before re-potting and/or spring growth starts.

Sometimes it is better to prune directly after flowering. This should be done with plants that flower in spring or early summer, as the new shoots which they then produce during the rest of the growing season will be the ones on which they flower the following spring. If you prune this kind in late winter, you will only cut off what would otherwise have been flowering shoots.

Plants that flower in mid summer or autumn can be safely pruned in late winter; some may even be pruned as soon as flowering has finished.

Palms & Ferns

The diversity of foliage shown by plants is probably not fully recognized by most people, even experienced gardeners. Professional botanists are the most likely to appreciate the range of leaf that nature has produced, but even their knowledge tends to be restricted to a particular family or group of plants.

The leaves of plants mentioned in the foliage chapter are mostly conventional in shape and function. Describe an object as being leaf-like in shape and colour, and one's mental picture is of a green, flat piece of plant tissue, longish but pointed at the end. Ferns and palms, however, do not fit into this pattern, any more than bromeliads and cacti do.

Fern leaves are, in general, greatly divided and these divisions in turn are also divided, so that the whole appearance is feathery, or pinnate. They are thus un-usually, even uniquely, elegant and graceful. However, even with this class of plant, nature has not been content with uniformity, so that there are also ferns with rounded leaflets, long narrow entire leaves, bisected, or even holly-like leaves.

Ferns which can be grown both indoors and outdoors are returning to popularity. The Victorians were greatly attracted by them and ferneries abounded in the garden. In the 1840s, a Mr Ward invented the Wardian case with glass sides and tops for growing ferns indoors. Ferns are inhabitants of shady places so you will be able to find a fern to fit most positions in your house, particularly if there is plenty of moisture about.

Ferns bring outdoor freshness to a room. Below: *Nephrolepis exaltata* and opposite the much-loved *Adiantum,* or maidenhair fern

A hanging basket is the ideal way to display the delicate fronds of an asparagus fern, especially against a light background

streams. But its fronds are complete and leaf-like, though still elegant as they unfurl in spring. Unlike flowering plants, fern leaves unroll from the base upwards and lengthen as they do so.

The leaves of *Asparagus setaceus* (syn. *A. plumosus*) and *A. densiflorus* are quite different, being reduced to a needle-like fineness. The stag's-horn fern, *Platycerium bifurcatum*, could not provide a greater contrast in form of leaf, and the holly fern, *Cyrtomium falcatum*, is barely recognizable as a fern, with its shiny and prickly-pointed leaflets. The maidenhair fern, *Adiantum capillus-veneris*, must be everybody's favourite fern, with its rounded, fragile leaflets and fronds and, again, it is difficult to believe that it is a member of the same group as the ones already mentioned.

As a group, ferns have common cultural needs which distinguish them from other houseplants, for instance, they must have shade. In their native regions, they grow in woods, jungles and forests, always beneath the canopy of foliage and branches supplied by trees, or in the shelter of rocks and banks, and always where there is moisture in the air and in the soil. So keep your ferns away from the light, whatever you do. They will grow in the most unlikely corners because, however dark, there is bound to be sufficient light for photosynthesis to go on in a fern.

But you must make sure the atmosphere is always moist, and for some species of fern, for instance, the maidenhair, it has to be very moist. More of these die every year through lack of humidity than any other cultural factor. Bathrooms, especially if heated, are marvellous places for ferns; if you have such a bathroom the stag's-horns and the bird's-nests could before long make it very difficult to get at the toothbrush.

Moisture at the roots is important, as with any plant, but perhaps slightly more is needed for the ferns. Use acid compost—ferns will not grow in an alkaline one—and use soft water whenever the plants need a drink.

A good many of the ferns which can be grown in the home like to be kept cool, and are virtually, if not completely, hardy, so there should be no difficulty over temperature with them. Others which originate from tropical forests, and which used to be grown in 'stove-houses', need a good deal of warmth and freedom from draughts. Central heating will only be suitable if you can ensure a lot of humidity at all times—the easiest and most effective way to do this is to obtain the humidifiers which are supplied for use with radiators, otherwise supply it by the methods suggested on pages 18–19.

Ferns have two special pests which can cause a good deal of trouble. One is scale insect (see page 26), but do

Some species you may not recognize as ferns at all, others, for instance, *Nephrolepis exaltata*, have the typical fronds. This is one of the prettiest and easiest to grow of the ferns, and you will be able to find several different forms of it, with doubly pinnate, wavy-edged or crisped leaves.

Pteris cretica, related to the common bracken, is another of these feathery forms, and in its cultivar 'Albolineata' the veins are outlined in white. The hart's-tongue is one of the British native ferns, often seen growing on shaded roadside banks and at the sides of

not use the conventional insecticides as they damage ferns; either pick or scrape off the scales or brush gently with methylated spirits.

The other pest is eelworm, which is extremely difficult to deal with. They infest the crown and leaves of the plant, so that the leaves are discoloured and the whole plant is stunted and sick-looking. Hot-treatment may deal with a mild infestation, but needs to be done precisely, otherwise it is ineffective. Wash *all* the compost off the fern, put the whole plant in hot water—50–52 °C (122–125 °F)—and keep it in there, at *exactly* that temperature, neither higher nor lower, for 5 minutes. (Remember that putting the plant in the water will lower its temperature to start with and it must be brought back up to the right one before starting to time the 5 minutes.) Then remove and drain, and pot in fresh compost and a different pot. Badly infested plants should be destroyed and the compost discarded.

The palm family, Palmae, is one of the most economically useful, containing the date palm, sago palm, rattan palm, coconut palm and raffia palm. Palms supply fibre for ropes, wax, oil, betelnuts, vegetable ivory, food of various kinds, material for building, thatching and basket making, and alcoholic drinks. Palms may have graceful, feathery leaves, like some ferns, or leaves like pleated fans. The palm of the 'palm court orchestra' was generally a species of *Howea* (*Kentia*), one of the tallest and most graceful under container conditions, and not difficult to grow. Palms were once very fashionable, and it looks as though it will not be long before they are popular again.

Palms are rather more amenable than ferns in their environmental needs. Growing slowly under the restricted root conditions provided by containers, they are not fussy about humidity, light or acid soil. Certainly humidity is advisable—if the leaflet tips start to brown, then the atmosphere is dry and must be dealt with accordingly—but palm leaves are much tougher than ferns, almost leathery, which is not surprising when you remember that many grow on tropical coasts regularly lashed by hurricanes and monsoons. They have a thick cuticle and a very waxy covering, both of which help to prevent moisture loss.

Though most grow in brilliantly sunny conditions—particularly the date palm, *Phoenix dactylifera*, and the coconut, *Cocos nucifera*—they will be almost as happy in a good light or slight shade.

Palms cannot tolerate cold and you should try to provide a temperature of at least 10 °C (50 °F) in winter for the majority, and as high as possible in the summer.

Compost can have some extra peat added to it, and if you can get them, the specially deep palm pots, which resemble ordinary pots but are very much longer than they are wide, will give the best results for the long roots.

Palms can, in time, grow into really large plants, 1.5–1.8 m (5–6 ft) tall and, if you look after them well, will be decorative inhabitants of your home for many years. The coconut palm can grow to 30 m (100 ft) in its desert island, so its size in a container will be in proportion, but don't panic, there are little ones, such as the Chusan palm, *Trachycarpus fortunei*, or the parlour palm, *Chamaedorea elegans*, which will even flower and set viable seed.

Decorative hanging baskets are appropriate to kitchen/dining rooms, looking good but leaving work surfaces clear

Bromeliads

A bromeliad is a member of the plant family Bromeli-aceae, and there is a genus in this family called *Bromelia*, after Olaf Bromel, a Swedish botanist of the seventeenth century. Many species were discovered and introduced in the 1800s, but they were not much grown in homes before the 1950s.

A bromeliad consists almost completely of a rosette of stiff, leathery, strap-shaped leaves, spraying out from a central crown at soil level. These leaves grow sheathed round one another to form a short vertical tube before they begin to fan out, and this tube or funnel serves to collect rain-water which runs down the leaves into it. The funnel contains water throughout the plant's life and is indeed its main source of water; the roots, unlike those of ordinary plants, absorb very little, and are mainly needed to attach or anchor the plant.

Most bromeliads are epiphytes, that is, they attach themselves to other plants, though they do not absorb food from them in the way that parasites do. Forest trees are the usual supports, and in South and Central American jungles you will see bromeliads growing high above you, on tree branches, and in the forks of trunks and branches, always at the point where rain-water and rotting vegetation are liable to collect.

But some bromeliads can also be found growing on the ground, in rocky and desert-like places where there is very little water and where the temperature may be quite low at night. The South American Andes are the home of many of these species and they also have the central funnel for collecting rain. They tend to grow

Below: *Nidularium fulgens.* Opposite: *Aechmea fasciata*

flat and close against the ground, looking like starfish, and the flower is insignificant and small, whereas the forest species are much more upright, with flowering stems 30 cm (12 in) or more tall.

All the bromeliads have handsome leaves, plain green, variegated yellow or banded in various colours such as red, silvery-grey or wine. Many have attractive and unusual flowerheads which last for many weeks. These flowerheads actually grow up through the water in the funnel, but they do not rot while doing this, as you might expect. Some, such as the *Nidularium* species emerge from the water just before the flowers develop.

Once they have flowered, bromeliads do not do so again; they eventually die, but the leaves will continue to be attractive for months before they start to wither, and in the meanwhile the plant will produce offsets, which can be used for increase.

You can grow bromeliads in standard pots, but pans, or any shallow container, are better because the plants do not have deep roots. An attractive alternative is to grow several bromeliads on a branch. Dead apple wood or driftwood from the beach is excellent.

Fill the hollows and forks where the side branches join with moist peaty compost and tuck the plants in. Wire the plants on inconspicuously and cover the wires with dampened sphagnum moss. If you get your support set up and then spray or trickle water down it then the places where the water collects are the places to put the plants for a natural effect.

Opposite: *Ananas comosus* 'Variegatus' presides over a collection of *objets d'art*. Inset: *Vriesea splendens*. Below: Close-up of the vase of *Neoregelia concentrica*. drained to show the flower-head forming

Surprisingly, bromeliads are rather like cacti in that they grow in places where they receive little water, either because they are sheltered by large trees or because the area where they grow has a tiny annual rainfall. So you should keep the compost just moist, but maintain the water level in the central funnel, topping it up with rain-water at room temperature at intervals of two or three weeks in the growing season.

Compost can be very peaty, and the soil-less composts are excellent, perhaps mixed with a little sphagnum moss and coarse sand. Bromeliads do not live in 100% soil by any means. Insects and leaves that have fallen into the water in the funnel provide a bromeliad with most of its food. You can give a weak liquid feed at half strength instead of water once a month while the plant is growing and flowering.

Humidity is not very important; some will grow well in a dry atmosphere, others are better with some moisture in the atmosphere, as noted in the individual descriptions. Nor are they fussy about warmth, though one or two do need quite a lot, and of course it does help them to ripen and flower.

A good light, but practically never direct sunlight, is preferred; some will grow in a little shade, others need light to give them their best colouring. Pests and diseases really do not seem to occur, though crown rotting is likely if you keep the compost too wet and the temperature low.

Increase is by detaching the offsets when about 15 cm (6 in) tall and potting in similar compost in a small shallow container. Put in a warm shady place until the offsets have rooted into the compost.

Bulbs

Nothing in nature could be better packaged than a bulb or an egg. Both are rounded for ease of handling, both are clean, both have a protective covering, and both have an internal supply of food ready for when growth begins. Of course, both will die in due course if warmth and moisture are not forthcoming when required. Bulbs are, however, very much tougher—they do not break when they are dropped.

Bulbs store a good deal of food in the form of carbohydrates which are manufactured after flowering and retained during the resting season. This rest occurs because many bulbs grow in places where there is little or no rain in summer, and they have therefore adapted so that they can go into a kind of hibernation until the cool, damp autumn. At the same time summer heat serves to mature the bulb so that it will flower in the coming spring. In autumn and winter it becomes active again but because no top growth is seen until late winter, most people assume, mistakenly, that a bulb is dormant in winter. In fact, the roots are growing rapidly and, once enough of these have been produced, the shoots start to grow. However, with quite a layer of soil to penetrate, they take some time to break through to the light.

Thus the standard life cycle of bulbs that flower in spring and early summer consists of flowering at these seasons, leaf growth to feed the bulb, then rest, then root growth, and finally elongation of shoots into the light in late winter to complete the cycle. Other bulbs do the same, but may have their rest in autumn and not flower until summer. The time for the various stages in bulb growth depends on the part of the world they come from. Occasionally there are deviations, which are mentioned under the bulb concerned in the A–Z section.

You can have one kind of bulb or another in flower, in succession all through the year, even in winter. The spring-flowering bulbs—scillas, crocus, daffodils, narcissus, tulips and grape hyacinths—can all be potted up for flowering in the house. The clivia which flowers in spring, will be a permanent inhabitant. Hyacinths, narcissi, daffodils and snowdrops can be forced for blooming from early to mid and late winter. Treated hippeastrums can be bought for flowering in early winter, and *Iris reticulata* flowers naturally in mid and late winter. In summer there are the later tulips, gloxinias

bring them out into gradually increased light and warmth to bring on the leaves and flowers. A standard compost is used, and the bulbs are then watered and fed until the leaves die down, when they are dried off and not given moisture for the rest of the summer. In autumn they are planted in the garden; they cannot be forced again but will flower at their normal season, probably not as well, but enough to make them worth keeping and growing.

You can grow bulbs in bulb fibre, which can be bought made up; it consists of 6 parts (by loose bulk) of peat, 2 parts oyster shell and 1 part crushed charcoal. Bulb fibre must be thoroughly wet when used, but with the surplus water squeezed out by hand first. Another method of cultivation is to put the bulbs in the mouth of a bulb glass which is filled with water. The base of the bulb is just above the water, and the roots will grow down into it, but bulbs grown this way and in bulb fibre will not flower the following year, and can only be put on the compost heap or thrown away.

In general bulbs require a well-drained, soil-containing compost. An extra part of coarse grit, or even a little fine shingle added to compost will do wonders for the drainage. You should also make sure that the base of the container, whether plastic or clay, has broken pieces of clay pot in it. Sour soil and standing water

and achimenes, and in autumn the nerines and autumn crocus will be at their best.

There are various ways of forcing bulbs for early-winter flowering. The commonest is to pot up prepared bulbs in late summer or early autumn, put them in the dark and cool for many weeks to grow roots, and then

Left: Narcissi will bloom in winter if nursed indoors. Top: Hyacinth 'Queen of the Pinks'. Below: *Muscari armeniacum* reaches 20cm (8in) and is very easy to grow. Right: the modest herald of spring, golden crocus

finish off a bulb, whose fleshy base is particularly vulnerable to rotting. Placing the bulb on a little coarse sand when potting, will help it to grow well—the lilies will be especially grateful.

Some humidity is needed, but is not crucial; the need for warmth and light varies from species to species, but in general the limits for both are fairly wide.

Bulbs are planted at depths which depend on their own height. For instance, a daffodil bulb which measures 5 cm (2 in) from base to tip will be planted so that there is at least 5 cm (2 in) of compost above the tip; in other words it will be 10 cm (4 in) deep. There are exceptions to this, as always; some are planted so that only half the bulb is buried, others so that the tip is showing, and so on.

Feeding at the right time is very important; it often makes all the difference between flowering and not flowering the following year. Feed until the leaf tips begin to yellow and wither naturally, and then stop. By doing this, the leaves can manufacture food and transfer it to the bulb for storage during rest and at the same time the roots can absorb food from the soil and do the same. In general, if you dry the bulb off as soon as it has finished flowering, don't expect it to bloom the following year.

Bulbs are fairly free of pests, except for mealy-bug and occasionally root aphis. As with ferns, however, eelworm can be devastating, and if you have a stunted bulb, and misshapen flowers, suspect them, destroy the bulb, and discard the compost.

Offsets taken off the parent bulb and potted will flower in two to four years.

Cacti & Succulents

You may already be a cactus convert; if so, there is no need to read the propaganda that follows. If you are one of the many who think of cacti as fat, dull, plain green dummies, flowering once every seven years at night, you are in for a very pleasant surprise.

There are plenty of cacti which flower profusely, easily, and regularly every year, in brilliant and exotic colours, sometimes fragrantly, either for weeks on end or twice a year. Even if they do not flower, they have beautiful leaves in varying colours. But one of the main attractions is the often comic shape of the plant itself, with flowers apparently just stuck on to the stems at random. The opuntias in particular shoot out 'ears' at the strangest places; the hairy cacti are extraordinarily

reminiscent of some of the present-day masculine representatives of our own species, and a collection of cacti at a show will be guaranteed to amuse and fascinate you.

Cacti are not difficult to look after, provided you remember that they are in fact alive: don't fall into the trap of thinking that, because they are cacti, they don't need any water. All in all, cacti are ideal houseplants, which are both ornamental and easy to care for. How many other standard houseplants are there that fall into this category?

The cactus family consists of plants that have had to put up with extreme drought, and often, though not always, extreme heat. Since plants usually die under such conditions, the cacti have been forced to adapt to survive, and this they have done very successfully. A spherical shape is the one with the least area for a given volume, which is why there are so many rounded cacti, as they transpire the least possible moisture. The cell tissue is modified to absorb the greatest possible quantity of water, and the hairs, prickles or bristles, and the thick skin cuticle and wax covering prevent water loss. The prickles discourage grazing animals.

The roots are shallow, but extremely far-reaching, so

Opposite page, top left: *Echeveria leucotricha*. Echeverias are one of the easiest succulents to cultivate. Top right: *Conophytum pearsonii* grow naturally amongst stones, which they somewhat resemble. Bottom left: *Rebutia haagei* freely produces flushes of brilliant flowers. Bottom right: keep *Echinocereus blanckii* completely dry from October to March. In June and July the vivid flowers appear. Above: The flowers of *Epiphyllum* x *ackermannii* can be up to 15cm (6in) across

that they can make use of whatever rain or dew comes along before it evaporates in the hot sun. Many cacti flower in one splendid burst at a particular time because that is when the rains come in their natural homes. They then lengthen and produce new leaves or shoots.

All cacti, except one genus, *Rhipsalis*, come from the New World, where they grow in places with virtually no rain, or only heavy mists or dew, or where very heavy rain falls for a few hours followed by months of drought. They have roots, leaves and shoots as other plants do, but also one characteristic in particular which distinguishes them, the areolae, which are the small bumps on the stem from which come the flowers, leaves and prickles or spines.

Above: *Mammillaria wildii* is prized for its beautiful spines as well as its bell-like flowers. Opposite: *Opuntia microdasys* with *Haworthia margaritifera*. Inset: *Astrophytum myriostigma* is popularly known as bishop's cap cactus

always have a little drainage material in the bottom, and a pan rather than a pot gives the best results, though pots will do. A layer of gravel on the compost surface round the plant helps to prevent the lower part from being in direct contact with moisture, which could result in rotting. This good drainage is extremely important for growing a healthy cactus.

The diameter of the pot should be such that a space of about 2–2.5 cm ($\frac{3}{4}$–1 in) shows all round the plant, depending on its size. Repotting is needed when the plant practically covers the compost.

Depending on the plant, repotting or potting-on will be needed every year in spring, though no harm will come if you have not the time to do it until mid summer. Some that grow very slowly can wait two seasons. If you are dealing with a prickly cactus, handle it carefully with tongs, or with a collar of paper wrapped round it, though tongs are better as they cause less damage to the prickles. Take off any old roots, and break up the old surface compost, but do not fiddle with the soil-ball more than is essential.

In general, keep your cacti in as sunny a place as possible and where they get the most heat in summer. It is vital not to forget to water them under these conditions, and you will find, too, that flowering will be much better if you feed, between mid summer and autumn, with a high-potash liquid fertilizer, as for other flowering plants. Humidity can be forgotten.

In winter, do not feed, and water only occasionally, perhaps once a month under cool conditions, slightly more often if in central heating. The object is to make sure the compost does not become bone dry, because if that happened then some of the fine roots would die. Conversely, too much water, especially when the temperature is low, will encourage rapid rotting.

Pests and diseases are very few; mealy-bug and root mealy-bug are the most likely, red spider mite and scale insect attack only occasionally. Brown patches on stems should be cut out, and flowers of sulphur applied to the cut area. Brown or reddish spots indicate cold or poor drainage and are permanent, though they do not usually result in rotting.

Increase of cacti is most easily done by offsets, cuttings or seed. The first two are put into a very sandy compost, in early summer, letting the cuttings dry off for a day or two first. Seed is sown in early spring, in a temperature of 21–27 °C (70–80 °F) on a moist, sandy compost and not covered with more compost; the surface should be very finely sifted compost or peat. Then cover with clear polythene and keep in a shaded place, even after they have germinated.

The cactus family, and many other plants that are not cacti, are often referred to as succulents—that is, they have thick fleshy leaves designed to conserve moisture. The leaves of succulents can be more beautiful than the average flower. The crassulas, echeverias, sempervivums (houseleeks) and aeoniums are some with the most colourful and ornamental leaves. For curiosity the 'living stones'—the lithops and conophytums—are outstanding: they are indistinguishable from the pebbles amongst which they grow. One of the nearest parallels to exact mimicry of this kind in the animal world is the stick insect.

The compost required for cacti is a standard soil-containing kind with coarse grit added at the rate of 3 parts compost to 1 part grit. The container should

A-Z OF
HOUSEPLANTS

To help you in your choice of plants to grow indoors, the name of each plant described is marked with a symbol: * means the plant is easy to grow; ** means a plant that requires more care; *** means a rather difficult and temperamental plant.

Achimenes (hot-water plant) */**

The cultivated species and varieties of *Achimenes* are pretty, upright or trailing flowering plants, which can be grown in pots, troughs, or hanging baskets. You can expect them to flower from mid summer to early autumn. The main colours are shades of purple, blue, violet, and rose-pink, but there are also red, yellow and white varieties, whose flowers are generally smaller, and rather shy to appear.

Achimenes have been grown on cottage window sills for at least 100 years —most were introduced in the early 1800s from Central and South America. For a long time it was thought that they had to be watered with hot water, hence the common name, but water at room temperature is quite warm enough.

There are lots of different hybrids and varieties now, and one nurseryman is naming his new plants after butterflies and gemstones, giving them such names as 'Red Admiral', 'Moonstone' and 'Tiger Eye'—all very expressive of the colour and charm of the flowers.

Achimenes grow from small tubers or tubercles, which look a little like caterpillars. At the end of the growing season, you will find each plant has produced a lot of new ones. Each of these will be the start of a new plant the following year.

When you get a plant, put it on a sunny window sill, but shade it from the midday sun, otherwise the leaves will become brown-spotted. Too much sun will always produce this result. Water using soft water and feed normally until the plant starts dying down naturally. Then gradually stop water-

Opposite: *Achimenes* 'Little Beauty'.
Above: *Adiantum*. Previous page:
Aspidistra elatior, crocuses, *Nephrolepis
exaltata*, *Zebrina pendula*, Azalea hybrid,
Cissus rhombifolia; hanging,
Schlumbergera x *buckleyi*

ing, take off the dead leaves and stems, and leave the tubers in the dry compost until late winter or early spring. Take them out, separate them from the clusters into single tubers, and put them in sandy compost or moist peat so that they are covered, but only just, about 5 cm (2 in) apart.

In a temperature of about 18 °C (65 °F) they will start to grow, though slowly; don't expect them to be through for three or more weeks. Not so much warmth will be needed after they have sprouted. When they are about 5 cm (2 in) tall, put about three in a 13 cm (5 in) pot of standard (lime-free) compost, spaced evenly. Water in and keep in the shade until obviously growing. The upright ones, height 30–60 cm (1–2 ft), will need supporting. Watch for red spider mite and greenfly.

A particularly easy variety to grow is 'Purple King', which is one of the oldest kinds. Others are 'Queen of Sheba', deep crimson, 'Tourmaline', pink with yellow and purple markings, and 'Cattleya', violet-blue, trailing.

Adiantum (maidenhair fern)**

The ferns are nothing if not varied in leaf form, and you can be forgiven for not realizing that the maidenhair is a fern. The rounded leaflets (pinnae) and thin wiry stems are quite untypical of ferns, but the clue is in the clusters of raised brown spots on the underside of the leaves of adult plants—these contain the fern spores. They are *not* a sign of disease or a form of scale insect!

There is one species of maidenhair which is native to Britain, *Adiantum capillus-veneris*. Although the slightest frost will damage the fronds, it will grow well and easily as a houseplant in a cool to moderate temperature. There are others native to Europe, and many from tropical areas such as Africa, Brazil and the West Indies.

Besides the British species, there is *A. raddianum* (syn. *A. cuneatum*), which is very similar but a little larger and taller, about 50 cm (20 in) in height; and *A. hispidalam*, whose young foliage is tinted red-brown, and this grows to about 30 cm (12 in) tall.

All the maidenhairs must have lots of humidity; this is absolutely essential for their fine, delicate fronds, otherwise they turn brown at the edges and wither up completely in a day or two. Misting them every day, and providing humidity from containers or humidifiers is vital.

They do well in a good light, but not in a dark place or a sunny one, with normal summer warmth, no draughts, and a winter minimum of 7 °C (45 °F). The rhizome grows quickly, and plants may need repotting during the season, as well as every spring.

Use soft water, and feed occasionally while growing. Pot into a lime-free compost, making sure that the rhizomes are on the compost surface, not buried. Increase by cutting the rhizome into sections, each with some roots and fronds, any time between late winter and mid-spring. *A. raddianum* will increase itself naturally from spores falling on to the compost surface, especially if this is a peaty one.

Aechmea (urn plant)*

The aechmeas (pronounced ek-me-a) are members of that curious but attractive plant family, the Bromeliaceae (see page 46), and they have a very pronounced central funnel or vase. They are mostly epiphytes, that is, they grow on trees, though there are a few found growing on the ground, amongst rocks. They come from South America.

Aechmea fasciata, (syn. *A. rhodocyanea*, *Billbergia rhodocyanea*), is one of the most ornamental, as well as one of the easiest to grow, of the bromeliads. Its greygreen white-banded leaves and bright pink flower spike, covered in blue flowers, combine to make an extremely handsome and colourful, long-lasting houseplant. It comes from Rio de Janeiro and was first cultivated, in greenhouses, as long ago as 1826, but has only become really popular for home growing since about 1960.

The leaves are slightly spiny at the edges, and channelled so that whatever rain there is does not run off, but down into the funnel where it collects. In particularly good growing conditions, the flowers may set to form small berries, but generally when the plants are grown in the home, the flowers do not open completely, and do not last long, so that pollination and fertilization, even if they occur, may not be complete.

Aechmeas will be happy in normal summer temperatures, 21 °C (70 °F) or more, and a good light, including sun, with shade from midday or very hot sun. In winter, the temperature can drop to about 7 °C (45 °F); lower temperatures will result in varying degrees of leaf discoloration.

Keep the water in the funnel topped up with soft water at room temperature during the spring, summer and early autumn, and feed occasionally via the funnel. The compost should always be slightly moist as well. In winter, give very much less water in the funnel, and do not give any if the plant is kept in low temperatures. Humidity is not important.

Once the flowerhead has died—it lasts for about four months—the plant will not produce another, but by then offsets will be appearing. When these are about 15 cm (6 in) tall they can be removed with roots attached, and potted into 7.5 cm (3 in) pots, moving them into larger ones as they grow. The parent plant will wither and should be discarded.

The offsets may be ready for potting in autumn, or not until the following

spring. During their first summer they should be kept in as warm and as light a place as possible, to ensure that they flower the following year.

Aeonium*
The aeoniums are succulent plants, one of the *Crassulaceae* family, and most of them come from the Canary Islands and North Africa. They vary a good deal in their habit of growth; some are herbaceous, others have several woody stems and form shrubs, but all have thick, fleshy leaves in rosettes at the end of shoots or branches.

Several aeoniums do well on sunny window sills in the home, for instance *Aeonium × barbatum*, which has masses of bright yellow flowers in late spring and early summer, as well as light green leaves all year. It grows about 30 cm (1 ft) high, but may be almost completely round. After flowering it will die, so cuttings should be taken before the flowers appear. The leaves of *A. undulatum* are spoon-shaped, wavy-edged and dark green, and it has a main stem about 60–90 cm (2–3 ft) high. It also has starry yellow flowers in early summer, and often produces new, taller stems after flowering.

Aeonium tabulaeforme, which grows naturally against rocks, forms flat rosettes of densely overlapping leaves, each as much as 30 cm (1 ft) across, and *A. arboreum atropurpureum* has metallic chocolate-purple leaves, especially in strong sunlight, on a plant with a tree-like form up to 90 cm (3 ft) tall.

Plenty of light at all times, normal watering in summer, but little in winter, just enough to keep the leaves plump and the soil barely moist, a minimum winter temperature of 10 °C (50 °F) and a gritty compost will keep aeoniums happy. Too little water encourages leaf drop.

African hemp, see Sparmannia

African violet, see Saintpaulia

Agave*

The agaves are succulent plants which grow wild in Mexico and the warmer parts of America in general. One species, the century plant, has been naturalized in southern Europe. The thick leathery leaves of agaves end in a point and form a rosette close against the soil, from the centre of which comes the flower stem. Mostly they are grown in the home for their ornamental leaves. The flowers take a long time to appear, and are not very interesting when they do.

The century plant causes a lot of interest because its flower stem can be at least as tall as 7.5 m (25 ft), often more. The leaves are in proportion, so that the rosette can be 1.8 m (6 ft) wide. It takes a long time to produce flowers, perhaps 30 or 40 years, and then dies; by this time, however, it will have produced plenty of offsets, and these will be flowering in their turn and setting seed, so it has no difficulty in spreading.

For pot cultivation, *Agave victoriae-reginae* is one which will not get out of hand. It does not grow offsets, and the rosette takes many years to reach its fully-grown size of 60 cm (2 ft) wide. The dark green leaves are triangular and fleshy, with white margins. *A. filifera* has 25 cm (10 in) long leaves, bright green, and leathery; long threads come from the edges, and there is in fact at least one species, *A. sisalana*, which is used for making hemp. *A.*

Left: *Aechmea fasciata*; below: *Aeonium arboreum atropurpureum*; opposite: strap-like leaves of *Agave americana marginata*

parrasana has blue-green leaves, 30 cm (1 ft) long, but much wider than is usual in agaves, about 15 cm (6 in).

For general cultivation of the agaves, see page 54. The main point to note is that the compost must be very well-drained. Temperature should not drop below about 10 °C (50 °F) in winter, as they need to be kept slightly warmer than the majority of succulents. Increase by taking off offsets in summer, and planting singly in small pots. Repotting will only be needed every four or five years.

Aglaonema**

These are foliage houseplants, and have large leaves, variegated in some way. They are members of the aroid plant family, the Araceae, which contains such plants as the philodendrons and dieffenbachias, and come from all over south-east Asia, so that they need quite warm temperatures, and high humidity.

Aglaonemas grow upright, fairly tall, and the leaves can be 23 cm (9 in) or more in length, and about 7.5–10 cm (3–4 in) wide, depending on the species. There is a very attractive one which is usually sold under the name *A. pseudobracteatum*, though it is probably a variety of *A. commutatum*. The leaves have a large central area of yellow. *A. costatum* has dark green leaves spotted white, and a bright white midrib, and *A. commutatum* has diagonal creamy lines running parallel to the side veins.

Aglaonemas need a fairly high temperature and humidity, especially in winter, with a minimum of 10 °C (50 °F) and no draughts. A good light, or even some shade, are suitable, though the variegation will be better in the light. Water and feed normally, resting in winter, and do not subject to gas or paraffin fumes. Use cuttings for increase.

Aluminium plant, see **Pilea**

Amaryllis, see **Hippeastrum**

Ananas (pineapple)*

Although it seems highly unlikely, it is quite possible to grow *Ananas comosus*, the pineapple, in a dwarf form, in the

home. It is a bromeliad, with narrow, spiny-edged green leaves in the usual rosette. There is a more interesting variety called 'Variegatus' whose leaves have a bright yellow margin. The pineapple plants grown to produce fruit are about 2 m (6½ ft) in diameter, with 1.2 m (4 ft) long leaves, but there are dwarf forms for decorative use.

The pineapple is a native of tropical America, first introduced in 1690, and the fruit was given its common name because it was thought to look a little like the cones of the Scots pine which were then called 'pynappels'.

The plant needs more warmth than most of the other bromeliads if it is to

fruit, otherwise it can be kept in moderate warmth of about 16 °C (60 °F) for most of the year, not lower than about 10 °C (50 °F) in winter. As a terrestrial bromeliad, it likes some soil in the compost; a good light and watering and feeding in the usual way are also acceptable. The variegated form is allergic to draughts.

In Victorian days it was much grown in hot-houses where it could easily be made to produce fruit.

Pineapple plants fruit at three years old, sometimes two in the home, but do need temperatures in the 20s C (70–80 °F) through the summer and well above 10 °C (50 °F) in winter, with

repotting in spring. Feeding while growing should not be forgotten. Increase is by detaching the offsets, or rooting the tuft of leaves at the top of the fruit in sandy compost, with warmth. As soon as the fruit is picked, slice the tuft off with one layer of pips, bury the layer in the compost, and put a plastic bag over pot and leaves until rooted (see also page 23).

Anthurium (flamingo plant) ***

The anthuriums are beautiful and unusual flowering plants, belonging to the same family as the wild cuckoo pint, or lords and ladies, which grows in hedgerows. The flower consists of a

available, giving the variety of colour. There is also one called *A. crystallinum*, which is grown for its foliage—the thick, olive-green leaves are large, 60 cm (2 ft) long, and distinctively outlined in white. This one needs plenty of space.

The anthuriums come from the tropical rain forests of South America, and the essentials for good growth are humidity, warmth of soil and air, a peaty compost and plenty of water when growing. Temperature in winter should be not less than 16 °C (60 °F), and as high as possible in summer, provided the atmosphere is humid. Use rain-water at room temperature for

Opposite top: *Ananas comosus*, the pineapple. Left: *Aglaonema commutatum.* Right: *Anthurium scherzerianum*

brilliantly red or pink, sometimes white, spathe (like a single large petal) and a coiled or straight spadix, on a stem 30–60 cm (1–2 ft) above the shiny green, spear-shaped or heart-shaped leaves. The main flowering season is the spring, but they can be had in flower for most of the year.

Anthurium scherzerianum and *A. andreanum* hybrids are the flowering kinds

both misting and watering, and supply a good light, but not direct sun.

The plants take well to hydroculture, provided they are fed with nutrients specially supplied for this form of cultivation; in compost they should not be fed as often as other plants, but only every three to four weeks, depending on the size and rapidity of growth.

Dry atmospheres and direct sun will

65

result in withering leaves and flowers, and infestation of red spider mite.

Increase is by dividing plants in spring, with great care, ensuring that the least injury possible is done to them, and that each piece has plenty of roots. Otherwise seed can be used, sown in spring in moist peat and a temperature of 27 °C (80 °F). With less warmth, the seeds germinate very slowly or not at all.

Aphelandra (zebra plant)**

It is easy to forget that the plants we grow with such care in pots in the home may be large and vigorous in their natural terrain. The zebra plant, for instance, is a bushy evergreen shrub in Brazil, where it grows 1–2 m (3–6 ft) tall.

Aphelandras are usually seen for sale in early winter; buy one whose bracts have only just started to separate, so that it lasts in flower as long as possible. When you get it home, water it every day; the leaves wilt in no time if the roots are short of water. Then they fall, and very shortly you are left with a bare stem and a tuft of leaves and flower at the top. It likes humidity, too; spray it every two or three days and supply evaporating water close to it by whatever means. It is one of the plants which does very well in a group of plants, all giving off moisture and making their own local micro-climate.

A lot of the difficulty comes because aphelandras are introduced to the home in early winter, when the atmosphere is dry and smoky, and plants tend to get forgotten anyway. Zebra plants are especially sensitive, so it really pays to keep an eye on them.

A good light, and a temperature of about 16–18 °C (60–65 °F) are advisable. Keep a zebra plant out of draughts, as they will make it drop its leaves.

When the flowerhead is starting to wither, cut it off with one or two pairs of leaves, to just above another pair, and continue to water. It will then produce sideshoots lower down the stem, and can be grown on and kept for the following winter. In spring, it should have a larger pot and new compost. Feed in summer and autumn.

Above: *Aphelandra squarrosa*. Opposite: *Araucaria heterophylla*, or Norfolk Island Pine

Alternatively, when the flowers have finished, the stem can be cut down to a stump of about 7.5 cm (3 in), less water given, the temperature lowered slightly and the plant forced to rest for a few weeks. Then it can be given more warmth and water, and when sideshoots start to grow from the leaf joints, it can be repotted and grown on. This will give a shorter but much bushier plant, though not as easy to produce.

Aralia, see Fatsia

Aralia, finger, see Dizygotheca

Araucaria*

Norfolk Island is an Australian island in the Pacific 1,280 km (800 miles) away from New South Wales. It is tiny, with an area of 3,367 hectares (13 square miles), and was discovered by Captain Cook in 1774. The Norfolk Island pine, *Araucaria heterophylla* (syn. *A. excelsa*), is a relative of the monkey puzzle, *A. araucana* but, unlike the latter, is not completely hardy. It is also found in eastern Australia.

As a houseplant, it is easy to grow and takes kindly to container cultivation in which it remains small, although in the wild it may reach 60 m (200 ft). It is evergreen, with horizontal shoots and branches radiating from the main trunk in regular tiers. The leaves are short and needle-like, but so arranged on the shoots that they look lacy and frond-like—the plant looks more like a fern with a trunk than the miniature tree it in fact is.

With good cultivation it will grow
1–2 m (3–6 ft) tall and more. A good
light or a little shade, cool conditions
in winter and moderately warm in
summer, and normal humidity, watering and feeding are all that it asks.
Repotting each spring will be needed,
in a standard soil-containing compost,
and be sure that there is a good quantity of drainage material in the pot base.
A dry atmosphere and lack of ventilation can result in leaf drop, and even
red spider mite in winter. At this time,
when it is kept cool, it should be barely
watered, only enough to keep the compost just moist.

Artillery plant, see **Pilea microphylla**

Asparagus 'fern'*

This is the plant with feathery leaves so
often used in corsages and wedding
bouquets. Its botanic name is *Asparagus
plumosus* or *A. setaceus* now, and the
small form of this, *A. p. nanus*, is the
best one to grow in the home, otherwise it becomes very tall. The fronds
are very like those of the edible asparagus, *A. officinalis*, which can quite well
be used in flower arrangements as well.

There is another kind of asparagus
'fern', *A. densiflorus* (syn. *A. sprengeri*),
which is very commonly grown; it has
very long trailing stems with rather
untidy, needle-like leaves, less fine, but
still feathery and decorative. Finally,
there is *A. asparagoides* (syn. *A. medeo-
loides*), the smilax used by florists.

All these come from South Africa,
but in spite of that are not difficult to
grow in temperate climates and do not
need great heat, as might be expected.
Temperature in winter can drop to 4 °C
(40 °F), and normal temperatures in
summer are quite satisfactory. Shade
or light (not sun) are equally suitable.
Plenty of water in summer, but sparing
amounts in winter, and feeding in summer, will produce thriving plants. If
any of the fronds become rather straggly and leafless, cut them back to soil
level. In a very dry atmosphere they
will lose their leaves, so supply humidity and spray every few days. New
plants are easily obtained by dividing
the old ones in spring, when repotting.

Aspidistra*

The aspidistra is as much a piece of Victoriana as fringed chenille table-cloths, glass domes with stuffed birds inside them and whatnots. In fact whatnots were probably invented for aspidistras, so that they could be sufficiently elevated to be a centre of attention.

So many aspidistras were grown that they eventually became rather boring parts of the furniture, a music-hall joke, and descended into oblivion. Now, however, the attraction of their large, glossy, gracefully arching leaves has been rediscovered, and the modern know-how on plant care ensures that they no longer become dusty and brown edged, but thrive to the extent that they even produce their curious flowers.

Aspidistra elatior comes from the lower slopes of the Himalayas in China, and was introduced to cultivation in 1822. The leaves grow on short stalks in a cluster straight out of the crown just below soil level, and the whole plant can be at least 45 cm (1½ ft) tall. Although grown as a foliage plant, it does have flowers occasionally, in late winter or early spring. Thick and fleshy, they emerge from the soil, without any stems, brownish-purple in colour, round and quite small. *A. e. variegata* has creamy-white striped leaves, and needs more light to maintain this variegation, but little feeding.

Part of the aspidistra's popularity was due to its constitution, which was thought to enable it to put up with more or less any treatment: no water, too much water, cigar ash, darkness, gas, draughts, tea, beer, and the same compost throughout its life. However, although tough and long-suffering, there are limits, and in any case, the right treatment will give a much more ornamental plant.

It is, however, quite true that it is not fussy about temperature or light: 4 °C (40 °F) in winter, shade or light and warmth in summer are all one to the aspidistra. Normal watering and feeding are in order; the occasional

68

spray overhead, and sponging to clean the leaves will keep them glossy. A dry atmosphere, however, will encourage browning of the leaf tips, and brown spots will appear if overwatered at the roots, or if sun shines through water drops on the leaves. Increase is by taking off suckers in spring, making sure that each piece has roots attached; a 10 cm (4 in) pot is a suitable size for one sucker.·

Asplenium nidus (bird's-nest fern)**

As with many bromeliads, this tropical fern is an epiphyte, living on the trees of the rain forests of Africa and Asia, and also in Australia. Its fronds are totally unlike the conventional fern, as they consist of a single segment forming a leaf blade like that of an ordinary flowering plant, glossy and light green in colour. They form a kind of funnel-shaped rosette, for the same reason that the bromeliads do, and can become enormous, up to 20 cm (8 in) wide and 90 cm (3 ft) long, in the right conditions of warmth and moisture.

The brown spore-containers form a kind of herringbone pattern on the underside of the adult leaves, and the spores will germinate, given a temperature of 27 °C (80 °F) and really damp conditions.

The bird's-nest fern is one for the warm bathroom; some shade, humidity and a minimum winter tempera-

Far left: *Asparagus setaceus* trails gracefully across a window, its frail fronds in marked contrast to the strong glossy leaves of an *Asplenium nidus*, or bird's nest fern (centre). Above: The Victorians loved *Aspidistra elatior*, which tolerates shade well

ture of 13 °C (55 °F) are preferred. Give it a peaty compost and the occasional spray so that water runs down the leaves into the centre. Use a nitro-

genous fertilizer while growing. It is an epiphyte and so will grow in peaty compost bound on to bark, hung from a support.

Azalea **

The lovely azaleas are one of the most glamorous of flowering pot plants; the pink or red double flowers are frilled so that they look like crumpled tissue paper—something out of a scene from Madame Butterfly. This is hardly surprising: very many of our azaleas, both outdoor and tender, come from Japan, from the tea gardens there. The Emperor's garden in Tokyo was the source of some of the first azaleas to be sent back to Europe.

The indoor azaleas are small evergreen shrubs, bred from the Japanese *Rhododendron indicum*, and from R. *simsii*, the so-called Indian azalea which in fact grows in China and Indo-China. They are nearly hardy, so do not need or like high temperatures: round about 16 °C (60 °F) is suitable while they are indoors, and a drop to 10 °C (50 °F) at night will not hurt.

You should aim for an airy (but not draughty), humid and moderately warm atmosphere. Stuffiness, too much heat and dry air will quickly lead to leaf and flower drop. A light place, but neither direct sunlight nor shade, will bring the buds out and ensure that the flowers last as long as possible. Daily misting is good, but not spraying as this marks the flowers.

A good deal of water is needed while in flower, and daily watering will be needed; a ring or watermark round the main stem will show the amount required. The higher this mark is, the less should be given, but if no mark is visible and the pot feels light, plunge the pot in a bucket of tepid water over the compost surface. Use lime-free water always, at room temperature.

After flowering, cut back all the old shoots by about one-eighth of their length, to just above a sideshoot; this will make the plant produce new shoots, which will flower next winter. Then pot into a slightly larger pot, using a peaty, *acid* compost, and put outdoors if possible in a slightly shaded place for summer, when risk of frost is past. Sink the pot in the soil of a border, feed every two weeks and remember to water. This is the plant's resting and ripening period. In autumn bring in before the weather becomes cold, stop feeding, water sparingly and increase the temperature a little. Flower buds will come on quickly, when watering can be increased. Cuttings of young shoots taken in summer, and rooted in warmed compost will give new plants.

Bead plant, see **Nertera**

Begonia*/**

The begonia family takes well to container cultivation in the home, and contains a very varied and attractive range of plants. Many grow from tubers, some of which are completely dormant

Opposite: Azaleas come in red and white as well as pink. Below: *Begonia semperflorens*

in winter, others are fibrous-rooted and can have shoots and stems all year, though growth is slower in winter. Some have extremely colourful leaves, particularly the *Begonia rex* hybrids. Some have massive, brilliantly coloured double, sometimes fimbriated flowers, others have small flowers, but in great quantities for many months, sometimes flowering continuously through the year. You could have a beautiful display of pot plants all year round by growing only different species and hybrids of begonias.

The double-flowered begonias grown from tubers need plenty of water while growing, a good light but not sun, a humid atmosphere and feeding from early summer until autumn. In late autumn they will die down of their own accord and watering should be gradually decreased. The withered stems are completely removed and the tubers left dry but frost-free until late

winter, then put into moist peat with the top just above the surface, and temperature of about 16 °C (60 °F). New shoots will appear from the top of the tuber, and when these are about 5 cm (2 in) tall, the tuber can be potted into fresh standard potting compost and a 13–15 cm (5–6 in) pot.

The *B. rex* hybrids have beautiful, pointed-heart-shaped leaves, coloured in shades of wine, pink, grey and green, spotted and lined in these colours. They are brighter than many flowering plants, and a group of them is quite dazzling. Height is about 30–60 cm (1–2 ft). Another good foliage begonia is *B. masoniana* ('Iron Cross'), whose corrugated light-green leaves have a dark purple-brown marking, shaped like a cross on the surface.

The rather thin leaves of the Rex hybrids need a good deal of humidity, no draughts and steady temperatures of about 18 °C (65 °F), otherwise they brown at the edges or in the centre. You must be careful with the watering: a teaspoon or two too much can make the difference between a healthy, enlarging plant, and one which diminishes and withers before your eyes. Give them a peaty compost when repotting.

Increase the Rex hybrids by removing a leaf, making cuts across the main veins, and laying the leaf flat on the surface of a sandy compost, weighing it down with one or two pebbles. Cover with a clear plastic bag and put in a warm shaded place, when roots and plantlets will appear at the cuts in a few weeks.

Begonias are often seen out of doors in summer as bedding plants, with a mass of small flowers, pink, red or white, with light-green or wine-red leaves. These are easily grown in pots, to flower from late spring until mid autumn, or through the winter—the semperflorens begonias. A good light, but no or little direct sun, water most days, and feeding, will keep them flowering until dried off and rested.

Another small-flowered begonia, of quite a different type, with a tuber, is *B. sutherlandii*. This has masses of small orange flowers in a kind of Victorian fringe dangling down round the outside of the plant; the leaves form a rounded mound out of which come yet more flowers and, apart from watering it every day when in full flower, it needs no other attention. The standard potting compost is quite suitable, and a good light. In winter it is dried off and kept frost-free.

There is now also a modern strain of flowering begonias, whose flower size is between the large hybrids and those just described. These are the German Rieger begonias, which are excellent indoor plants, flowering continuously from spring until well into winter. Red, orange and salmon are the colours, and 'Fireglow' is one of the best.

Mildew can be a trouble with begonias, in stuffy conditions, when plants are short of water at the roots.

Beloperone guttata (shrimp plant)*

The shrimp plant will flower all the year round if you let it, but it is better to force it to rest for a few weeks, in winter, otherwise it becomes weak and does not live long.

It comes from Mexico, where it grows into a bushy evergreen shrub, about 90 cm (3 ft) tall. The 'flowers' are pinky orange and more or less the same shape as shrimps; their 'petals' are actually bracts. The real flowers are small and white, spotted with purple, and protrude from between the bracts. There is a variety with yellow

bracts called 'Yellow Queen'.

Beloperones are both highly ornamental and amenable. Sun, shade or a good light, normal watering and standard potting composts are suitable. Feed from early summer until late autumn, but then cease feeding, and give less water so that growth slows down and the plant just ticks over for a few weeks. A lower temperature will encourage it to rest, as well. At the end of winter it can be cut back by about half, potted into new compost and started off again. Cuttings a few centimetres long, taken from new shoots before flowers appear and put into peaty compost and warmth, will supply new plants.

Billbergia nutans*

This bromeliad is one of the easiest to grow. J. G. Billberg was a Swedish botanist of the late nineteenth century, and this namesake is a terrestrial bromeliad from Brazil and Central America.

Its long, leathery, grass-like, narrow leaves are spiny on the edges growing in funnel-shaped clusters to produce a plant about 30–45 cm (1–1½ ft) tall and wide. The flowerhead is very curious; it dangles at the ends of the 25 cm (10 in) stems, and consists of bright, rose-pink bracts like a bud, out of which grow elongated flowers, coloured navy-blue, yellow, green and pink, all together. Flowering occurs in spring over a period of several weeks.

Give billbergia a peaty soil compost and put it in the shade; too much light will turn the leaves a nasty yellowish green. Moderate warmth in summer and a minimum winter temperature of 7 °C (45 °F), together with normal bromeliad watering and feeding will suit it. Repot in mid summer using a pan if possible, and water sparingly until it has settled down. At the same time you can detach some of the offsets which will have formed and pot them separately into small 10 cm (4 in) pots, and they should flower the following spring or early summer.

Bird's-nest fern, see **Asplenium**

Black-eyed Susan, see **Thunbergia**

Boat lily, see **Rhoeo**

Bread plant, Mexican, see **Monstera**

Bunny ears, see **Opuntia**

Busy Lizzie, see **Impatiens**

Cacti, see **Chamaecereus, Gymnocalycium, Mammillaria, Opuntia, Rebutia, Rhipsalidopsis, Schlumbergera**

Caladium***

The jungles of Brazil and the Amazon are the home of the caladiums. They are not easy plants to look after in home conditions, but they are some of the most beautiful foliage pot plants. Most of them are hybrids from *Caladium bicolor* and the leaves can be large, as much as 50 cm (20 in) long, paper-thin and silvery green, delicately spotted, mottled or veined with dark green, wine-red, crimson, purple or white. In the right conditions, depending on variety, they can grow into quite large plants, 60–90 cm (2–3 ft) wide and nearly as much tall, but the varieties grown indoors are usually much smaller.

The caladiums are not evergreen: the leaves die down in autumn, and the plants have a rest, during what would be the dry season in their natural home. They are tuberous-rooted, and the roots of *C. bicolor* are edible, known as cocoa roots in the tropics. As members of the *Araceae* or aroid family, they have arum-like flowers, but these are insignificant and are usually not produced in container cultivation.

A high degree of humidity is essential, combined with considerable warmth. Even while resting the temperature should not fall below 13 °C (55 °F). Give them light, but not direct midday sun, for best leaf colouring. Keep them very warm in spring, summer and autumn and mist them and the atmosphere frequently, as well as providing humidity in other ways. Otherwise the leaves will brown rapidly at the edges and wither. Cold draughts are, of course, unthinkable. Caladiums

Left: *Beloperone guttata,* the shrimp plant. Opposite: *Billbergia nutans,* or angel's tears

drink a lot while growing and also need a good deal of food, therefore, as well as rich peaty compost, feeding once a fortnight is required.

In late summer as they die down, give less water, and a lower temperature, and leave them in their containers through the winter, keeping the compost just moist. Then repot in spring, and start watering again. Increase by taking off the offsets, but not until they have formed their own leaves and roots.

Calamondin, see **Citrus**

Campanula isophylla (Italian bellflower)*

The campanulas are those pretty plants grown in herbaceous borders, with blue or purple bell-like (campanulate) flowers in summer; the one called Canterbury bells is a biennial form. This one, which is grown as an indoor plant, is nearly hardy, but does not survive frost, and is a native of northern Italy. The stems are long, with a tendency to trail. The blue flowers 2.5 cm

Top: *Caladium bicolor* 'Angel's Wings'; right: *Campanula isophylla* and *C. i. alba*; far right: fruits of the *Capsicum*

74

(1 in) wide start to appear in mid summer and continue successively until late mid autumn. There is a white variety called *alba*, which is equally enthusiastic about flowering. There is a variety with woolly leaves variegated in white called *mayii*, but it is difficult to obtain.

The Italian bellflower is easy to grow, and is very satisfactory in hanging baskets. With a standard potting compost, a good light or some sun, and plenty of warmth in summer, it will flower as described. A cool season means no flowers until late mid summer and it may then stop flowering in early autumn. It will drink a good deal at this time. Take off the flowers as soon as they have finished, unless you want seed; this will help to keep up production of bloom.

When growth has finished for the season, cut off the trailing stems, back to where there will probably be new leaves and little shoots appearing, keep it cool for the winter, and water sparingly. If you keep it too warm it will try to grow and weaken itself. Increase is easy, by division in spring or by taking 5 cm (2 in) cuttings in late spring or early summer before flowers appear, and rooting them in warmth, shade and a peaty compost.

Cane, dumb, see **Dieffenbachia**

Cape primrose, see **Streptocarpus**

Capsicum (Christmas or ornamental pepper)*/**

All sorts of peppers or capsicums have become popular in the last few years, either as vegetables, or as spicy flavourings for food. Strains of these have been selected which are particularly ornamental in fruit and are now available for home cultivation. *Capsicum frutescens* and *C. annuum* are the two main parents; they are tropical plants mostly grown and used in India, Thailand, East and West Africa and Spain.

You will usually see them for sale during early to mid winter, with bright red, orange or yellow fruits, the colour depending on the stage of maturity. The fruit is long-cone-shaped, about 2.5 cm (1 in) long, held upright on a bushy little plant about 23 cm (9 in) tall, and if you make sure the atmosphere where the plant is growing is moist, the fruit will last a long time before they begin to wrinkle, and finally drop off.

They are edible, although because they have been selected primarily for their appearance, they will not be as well-flavoured as those grown for spicing food. However, they are very hot, so be warned.

When grown as a pot plant, they need warmth in winter, over 10 °C (50

°F), normal watering while the fruits are still plump, a daily overhead spray, and humidity at all times.

Although the plant is often thrown away after fruiting, most can, in fact, be kept and will flower and fruit again, with the right treatment. When the fruits have fallen, the plant can be rested by reducing the temperature and watering. Then, in early spring, cut last year's new growth back by about half, repot the plant into fresh compost, using a fairly rich one, and give more warmth and water. Put outdoors once frost is unlikely, in a sunny place, and flowers will appear in early summer. Spraying the plant, especially on hot days, will encourage fruit to set, and from then until mid autumn, it should be fed once a fortnight. Bring in when the weather begins to get cold.

Watch for red spider mite, which are very partial to peppers, as are whitefly.

Castor oil plant, false, see Fatsia

Ceropegia woodii (hearts entangled)*

Ceropegias are trailing plants and grow so easily and quickly that they are first-class plants for using as room dividers or hanging down a window as living curtains. Literally metres of stem will hang down, festooned with the heart-shaped, thick, puffy leaves, each with white marbling on grey-green, and purple markings at the edges.

Although it grows from a corm 5 cm (2 in) wide, and has long stems, cero-pegia is a succulent, and is in the same family as hoyas. It comes from South Africa. Small brownish-purple, lantern-shaped flowers appear in summer and

autumn, from between the paired leaves, down the whole length of the stem, but they are not very spectacular, and the plant is really grown for its long leafy stems.

Temperature in winter can drop as low as 7 °C (45 °F), though if kept a little warmer it will produce new shoots. In summer it is happy in normal temperatures and will do well outdoors in a hanging basket. Light or some shade are equally suitable. Feed occasionally in summer. It takes well to the soil-less composts; in the standard soil composts, it should be watered only sparingly in winter, normally at other times. Increase is by cuttings put in sandy compost in spring, with a temperature of 18 °C (65 °F), or by corm-lets produced on the stems. Humidity is not very important. If any of the stems start to wither, they should be removed.

Chamaecereus sylvestrii*

The cacti are exceedingly varied in shape and flowering ability; chamae-cereus is one of the most easily grown, and one of the readiest to flower. It is a small plant from western and northern Argentina, being only 7.5–10 cm (3–4 in) tall, in a kind of mound of fat, worm-like, bristly stems about the length of a finger. Each stem can erupt into one or more vividly red flowers 2–3 cm (1 in or so) wide in late spring or early summer.

Chamaecereus quite quickly becomes a tangle of these thick stems, and needs repotting each spring, or some of the shoots can be taken off and potted singly in 5 cm (2 in) pots in mid summer. In fact, they usually fall off when the plant is being repotted. These should themselves flower the following year. All that need be done with each shoot is to ensure that the base is firmly in touch with the compost surface, which should be moist but not soak-ing, and leave it in as much heat and light as possible. They root very easily; there is no need to bury the base and if you did this, it would rot. A little propping up with compost so that it does not fall over is permissible.

Give your chamaecereus the standard

cacti care (see page 54), that is, a gritty compost, warmth and sun all through summer, normal watering and feeding at that time, no feed and practically no water in winter (about once a month) and a dry atmosphere. *Chamaecereus sylvestrii* is even more accommodating: in winter the temperature can drop to freezing and, provided it is dry, it will not be harmed, although it may shrivel a little, and will actually flower better.

Chamaedorea elegans (syn. *Neanthe bella*) (parlour palm)*

If you want a tall, graceful plant for your living-room, then a palm is usually a good choice. Their arching stems and fronds are elegant and airy, and chamaedorea is one of the smaller palms with these qualities. Each leaf blade is wider and shorter than those of many palms, giving it a more obviously pinnate look, and it does not very often grow much taller than about 75 cm (2 ft).

It is the only one likely to produce flowers – small yellow blobs dotted along the flower stem in a kind of plume which, if they set, are followed by pea-like, shiny fruits. The hotter and sunnier the weather is during summer, the more likely is chamaedorea to produce these flowers, usually when three or more years old, and the fruits can be used for increase.

The origin of this palm is Mexico, where it grows in the shade of taller trees. Provided you supply reasonable warmth, a little shade, and plenty of water in summer but only a little in winter, it will grow well, though slowly. Occasional feeding in summer will be welcome, and some humidity if the temperature becomes very high. In winter it prefers to be on the cool side, 7–10 °C (45–50 °F). Young plants need repotting every spring, older ones every two or three years.

If your plant sets fruit, the seeds from these can be used for increase, sown in early spring. They germinate slowly, even in the high temperatures of 20–24 °C (70–75 °F) required, in warm, peaty compost. Three seeds are sufficient for a small deep pot, and only pot the young plants separately when a few centimetres tall, taking extreme care not to injure the roots. Keep them out of the sun until they have settled down and are growing.

Cherry, Christmas, see **Solanum**

Chionodoxa (glory of the snow)*

The chionodoxa is a hardy plant grown from a bulb. It is so charming that it is worth potting a few in a pan in autumn, and bringing them on a little early, to flower just as you're beginning to think that winter is never going to end. It comes from the eastern Mediterranean and the mountains of Crete and western Turkey, and flowers as the snow melts. In summer it dies down completely and remains dormant in ground baked hard by the sun.

The brilliant blue starry flowers are in a loose cluster, 15 cm (6 in) or more tall, with narrow leaves surrounding them. Large bulbs produce several flowering stems. There are varieties in

Opposite below: *Ceropegia woodii*; above: *Chamaecereus sylvestrii*; left: *Chamaedorea elegans* and below: *Chionodoxa sardensis*

different shades of blue, and also pink or white-flowered kinds.

Pot the bulbs in well-drained compost in very early autumn, 2.5 cm (1 in) or so deep, about six in an 8 cm (3½ in) pan, put them in a cold place, outdoors if possible, until early mid winter, to grow roots, and then gradually give them a higher temperature. Don't forget to look after their water needs while they are rooting. Water and feed after flowering until they die down, and then leave them to dry until autumn, then repot in new compost. Increase by offsets.

Chlorophytum (spider plant)*

The spider plant could be said to be the modern equivalent of the aspidistra; its ease of cultivation is outstanding, and

it will even survive slight frost. The white roots are thick and fleshy, almost tuberous, and are produced in great quantities. It grows plantlets at the ends of long arching stems which soon put out their own roots, even in mid air. With all this vitality and vigour, one trembles to think what it must be like on its home ground in South Africa.

A variegated form, *Chlorophytum comosum variegatum* is the one commonly seen. Its grass-like leaves have a central white band. The stems are deep cream coloured and may produce small white flowers along the end few centimetres, followed by rosettes of small leaves

which form the new plantlets. A well grown plant can be 45 cm (18 in) wide by 37 cm (15 in), with stems hanging down all round it and masses of new little plants at the ends.

There is a form with plain green leaves, which is not as vigorous, and also one with variegation on the margins of the leaves, but in creamy yellow; this is called *C. elatum variegatum*. Both the variegated chlorophytums will be much more distinctively variegated if kept in a good light, near a window, but not in direct sunlight. Put in a corner away from the light, they will become rather anaemic green all over, very dull and uninteresting.

The main point about these plants is that they grow fast, and will need repotting in spring, and again in early or mid summer. Standard potting compost, normal watering and feeding, and ordinary summer temperatures will suit them; winter temperatures can go quite low, as already mentioned. If the tips of the leaves turn brown, the atmosphere is too dry, or you may have let the roots get dry, through not realizing

that it needs a good deal of water in summer.

Take off the plantlets when they have grown some root, and pot singly into 7.5 cm (3 in) pots, because they will grow quickly.

Christmas cactus, see **Schlumbergera**

Christmas cherry, see **Solanum**

Christmas pepper, see **Capsicum**

Chrysanthemum*

The chrysanthemum is a glorious flower which has a history of cultivation stretching back at least 2,000 years. It is said to have been grown in China in 500 B.C., and in A.D. 400 its breeding and cultivation spread to Japan, where it soon became an Imperial flower, in much the same way that swans are a royal bird in England.

The large-flowered kind was not sent back to England in any quantity by plant hunters until 1796; previously only 'Blancard's Purple', introduced about 1790, from Marseille, was grown.

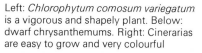

Left: *Chlorophytum comosum variegatum* is a vigorous and shapely plant. Below: dwarf chrysanthemums. Right: Cinerarias are easy to grow and very colourful

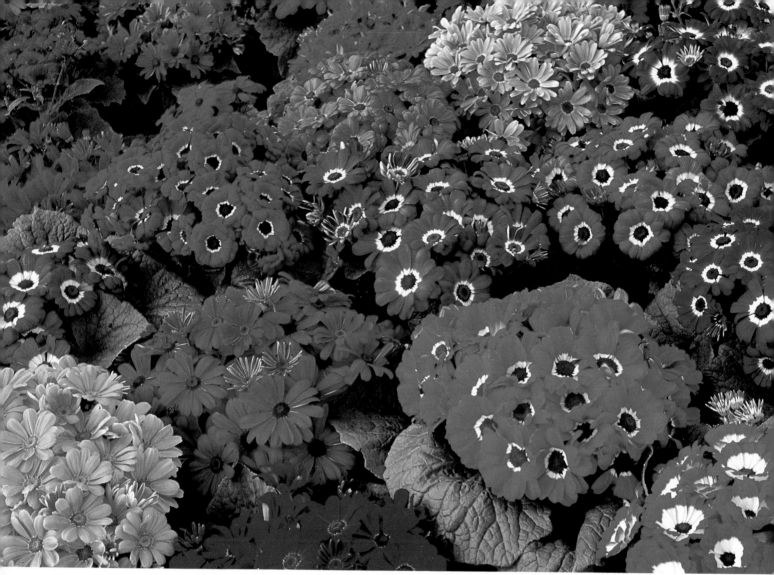

Since then, a great deal of breeding and selection have gone on, so that there are now not only the large-flowered reflex and incurve kinds, but also sprays, pompoms, singles, cascade, Korean, charm, and other kinds. Some are hardy, some need greenhouse protection, and others are at their best in container cultivation.

The type of chrysanthemum now sold all year round, as a bushy small plant, with a mass of flowers in the glowing autumn colours so typical of the chrysanthemum, has been given 'short-day' treatment to ensure that it will flower in succession through the year. It has also been watered with a chemical solution which has the effect of making it flower when small. When you buy or are given one of these plants, it should flower for nearly two months. Look for a plant which has perhaps three or four flowers out and a mass of flower buds. If any of these have black centres, don't buy the plant; the buds should be green and quite near to flowering.

Water the plant daily, keep it cool and in a good light, and take off the flowers as they finish. When flowering is over, if you continue to feed and water the plant, and cut the stems back a little, it will produce sideshoots, and the ones nearest the soil can be used as cuttings. These will produce normal-sized plants eventually, which flower in autumn or early winter. The parent plant is thrown away after flowering or being used for cuttings.

Cineraria*

The florists' cinerarias have been selected during the last 60 years or so from a species of *Cineraria* (syn. *Senecio*) which inhabits the Canary Islands. The result is plants which are a mass of daisy-flowers, some single, some more or less double, in the most exquisite jewel-like colours. A display of the multiflora kinds in pots looks as though several rainbows at once have fallen on to the table. The royal blue and white kinds and the old rose-pink ones are especially distinctive.

You can buy pot specimens in winter, usually between early winter and spring. When growing them as pot plants, bought in flower, they will do best in a cool place, about 7–10 °C (45–50 °F); give them plenty of water as they drink a lot when in full flower, and lose a lot through their large leaves. A good light or a little shade, but never sun, is preferred, and a humid atmosphere. Cinerarias are to greenfly what rump steak is to us, so keep a very sharp eye open for them; they collect first in the tips of shoots and round unopened flower buds, and seem to multiply faster than the speed of light. Another trouble can be leaf-miners, which also seem to think that cinerarias were specially invented for them.

Growing cinerarias from seed is not difficult. They can be sown from mid spring to end of early summer and will flower the following early winter to early spring, depending on the sowing time. Sow the seed thinly in seed compost, finely sieved, and barely cover with polythene or glass and keep moist and shaded until germinated. Then remove the cover, and move the seedlings, when three leaves have formed, into a box, spacing them at 5 cm (2 in) intervals each way. Later they can be moved singly into 11 cm ($4\frac{1}{2}$ in) pots and then 15 cm (6 in) as they grow, in standard potting compost, keeping them always on the cool side, out of the sun, and well watered. Feeding is advisable from autumn until flowering.

Cissus antarctica (kangaroo vine)*

Don't worry, this plant doesn't leap about the house all the time. *Cissus antarctica* is in fact Australian, a climbing plant which hoists itself up other plants by coiling tendrils round them. Growth may be 15–30 cm (6–12 in) a year, and supports will be needed. It is evergreen, grown for its glossy leaves, which are rather like large beech leaves but darker green, and which clothe the stems all the way up. The name comes from the Greek *kissos*, ivy, a reference to its climbing habit.

The grape ivy is sometimes called *C. rhombifolia*, though at present it is usually known as *Rhoicissus rhomboidea* (see page 123). *C. discolor* is another species which is one of the most beautiful of foliage plants, with 15 cm (6 in) long, pointed, velvety leaves, coloured silvery white, olive-green, red and purple. It does, however, need a very high temperature, no lower than 16 °C (60 °F) in winter and as high as possible in summer, and an almost saturated atmosphere.

Cissus antarctica will grow well and easily in cool, slightly shaded places. It is a good plant for halls, window sills on north-facing landings, corners of bedrooms away from the light, or

Above: *Cissus antarctica*. Opposite top: *Citrus mitis*, the calamondin orange. Below: *Clivia miniata*

living-rooms, provided they are not centrally heated. A dry atmosphere makes the leaves curl up, turn brown and wither. In too much light, especially sun, transparent blotches appear on the leaves and then turn yellow and brown. An occasional spray, as well as some humidity, is helpful. Feed normally but do not water too much in summer, otherwise the leaves will turn brown, and be careful with winter watering as well. *C. antarctica* must always have good drainage material in the base of the pot. Cuttings of 3.5–5 cm ($1\frac{1}{2}$–2 in) length, with one leaf, will root in warmth, in spring or early summer.

Citrus mitis (calamondin)*/**

This neat little orange tree has only been easily obtainable from garden shops and stores since about 1965, but it has become very popular, in spite of its high price. To grow your own oranges in your own home is enough of an achievement, and miniature replicas are always fascinating, so a dwarf orange is bound to enchant a lot of people.

Full-size orange trees have been grown under cover, in orangeries, in winter throughout Europe for several centuries. Surprisingly, orange trees are almost hardy. The difficulty comes in summer when they need more heat and sun than Britain and northern Europe generally experience, to ripen the fruit.

However, the calamondin is not difficult to grow indoors. The height of this small bushy evergreen from the Philippines can be 30–45 cm (1–$1\frac{1}{2}$ ft), and the fragrant white flowers will open in spring and continue at intervals until the autumn. The edible fruit are 3.5 cm ($1\frac{1}{2}$ in) across, but are not sweet, rather sharp in fact. They make good marmalade. A plant can have flowers and ripe fruit on it at the same time. Ripening starts in late summer, and individual oranges can continue to change colour through the winter until the following spring's flowering.

A winter temperature of about 10 °C (50 °F) is needed and normal temperatures in summer, when the plant can be put outside in a sunny place, otherwise left on a sunny window sill. Spray it overhead occasionally—this will help the flowers to set—and supply humid air. Watering needs care because the roots are rather temperamental. The drainage should be good. Do not give too much water in summer and keep the compost slightly on the dry side in winter. Be careful when repotting not to damage the roots, and do not pot more often than is essential. Feed while growing. Increase can be from cuttings, rooted in warm, peaty compost, and an air temperature of 21–24 °C (70–75 °F). They should be about 10 cm (4 in) long, from new shoots in

spring, and plants will fruit in about two seasons (see also page 142).

Clivia miniata (kaffir lily)*

From the mountain valleys of Natal in South Africa, where it grows in a humus soil on top of a freely draining subsoil, the kaffir lily is one of the best behaved of pot plants. Bright orange, funnel-shaped flowers in clusters at the end of a single stem, 30–60 cm (1–2 ft) long, appear in spring, pushing up from between the narrow evergreen leaves, which themselves come straight out of the soil in a rosette, from a rather bulbous base. Clivias do not form proper bulbs, but build up layers of fleshy leaf bases which become rounded and bulb-like in time. New leaves develop in pairs, so that, in the end, a kind of central system is formed from the leaves. A ten-year-old plant can have as many as eight or nine flower-heads, each with a dozen flowers.

There are now varieties of clivia which have red-orange or yellow flowers, as well as orange, but all have yellow throats.

Temperature and watering are the two cultivation points to take particular care with. In winter the temperature should not rise above 14 °C (58 °F), and is better if kept nearer 10 °C (about 50 °F). It can drop to 7 °C (45 °F), if the plant is kept slightly dry. In summer moderate warmth is preferred, in the 16–21 °C (60–70 °F) range.

As you will have realized from the opening sentence, clivias are very sensitive to too much water; make sure the compost really does allow extra water to run through, and that it does not collect in the bottom of the pot. Give plenty of water at any one time, but then wait until the compost surface is really dry, and between autumn and mid winter, give very little, especially in cool conditions.

Otherwise, clivias are indifferent to humidity, like a good light with some sun at some time during the day for best flowering, and can be left in the same pot for several years, provided they are fed from spring until late mid summer. Leaving the pot in exactly the same position all the time gives the best

81

flowering results. Occasional spraying, and sponging of the leaves, gets rid of the dust and grit.

Watch for scale insect, which can get down between the leaf bases, and is then difficult to deal with. Increase by removing offsets when they have formed four to five leaves, and pot singly into peaty compost in 7.5 cm (3 in) pots. Use standard potting compost for older plants, and repot in later winter if necessary.

Clog plant, see **Hypocyrta**

Cobaea scandens (cup-and-saucer vine)*

The cup-and-saucer vine is a flowering plant climbing, with the help of its tendrils, to a height of anything up to 7.2 m (24 ft). Its home is Central and South America where it is a perennial plant, but in temperate regions it is grown as an annual from seed each year. The name comes from that of a Jesuit priest and naturalist, Father Cobo, of Elizabethan times.

The bell-shaped flowers have a ruff round the base; this is pale green on the outside and violet on the inside. The flowers are apple green when they first open, but turn white and finally violet, so that when the plant is in full flower in summer, it is extremely pretty with all these differently coloured flowers, all constantly changing. There is a form with white flowers, called 'Alba'.

The cup-and-saucer vine is quick growing and prolific to flower, but will need a good deal of climbing space, and a good light. Close to a floor-to-ceiling window, or glass door, is one of the best positions. It must be given strong canes for support and a large container.

If you are growing the plant yourself, sow the seed in late winter and early spring edgeways on, in a temperature of 16–18 °C (60–65 °F). Use a sandy compost and make sure the seed is fresh for reliable germination. Pot the seedlings into small pots as soon as they are large enough to handle, and

move the plant again as soon as they have filled their small pots with roots, into 15 cm (6 in) pots, in which they can flower; early summer should see the first of the buds.

Use a standard potting compost and always put the plant in a good light; this is important both for the number of flowers and intensity of colour. In a bad light, the flowers will be rather wishy-washy. Supply some humidity, and keep in normal summer temperatures. Feed towards the end of the summer to keep the flowers coming well.

Plants can be kept from year to year; allow them to rest between autumn and spring, with a lower temperature, 10 °C (50 °F), and less water. In late winter cut back the main stem hard, so that they sprout new shoots on which to flower, and cut out weak shoots completely. Then repot in fresh compost, and a larger pot if necessary.

Codiaeum (croton)***

The crotons are magnificent evergreen shrubs. They grow several metres tall in their native Indonesia, Polynesia and Malaya, and are now widely grown in the tropics as hedges. Their brilliant, beautifully coloured, rather tough leaves are the main reason for cultivation, each plant usually having three- or four-coloured leaves, in various combinations of green, yellow, pink, orange, red, white and brown, either spotted, lined, blotched or marbled, depending on variety. All are descended from *C. variegatum pictum*. Besides the tremendous variation in colour, the variation in leaf shape is also considerable, from narrow and grass-like to broad, lobed, crisped, fern-like and so on.

Steady warmth and humidity are the main needs; lack of either or subjection to draughts or a sudden drop in temperature results in rapid leaf drop. A minimum winter temperature of 16 °C (60 °F), and as high as possible in summer, combined with plenty of air

Left: *Cobaea scandens* flowers throughout the summer. Opposite top: *Coleus blumei*. Right: *Codiaeum* 'Madame Mayne'

humidity and overhead spraying, and plenty of water in summer, will give a thriving well-coloured plant. A good light, or little shade, or some direct sun will ensure good colouring, though be careful not to scorch them with too much sun.

In pots, crotons are usually 45–60 cm (1½–2 ft) tall, and need feeding once a week while growing; if they get much larger they will need feeding at a greater strength than recommended by the fertilizer supplier, and are probably the only exception to the rule of never ignoring fertilizer dilution recommendations.

Use standard potting compost when repotting in spring, and watch for scale insect and red spider mite. Increase is by cuttings—of leading shoots, not sideshoots—about 10–15 cm (4–6 in) long, put in a sand/peat mix with plenty of humidity and a temperature of about 24 °C (75 °F), using warmed compost. Singe the end of the cuttings before inserting, as they produce a white liquid, typical of their family, the spurge family or *Euphorbiaceae*.

Coleus (flame nettle)**

The flame nettle has rainbow leaves with fantastic colouring and leaf shape. The leaves of the species, *Coleus blumei*, and the early cultivars were all more or less nettle-shaped, but with rounded instead of pointed teeth on the margins. Now they have become fringed, fern-leaved, fingered, parsley-leaved, and antler-like in shape. They are blotched, veined, spotted, edged or marbled in various combinations of such colours as red, wine, pink, orange, bronze, green, cream, yellow and black.

Although they are grown for their highly coloured leaves, as codiaeums are, they do not resemble them in plant growth or cultivation. They are not really worth keeping through the winter, as the light is so poor then that they lose the brilliance of their colouring and become faded and sludge-coloured, as well as weak plants, likely to be infected with grey mould. The leaves are softly hairy and thin in texture. Instead of falling off, they wilt in cool or dry conditions.

As summer and autumn pot plants, however, coleuses are exceedingly attractive. Give them plenty of water and light, especially in warm weather, though too much sunlight will bleach the leaves. Shade will produce dull-coloured leaves. Remove flowers if they begin to appear. Provided a standard potting compost is used, of the second grade, no feeding will be required, and would actually tend to make the leaves all-green.

Coleuses are easily grown from seed sown in the dark in late winter at a temperature of 18–21 °C (65–70 °F). They are transplanted to boxes at 5 cm (2 in) apart each way, and then into 11 cm (4½ in) pots. Take out the growing tips when the plants have four or five pairs of leaves, and also the tips of the side-shoots at two pairs of leaves, for extra bushiness.

If you want to grow coleuses through the winter, keep the temperature above 16 °C (60 °F) and give them as much light as possible, even artificial light. Then repot in early spring and eventu-

ally grow as small shrubs. Watch for greenfly. Cuttings taken in early summer will root in water.

Columnea*

Although the columneas are named after an Italian botanical writer, Fabio Colonna, of the sixteenth to seventeenth centuries, most of the species now grown were not discovered and introduced until the early part of this century. They come from the tropical forests of Central America, the Panama Canal Zone and the West Indian islands, where they grow as epiphytes, some shrubby, some herbaceous, and mostly climbing or hanging down from the trees of the forest.

Columneas are spectacular flowering plants, with large, tubular orange, red or yellow flowers, along the length of the stems. Those grown in the home are winter-flowering species. *Columnea × banksii* has 5–7.5 cm (2–3 in) long, brown-orange flowers, lasting from late autumn to late winter, all down the hanging 60–90 cm (2–3 ft) stems. *C. gloriosa* 'Purpurea' has bright red, yellow-throated flowers, and leaves that are purplish when young and bronze when mature. *C. schiedeana*, which is slightly different, has red-flecked brown flowers, yellow inside, 120 cm (4 ft) long stems with a tendency to climb, and a flowering time from spring to early summer.

All the columneas might have been made for hanging baskets; their cascades of brilliant colour in winter have no equal, and hanging in mid-air suits them perfectly. The peaty compost suggested for the epiphyllums or bromeliads will be ideal, and the baskets (or pots) should be hung in a good light, but away from direct sun.

A very damp atmosphere is most important—central heating is not suitable unless humidifiers can be supplied—and a winter temperature of not less than 13 °C (55 °F) is needed for the winter-flowering kinds. *C. schiedeana* will be happy with 10 °C (50 °F). Tepid soft water should be given to keep the compost evenly moist at all times—more will be required in summer when they are growing new shoots. Feed in summer once a week and also repot at this time.

Once a length of stem has flowered, it will be more or less leafy thereafter, but flowers only come at the end of new growth so to prevent lengths of unflowery stem, cut the flowered ones back by about half, or even more, directly after flowering, so that the remaining stem is forced to put out new shoots near its base. Even so, you will need new plants within about three years, as there is a limit to how often this can be done.

Stem cuttings 7.5–10 cm (3–4 in) long will root in sandy compost if put into a moist warm atmosphere during late spring or early summer, with a temperature of about 18–21 °C (65–70 °F).

Conophytum (living stones)*

There are several kinds of succulent plants which have the common name 'living stone' (see also *Lithops*) because they are virtually indistinguishable, out of flower, from the pebbles, rocks and stones amongst which they live. Conophytum comes from West and South Africa, and scrapes a living from almost completely bare rock, where it grows in clumps.

The seasons for resting and growing vary according to species; when they are resting, no water is given at all—they must be completely dry.

Above: *Conophytum pearsonii*. Below left: *Columnea gloriosa* 'Purpurea' in full flower

Conophytum ficiforme has pink-lilac flowers 2.5 cm (1 in) wide which open at night, between autumn and spring. While flowering, it needs to be sparingly watered and given a good light and a temperature no lower than 13 °C (55 °F). At the same time as the flowers appear, new growth will also come and watering should continue until some time in spring when the plants begin to look dull coloured and have ceased to grow. Then they must rest completely, while the skin shrivels, for the summer months, in as hot and sunny a place as possible, until they start to look 'alive' again.

There is a selection of species available with flowers varying in colour—yellow, orange, purple, magenta or pink. They flower at different times, sometimes even in summer, so all must be treated individually as regards resting and growing. The conophytums increase naturally, forming larger and larger clumps. Individual plant bodies can be detached, with the stem, the skin removed, and then put into the standard well-drained compost for succulents, into which they will root.

Cordyline*/**

Eastern Asia, New Zealand and Australia are the homes of the cordylines, where they grow as decorative evergreen shrubs and trees. Like crotons (*Codiaeum*), they have dazzlingly coloured leaves, but in less variety, and a different range of colour, for instance wine-reds, pinks, rose, purple, dark green and cream flushed with pink.

The leaves of *Cordyline terminalis* kinds are oval, sometimes grow as

long as 30 cm (12 in), and the plant's central stem grows 60–90 cm (2–3 ft) tall, in containers. These cultivars are the more exacting in their requirements but also the prettier. *C. indivisa* is much hardier and rather palm-like, with long narrow, bronze-red-green leaves up a centre stem, perhaps 90 cm (3 ft) or more tall. It comes from New Zealand where it grows to 7.5 m (25 ft), and in Britain can be grown outdoors in the extreme south-west.

A good standard compost, and feeding through the summer, combined with plenty of soft water, a good light, and some humidity, will give strong, attractive plants. Normal summer temperatures for both, but no lower than 13 °C (55 °F) in winter for *terminalis* kinds. *C. indivisa* will take 4 °C (40 °F), provided the compost is only just moist.

One method of increase is unusual, as pieces (cuttings) of the fleshy roots can be used. Make them about 5 cm (2 in) long and put them in sandy soil

Above: *Cordyline terminalis* 'Firebrand'.
Below: *Crassula corymbulosa*

lengthwise, about 2.5 cm (1 in) deep, in spring. Provided they have a temperature of 24–27 °C (75–80 °F), they will root. A small, electrically heated propagator is very useful for this, and can also be used for plants whose seeds will only germinate at high temperatures. If you haven't got a propagator you can still take offsets from cordylines at any time, and they do not need such a high temperature to establish.

Crassula*

The crassulas are succulents, mostly from South Africa, though some come from tropical Africa, Arabia and Madagascar. Their habits of growth and leaf shapes are very varied, from shrubby to herbaceous. They can have fat succulent leaves, pointed, rounded or prickly ones, or thin leaves pressed close against the stem. They are so different to look at that, without the flowers, it is difficult to believe that they belong to the same family. However, since flowering plants are classified according to their floral characteristics, all these apparently unrelated plants belong together because their stamens, pistils, ovaries and so on are like one another but not like those of other plant groups.

Crassula arborescens is often seen as a pot plant not doing as well as it might, because it hasn't been watered. It is a small bushy plant, slowly growing to 90–120 cm (3–4 ft) after many years, with thick, spoon-shaped shiny leaves, and clusters of white starry flowers in late spring and early summer. *C. lycopodioides* is another commonly grown species, with small leaves pressed flat against the stems in layers, so that it looks like a collection of small green snakes.

Crassula falcata is a really beautiful succulent with thick, silvery grey leaves, shaped like sickles, and clusters of tiny red flowers on short stems in late spring; it is sometimes called the South African alpine rose. As it is inclined to lie down and turn into a prostrate plant, a support is a good idea. *C. lactea* has dark green, fleshy leaves and a cluster of fragrant white flowers on 15 cm (6 in) stems in late winter.

The crassulas are easily grown, provided you give them the water they need; without it the leaves gradually shrivel and fall off, the flowering kinds never do bloom, and the plants die slowly after a miserable existence. They need normal water (see page 17) while flowering, and during the growing time that follows, but from then until mid or late winter very little is needed —just enough to keep the compost barely moist. Give them perhaps one watering a month if the temperature is about 4–9 °C (40–49 °F), but every two or three weeks if about 10–15 °C (50–59 °F).

If, after the resting period, the compost is very dry, the addition of 5 ml of liquid detergent to 4.5 litres of the water used for watering (1 UK teaspoon to 1 UK gallon; 1 US teaspoon to 1¼ US gallons) will help it to penetrate all the way through.

Do not worry about humidity for these plants. Put most species in as sunny a position as possible, though some become tinted red or brown in too much light, and feed once a month while growing. Repot every two years or so, just as they start to grow again; this may be spring or mid summer depending on the species.

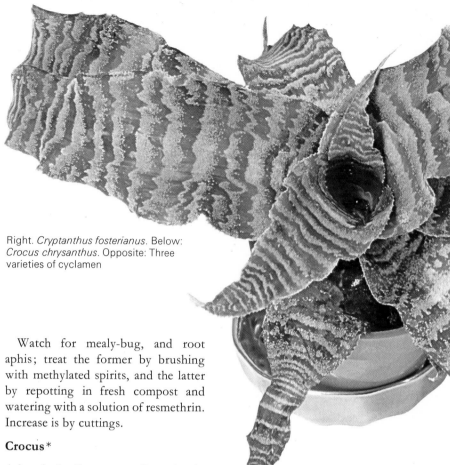

Right. *Cryptanthus fosterianus*. Below: *Crocus chrysanthus*. Opposite: Three varieties of cyclamen

Watch for mealy-bug, and root aphis; treat the former by brushing with methylated spirits, and the latter by repotting in fresh compost and watering with a solution of resmethrin. Increase is by cuttings.

Crocus*

A bowl of yellow crocus flowering in mid winter for several weeks is, like the chionodoxas, good for the morale. Yellow is a lovely cheerful colour, and is supposed to be the sign of hope. There are crocuses in other colours as well as shades of purple, violet and almost blue, some most delicately veined and feathered with purple on white, some with petals bronze on the outside and white inside, others whose stamens are bright orange inside a deep purple cup. Some crocuses have pointed

petals, some are rounded, so that they look like an elongated egg before they unfold.

The best ones for gentle forcing are the Dutch kinds, which flower in early spring, but the prettiest are those flowering naturally in mid to late winter, which come in the *Crocus chrysanthus* group. Don't forget the autumn-flowering species such as the purple-blue *C. speciosus*, and *C. sativus*, the source of saffron, with its purple flowers. A specialist bulb catalogue will list a choice of named sorts, whose descriptions are sure to make you want to grow them all.

Crocuses need a gritty compost, and are planted 5 cm (2 in) deep and 2.5 cm (1 in) apart in early autumn, except for the autumn-flowering kinds, which are planted in mid summer. Those for forcing are put outdoors in a cool place, plunged in soil and covered with bracken, ashes or leaves. Take precautions against mice. Bring in in early

wine, pink and so on, depending on species. *Cryptanthus bivittatus* is the one most often grown, a small plant perhaps 15–20 cm (6–8 in) or so wide, very flat growing and with a broad creamy stripe down the leaf margins, which flushes pink in a bright light. *C. zonatus* is a handsome plant, much larger, with wavy-edged leaves, horizontally banded with grey and wine-red. This also changes its colour, depending on the light, and is much greener in the shade. *C. bromelioides* 'Tricolor' is more like an ordinary bromeliad with a funnel, and the leaves are broadly striped creamy yellow and green, tinted pink from the centre. *C. fosterianus* has thick leaves which lie in flat rosettes up to 45 cm (18 in) across.

The cryptanthus like the same sort of cultivation as the billbergias, except for lighting. A peaty compost, occasional watering in the centre of the plant, and liquid feeding via the centre also, temperature no lower than about 8–9 °C

(46–48 °F) in winter and normal in summer, will produce a healthy cryptanthus. They are indifferent to humidity. In good light though not necessarily sun, they are more interestingly coloured.

Use the offsets to increase your collection of earth-stars. Although they produce flowers when growing naturally, the small flowerheads are the same colour as the leaves, and do not emerge from the centre of the plant.

Cup-and-saucer vine, see **Cobaea**

Cyclamen * *

The cyclamen is a comparatively modern plant, most species having been introduced since the end of the last century from North Africa, Cyprus, Turkey, southern France and the Lebanon. The name is taken from the Greek *kyklos*, circular; the rounded seedheads of some species are drawn down onto the soil by the coiling of their stems, like a spring.

The cyclamen species all have small flowers about 1.3 cm ($\frac{1}{2}$ in) long. Their colours are shades of pink, rose, red and purple, also white, and some are scented. Flowering can be in autumn,

winter and introduce them gradually to extra heat and light, but not too fast or they will be all leaf and possibly no flower. A final temperature around 17 °C (63 °F) will be suitable.

When flowering has finished, feed and water until the leaves have died naturally, then leave dry until planting outdoors the following autumn.

Crocus, Himalayan and Indian, see **Pleione**

Crown of thorns, see **Euphorbia**

Cryptanthus (Earth-star) *

This is a bromeliad, one of the stemless terrestrial species, though occasionally it is found on trees. Mostly it lives on dry stony soils, like a groundcover plant, in eastern Brazil and other parts of South America, and is tough and adaptable.

Cryptanthuses are grown in the home for their decorative leaves which are green, variegated in cream, yellow,

winter or early spring. The rounded leaves are either plain green, or marbled and mottled with white, or sometimes a silvery green, particularly attractive when contrasted with the flowers, though in some the flowers appear without the leaves.

The large-flowered florist's cyclamen have been selected and bred from *C. persicum*, a fragrant plant which flowers in winter and spring, is evergreen, and comes from the eastern Mediterranean. The weather in that area in winter is like a rather mild British winter, so your pot cyclamen should not be given a high temperature—up to 18 °C (65 °F) is sufficient, and a humid atmosphere. It will need lots of water, given every day at room temperature at the top of the pot when in full flower. Smokey atmospheres and draughts result in leaves discolouring and collapsing. Shade from bright sun is important as well.

If you overwater, the leaves quickly turn yellow and the corm may begin to rot or grey mould may infect the leaf and flower stems, especially if you water between the stems. Try to pour the water onto the soil round the corm, the top of which should be slightly higher than the compost surface. A dry compost, too much warmth or a dry atmosphere will also cause yellowing leaves.

When the plant has obviously finished growing for the season, remove any remaining dead flowers and leaves, and let it dry off completely. Leave the corm in the pot and put it on its side out of the way. In mid or late summer, you will find new shoots appearing of their own accord and the corm should at once be repotted in fresh, acid potting compost, slightly higher than the compost surface. Water it moderately at first. Increase the amount of water when the plant is growing strongly. Feed from then until the flower buds begin to show and again when flowering has finished.

Cyperus (umbrella plant)*

The umbrella plant lives up to its name in appearance: the narrow pointed leaves radiate out from the centre of

the top of a stem, and curve over slightly like the spokes of an umbrella. One plant will consist of a cluster of these umbrellas of varying heights up to about 90 cm (3 ft) in the species *Cyperus diffusus*, 1.8 m (6 ft) or less in *C. alternifolius*. In spring and early summer clusters of brown and white flowers are produced from the tops of the umbrellas.

The cyperuses are related to the sedge family and grow in all parts of the world except the very cold areas. *C. papyrus* is the Egyptian reed or papyrus, which is a much larger plant, growing to 3 m (10 ft) tall. The ancient Egyptians used to cut the pith-like tissues of the flowering stems into strips, lay them to cross with overlapping edges, then press them together to make papyrus for writing on.

Cyperus alternifolius comes from Madagascar, but in spite of this, does not need high temperatures; a minimum of 10 °C (50 °F) in winter and normal summer temperatures will suit.

The one thing it really needs is plenty of water all the time, because it lives in marshes in its home country. The container should actually be stood in water all year, so that the compost is permanently wet. Liquid feed should be given from late spring until late summer. A little shade is preferred.

The umbrella plant grows fast and will need repotting in spring and probably again in early to mid summer, in good standard potting compost. Increase is by division at potting time. If the plant is kept too warm, or in a dry atmosphere, it will be infested with greenfly; the tips of the leaves may also turn brown.

Cyrtomium falcatum*

This plant is a fern from south-east Asia, which is nearly hardy and tolerant of a good many conditions. The holly fern is *Cyrtomium falcatum* 'Rochfordianum' and this has glossy, dark green, pointed leaflets in pairs, making a frond up to 30 cm (12 in) long, not at

all fern-like to look at, but nevertheless an attractive foliage plant for indoor cultivation. When the leaves are adult, tiny pale-green spots appear on the underside of the leaves; these are not a disease, but clusters of spores which turn brown as they mature.

The holly fern is best kept in warmth, shade, and humidity but it will grow in a good many different conditions, and is indifferent to draughts and smoke. It does best where the atmosphere is humid and the temperature is 10 °C (50 °F) or above in winter and normal in summer. However, it will survive a minimum temperature of 4 °C (40 °F) and a dry atmosphere for a short time. Give it plenty of soft water in summer, but allow it to rest in winter by watering sparingly. A little weak liquid feed given occasionally while growing will be sufficient in the way of nutrients. The leaves will die naturally at intervals and should be removed. The remainder will appreciate an occasional sponging with water to clean them.

Increase is by division at potting time, in spring, or by spores, which may germinate spontaneously as they fall on the compost. When potting, remember that holly fern prefers a rather loose, fibrous, acid compost; too firm potting will produce an unhealthy plant.

Daffodil, see **Narcissus**

Devil's ivy, see **Scindapsus**

Dieffenbachia**

There are more than fifty-five varieties of *Dieffenbachia*, one of which, *D. seguina*, has been given the common name of 'dumb cane' because its poisonous bitter-tasting sap will render speechless anyone whose mouth it touches.

They are splendid foliage plants with large leaves, up to 23 cm (9 in) long, so heavily spotted and marked with cream that the only green left is at the edges, and odd spots on the blade.

Opposite: *Cyperus alternifolius.* Left: *Cyrtomium falcatum,* the Japanese holly fern. Below: *Dieffenbachia picta* hybrid

The variety *D. exotica* 'Perfection', commonly known as the Leopard Lily, is a handsome example of this family. Like other members, its leaves may irritate the mouth and throat if eaten.

These plants are aroids but rarely produce the typical aerial roots of the arum family. The stems are stout and fleshy, with the leaves produced all the way up them, closely spaced. Height can be 1.5 m (5 ft) or more, with leaves in proportion, so don't buy a dieffenbachia if you are looking for a small plant; it will need a lot of space.

It may produce flowers, like an arum lily in shape, when it is several years old, but they are not particularly attractive and they absorb some of the plant's energy, so they should be cut off cleanly with a sharp knife. Wash your hands as soon as you have done this, or handled the plant in any other way, so that there is no risk of the sap getting to your mouth; if it does, it will be extremely painful.

Dieffenbachias need warm, humid conditions and steady temperatures to grow well. Shade in summer is necessary. In winter they will need all the light available, except for days when the sun is very bright and scorching, as on a fine day when snow has fallen, or when winter ends and the sun rises higher in the sky. Keep the temperature above 10 °C (50 °F) in winter, and normal in summer. Water and feed normally, and spray overhead occasionally with clear water. Use only soft water for spraying and watering.

If the leaves turn brown at the edges, the atmosphere is not humid enough, or the compost has become dry. Leaves will fall because of lack of water, low temperatures, draughts, and temperatures see-sawing up and down.

Plants are repotted in spring, using peaty compost, with good drainage in the lower part of the container. If, in spite of your care, you have a bare stem with a tuft of leaves on top, the stem can be cut back to a stump about 10 cm (4 in) high, then sideshoots will eventually grow from lower down, especially in spring. The cut-off top can be used for increase, and will root, provided a temperature of 24–27 °C (75–80 °F) is given.

Dionaea muscipula (Venus's fly-trap)*

The insectivorous plants have a horrid fascination for many people. Plants which live like this have adapted various parts of themselves to trap the animal protein that they need, but it is possible to keep thriving plants of this kind by feeding them ordinary mineral or vegetable nitrogen and other nutrients.

The Venus's fly-traps come from South Carolina, in America, where they grow only in a rather narrow strip of land, sandy, damp and mossy. Dionaea was one of the classical names for Venus, and the genus only has this species in it. How long it will survive as a wild plant is problematical, though it should continue in cultivation as long

as there are gardeners.

Dionaea has adapted the end half of its leaves so that there are teeth on the margins and bristles in the leaf centre. The leaf is divided into two, and when the central bristles are touched, by a fly or other insect, the two parts of the leaf fold together so that the teeth interlock and the insect is trapped inside, to be digested at leisure by the plant.

It is a small plant, no more than 15 cm (6 in) tall when in flower, and consisting of a rosette of leaves close to the soil for the rest of the year. The flower is white, quite pretty, and blooms in mid summer. In sunny conditions, the leaves turn red, with the winged stalks yellowish-green, but in shade, the whole plant is green.

Compost should be a mixture of peat and living sphagnum moss, which can be bought from garden shops and some florists. Plant in a pan, and keep it partly immersed in water, and always keep the compost well watered. Coolness in winter and summer alike will give a good plant. Repotting is in spring.

Dipladenia***

The dipladenias are climbing plants with glossy, evergreen leaves. They climb by twining their stems round a support, but only when they are no longer young plants. When young they are inclined to be bushy. The funnel-shaped flowers are large, with a yellow throat and petals in various shades of rose-pink or red, depending on variety. The flowers are produced in succession from late autumn if the plants are given the right environment. Dipladenias come from the rain forests of Brazil and Bolivia and need a good deal of warmth and humidity if they are to do well. They like a little shade or a good light, but not direct sunlight.

Give normal watering while growing and feeding, and allow the plant to rest in mid and late winter by watering very moderately and lowering the temperature to about 13 °C (55 °F).

Humidity is very important during spring and summer: spray every day, and supply a moist atmosphere with trays of water, humidifiers or outer containers of wet peat. Temperature should be at normal summer levels, preferably 24–30 °C (75–85 °F) or more.

Dipladenia splendens is the species most often available, with pink flowers, but there is now also 'Rosea', with larger flowers, coloured salmon-pink and there are one or two other varieties, in paler or deeper shades of pink.

Repotting is in spring, and dipladenia needs quite large pots, as it is a vigorous plant. It is generally sold in about 15 cm (6 in) pots, but be prepared for it to need 30 cm (12 in) pots or even small tubs, if it is happy. Pruning will encourage flowering; this is done when flowering has finished, which may be mid or late autumn, removing the shoots on which there were flowers so as to leave about 5 cm (2 in) of stem. The stubs remaining will sprout sideshoots in the spring, on which there will be the new season's flowers, and the same thing can be done to these the following autumn. If you wish to have a climbing rather than a bushy plant, however, the old shoots need only be cut back so as to leave half the growth they produced that season.

If you want to increase your plant, you will need a good deal of warmth, especially in the compost; tip cuttings can be taken in spring and put in peaty compost in a temperature of 27 °C (80 °F).

Dizygotheca elegantissima (finger aralia)***

The aralia family mostly hail from Australasia and the islands of the Pacific, and the finger aralia is a particularly attractive and unusual foliage specimen. The leaves are frond-like, with a tendency to wave about in the air like long narrow fingers. The leaf margins are much serrated, and the leaves themselves are very dark olive-green.

Dizygotheca is truly an elegant plant, turning into a small tree with a main stem about 1.5 m (5 ft) tall, but it is a slow grower, and will take about twelve years to reach full height. From then on, the leaves become broader and coarser, and it is less attractive, though still unusual.

What usually happens to a dizygotheca in a home is that the leaves drop rapidly, one after another, quite soon after it is acquired and nothing is left except a bare pole. This is because it has either been put where draughts occur, given too low a temperature, a dry atmosphere, or see-sawing temperatures. It is rather particular and you will have to make sure that there is plenty of humidity and that the plant and its compost are constantly warm, with a winter temperature no lower than 13 °C (55 °F) and a higher summer temperature.

A dizygotheca will need misting or spraying daily, as well as other sources of atmospheric moisture, and is happiest in a group of plants. Give sparing amounts of water in winter and not too much while growing. Leaf drop will occur with wet or cold compost. A good light, but not sunlight or shade, is preferred.

Feed occasionally while growing, and repot in early spring, every year for young plants, every two or three years when older, using standard potting compost. Watch for red spider mite and scale insects which will appear in dry conditions. Increase is best by seed, but this is difficult to obtain.

Dracaena**

The dracaenas are members of the lily family, and are grown for their ornamental foliage, which varies considerably in form and colour within the group. They are found throughout the tropical regions of the Old World, especially India and Africa. The name comes from the Greek *drakaina*, meaning female dragon—one of the group

Opposite: Leaves of *Dionaea muscipula*.
Top left: *Dipladenia splendens*. Below left:
Dizygotheca elegantissima. Above:
Dracaena terminalis

is *Dracaena draco*, the dragon-tree, from the Canary Islands, which has red sap that was thought to resemble dragon's blood.

As you will realize from the countries of origin, warmth and humidity are essential, otherwise there will be the usual trouble with falling leaves when you have hardly got the plant home. However, the species available are very different in appearance, and cultural needs vary slightly also, although in general they are rather like the codiaeums.

Dracaena sanderiana is an upright, graceful plant, whose long narrow leaves sheathe their bases round the central stem. They are grey-green,

striped longways with creamy white. The plant is inclined to produce new shoots from the main stem. It is not quite as tender as the others and will take a winter minimum of 7 °C (45 °F), though it is happier if warmer.

Dracaena godseffiana is quite different to all other dracaenas, as it is naturally a low-growing shrubby kind of plant, with oval, dark-green, thin-textured leaves, heavily spotted with cream. The variety 'Florida Beauty' is so heavily spotted as to be nearly white.

Dracaena marginata 'Tricolor' is a recent introduction, which is most attractive and elegant. It has a central trunk, which gradually grows to about 1.2–1.5 m (4–5 ft) tall, on which there is a large rosette of narrow leaves up to 37 cm (15 in) long, but only 2 cm ($\frac{3}{4}$ in) wide, coloured green, light green and cream, with rose-pink margins.

Dracaena fragrans is much more broadly leaved, and tree-like. It grows to 6 m (20 ft) in Guinea. As a pot plant it is mostly leafy, with 10 cm (4 in) wide leaves, with a central yellow band in the variety 'Massangeana', provided it is always kept in a good light. Finally, you may come across a florist or garden shop which is selling an apparently dead piece of trunk, and calling it a ti-plant, sometimes also called the happy or good-luck plant. This is actually a species of dracaena, and if you put the bottom end in some moist compost, and put the pot in a warm humid place,

the trunk will come to life and sprout clusters of attractive leaves without more ado.

You will have healthy dracaenas if you give them the conditions which apply to codiaeums (page 82), though they are not so particular about light. Increase by stem cuttings, partially buried horizontally, or by root cuttings—'toes' of the fleshy roots—put in sandy peat in spring, all in considerable warmth.

Earth-star, see Cryptanthus

Easter cactus, see Rhipsalidopsis

Epiphyllum (water-lily or orchid cactus)*

Although the epiphyllums are cacti

they are epiphytic, like bromeliads, and grow on branches of forest trees. They are sometimes called the leaf cactus, and the specific name when translated means 'on the leaf', a reference to the fact that the flowers emerge straight out of the edge of what appear to be stem-like leaves but are in fact leaf-like stems.

The large flowers are gorgeous; they can be single or double, mostly in various shades of red, rose and pink, but also some white, orange and yellow. Stems must be two years old before they can flower, but thereafter flowers will be produced every year, though at different places on the stem each time. As well as being beautiful, some flowers are fragrant. Flowering time is late spring to early summer and the modern hybrids flower again in mid autumn. Out of flower, epiphyllums are ungainly plants, with a tendency to droop awkwardly about the place. They usually need attaching firmly to supports.

In order to flower well, epiphyllums must have plenty of light, even some sun, though not the really hot midday sun of high summer. Small fat buds will start to appear on the stem edges in early or mid spring and will open in late spring. Don't move the plant at this time or when flowering; the buds develop facing the light, and moving or turning the plant will result in bud

Top left: *Dracaena* 'Massangeana'. Right: *Erica x willmorei*. Below: Epiphyllums bloom in spring and early summer

joint so that the cutting is about two or three joints long. Let the cutting dry for about three days—the end will callous—and then put it about 2.5 cm (1 in) deep in moist coarse sand, with a little support, and cover with a plastic bag, for quicker rooting. Warmth helps as well.

Erica (heath)***

The Cape heaths are related to the British heaths, but come from South Africa. Those which are sold as pot plants flower in winter and spring, and are mostly available from florists in early winter. They look very like the hardy heathers, with the same needle leaves, but are altogether bigger plants, 30–60 cm (1–2 ft) tall, and the flowers can be up to 2.5 cm (1 in) long.

There are more than five hundred species of *Erica*, and only sixteen or so come from Europe; the rest are practically all South African and so are tender in temperate climates. Temperature in winter while flowering should be about 10 °C (50 °F) but can be a little more in summer. If it goes up and down during day and night, trouble will ensue.

Grown in the home, Cape heaths dislike dry, stuffy atmospheres and will rapidly drop all their leaves, followed by their flowers, if put into such conditions. Misting at least once a day is necessary. The atmosphere should also be moist, airy but not draughty, and soft, tepid water should be given, daily while flowering, less often at other times. Be careful never to let the compost become completely dry, even when resting. The leaves will drop at once if this happens. A good light at all times is important.

After flowering, the flower spikes should be cut off. Pot the plants into a pot one size larger in early mid spring, using a mixture of two-thirds moist fibrous peat and one-third silver sand. New shoots will start to grow, which can be pinched back for extra bushiness, and if you can plunge the plants outdoors in a place where they will get the late afternoon sun, so much the better. Don't forget to water in dry periods, especially if the weather is hot.

drop. Flowers may also drop for no apparent reason—it is usually nature's way of getting rid of too many.

Water normally, using soft water, until flowering has finished, then allow the plants to rest by giving less water and a lower temperature for a few weeks; they can go indoors in a slightly shaded place for the time being. Then water normally and new growths will appear. Provided they receive sufficient light, some plants will flower again in autumn. After this, let the compost become just moist; the temperature can drop to about 7 °C (45 °F) but the plants need all the light possible at this

rather dull time of the year. In late winter start the plants growing again, if they have not already started themselves.

A standard potting compost with extra peat and good drainage is preferred, as are pans rather than pots, for their shallow roots. A 12.5 cm (5 in) size will do for one plant, and don't forget the supports, otherwise you'll have an overbalancing plant. Repotting is done after the first flowering of the season, at the end of the rest.

Plants are increased from cuttings: use the tip of a new shoot, in early summer, and cut it off at a convenient

Bring in in autumn as the temperature falls to about 7 °C (45 °F) and introduce them to higher temperatures gradually, to avoid leaf drop.

You will see several kinds for sale in florists. *E. hyemalis* grows to about 30 cm (12 in) tall, with rather stumpy spikes of deep-pink flowers tipped with white from mid winter until late winter. *E. gracilis* has small purple, much more bell-like flowers in very long spikes, about 23–30 cm (9–12 in) tall, between early autumn and mid winter. *E. nivalis*, which is exactly the same except for the flowers which are white, may be a variety of it, and *E. × willmorei* is a large hybrid, growing to 60 cm (2 ft) tall, and flowering in spring, with white-tipped, rosy, tubular flowers 2.5 cm (1 in) long.

Increase of these Cape heaths is not easy, and it will probably be best to buy new small plants and start afresh, or keep the older plants going, with careful cultivation.

Euphorbia */**

Besides the poinsettia, there are some other euphorbia species which are grown indoors, *Euphorbia fulgens*, which has willow-like, grey-green leaves, and small orange flowers tightly wreathing the arching stems, and some succulent kinds which look exactly like cacti and are grown in the same way, such as *E. caput-medusae*.

The crown of thorns, *E. milii*, is a succulent with thick, fleshy stems, covered in a tough greyish skin, almost bark, and with intimidating spines projecting from the stems, guaranteed to put off goats and other foraging animals of stony and desert-like places.

However, these murderous prickles are hidden by a mass of rounded fresh green leaves, and small bright red flowers in clusters, mostly from the ends of the stems. It is a pretty plant and flowers nearly all year, especially in late winter and spring, if treated in the right way.

The crown of thorns comes from the high regions of Madagascar and likes a warm sunny place, without humidity, all year. Temperature should never drop below 10 °C (50 °F), otherwise

the leaves fall and the stems shrivel, and then die from the tips. Water very sparingly in winter, not with cold water —this or too much water will result in falling leaves, as will moving the plant.

Use a standard potting compost and feed occasionally in summer; repot in spring if required, and support as the plant grows, up to 90 cm (3 ft) or more. Increase from cuttings, 10 cm (4 in) long of the older shoot tips in spring, let the shoots dry for a day or so and then put in a very sandy compost and warmth. Then, when rooted, pinch out the tips to encourage bushiness.

Euphorbia pulcherrima
(poinsettia)**

The poinsettia is a member of the spurge family, one of whose characteristics is that the stems contain a white liquid, which oozes out when they are cut and in some species is poisonous, though not in the poinsettia. It is an evergreen shrub, about 3 m (10 ft) in height. It comes from Mexico and was introduced to Europe in 1834. It has been grown as a houseplant since about 1950.

The poinsettia was not easy to grow

in the home to start with, but breeding and selection have now produced varieties which are shorter and more bushy, with several heads of flowers. They are much less temperamental, less inclined to drop their leaves and are longer lasting in flower. The red 'flowers' are not petals, but bracts. The real flowers are tiny and yellow in a cluster in the centre of the bracts. Besides the familiar red poinsettia, there are varieties with pink or white bracts. All have attractively lobed, light-green, quite large leaves, and will be in the shops from early to late winter.

In order that you are not left with several bare stems with a tuft of red on the top of each, a few days after you obtain your poinsettia, you must ensure the following conditions: a steady, warm temperature of about 16–18 °C (60–65 °F), no draughts, humidity, a good light including sunlight, and careful watering to ensure that the compost is moist but not soaking. Let it become more or less dry, then water well; you will know if it becomes too dry as the leaves wilt quickly, and you should watch closely for the very first sign of this.

After flowering, cut off the flowers and, as the leaves turn yellow, gradually decrease watering. Let the plant rest, with barely moist compost for two or three months, then water heavily, cut the stems back to 10 cm (4 in), dust the cut surface with cigarette ash or charcoal, and give more warmth and light.

When new shoots appear, repot the plant in fresh standard potting compost and the same size pots. Pot on later if necessary and start feeding with a high-potash fertilizer from the end of mid summer until flower buds start to show. From the end of summer, through autumn and into early winter, allow the plants the natural day length. Do not give them artificial light in the evenings otherwise they will not produce bracts or flowers.

Left: *Euphorbia milii*. Below: *Euphorbia pulcherrima*, better known as poinsettia. Right: *Exacum affine* is deservedly popular

Exacum affine*

The gentian family is renowned for its brilliantly blue flowers, covering mat-like plants which are found growing in the mountains of Europe. No one would associate the purple-flowered, bushy little exacum with such exotics —that is, no one except the botanists, who are a race apart. Nevertheless, *Exacum affine* is a member of the Gentianaceae. It grows to about 23 cm (9 in) tall, and is compact and covered in shiny green leaves, and purple, yellow-centred, fragrant flowers, which develop continuously from early summer until mid to late autumn.

Exacum comes from Socotra, an island in the Gulf of Aden, and although a perennial there, is grown as an annual for the home or greenhouse, and discarded in late autumn. Steady, warm, well-lit conditions with some humidity, will keep it flowering; too much light, especially hot sun, will brown the edges of the leaves, and the flowers will fade very quickly. It needs moderate watering and feeding from mid summer onwards with a high-potash fertilizer to keep it blooming well.

You can propagate from seed yourself, by sowing it in late winter to early spring in a temperature of 18–21 °C (65–70 °F). Use a fine sandy compost, and prick the seedlings out when large enough to handle into 5 cm (2 in) pots of standard potting compost and then, as they grow, into larger pots as required. Keep them in a humid atmosphere while being grown on like this. Flowering should start in mid summer if sown in late winter.

Fatshedera lizei*

This is what is known as a bigeneric hybrid; it is a plant produced as the result of crossing *Hedera helix* 'Hibernica' (Irish ivy) and *Fatsia japonica moseri* (see *Fatsia japonica*). It has a tendency to climb, though not a very strong one, and has leathery palmate leaves, about 5 cm (2 in) wide, deep green and glossy. A foliage houseplant which is hardy, it needs coolness in winter, and will grow in light or shade, though light is best for the variegated form, the edges of whose leaves are white. Height seems to have no limit, and it will need a support, but if you pinch out the growing point, you will have a bushier plant.

Standard compost and normal watering and feeding are suitable; repotting is in spring. You can increase fatshedera from cuttings of sideshoots in mid summer, or by using the pinched-out top of the main stem.

Fatsia japonica (aralia, false castor oil plant)*

The aralia, as it is often known, is an indoor plant grown for its leaves, which are large and handsome, glossy and markedly palmate with deeply cut lobes. These arrange themselves artistically up a quickly growing plant, which is all but hardy—it will only succumb to prolonged hard frost. In autumn it produces spikes of white flowers, which gradually expand into a large umbrella-like spray lasting for several weeks, followed by black berries.

In Japan it grows into an evergreen shrub 2.4–4.5 m (8–10 ft) tall, but grown indoors height will probably only be about 1.2 m (4 ft), outdoors about 1.5 m (5 ft). It will eventually need quite a large pot about 30 cm (1 ft) wide. There is a variety with white tips

to the lobes of the leaves *F. j. variegata*, sometimes sold as *Aralia sieboldii*, which grows less quickly and needs more light.

Fatsia is a tolerant plant; provided it has coolness in winter, it has no particular needs, and standard compost, watering, feeding, lowish temperatures and light or shade will suit it. The large leaves need sponging to keep them glossy. When the flowerhead has finished it should be removed, back to the nearest leaf.

It can be increased from cuttings, but seed will germinate quite quickly in a temperature of 18 °C (65 °F), sown in early spring.

Left: *Fatshedera lizei.* Above: *Fatsia japonica.* Below: *Ficus elastica,* the rubber plant. Opposite: right, *Ficus benjamina,* far right, *Fittonia verschaffeltii*

Fern, see **Adiantum, Asplenium, Cyrtomium, Nephrolepis, Platycerium, Pteris cretica**

Ficus (fig, rubber plant)*/**

The group which contains the rubber plant also includes the garden fig, *Ficus carica*, which grows wild in western Asia. The ficus species grown as houseplants are trees and shrubs from the warmer parts of the world, whose foliage is ornamental for one reason or another.

The rubber plant, *F. elastica*, was originally a source of the rubber used for erasers, but for commercial rubber extraction it has been superseded by *Hevea brasiliensis*, a tree member of the spurge family. The large oval leaves and ease of cultivation of the tree-like rubber plant have made it as popular as the aspidistra was in Victorian times. 'Robusta' is the form usually grown, but there are varieties such as the very handsome 'Black Knight', whose leaves and growing tip have a deep red tinge,

making them a black-green, and 'Doescheri' ('Variegata'), whose leaves are grey-green, with dark-green patches and creamy yellow edges.

The rubber plant and its varieties are fairly amenable. Winter temperature should not be lower than 4 °C (40 °F), otherwise the leaves yellow and drop. In summer normal temperatures are suitable. Give it a little shade or a good light and some humidity. The leathery leaves need sponging fairly frequently. In summer water normally, but in winter water much less, otherwise the leaves again turn yellow and fall. However, in central heating it will need water every three or four days.

Rubber plants do best in smaller pots than might be expected, for instance, a 60 cm (2 ft) specimen will be happy in a 15 cm (6 in) pot, and potting need only be done every two or three years, provided it is fed in summer about every three weeks.

Other species of ficus, all evergreen, include *F. benjamina*, a charming weeping tree with small pointed leaves, *F. pumila*, a trailing or climbing plant, *F. radicana* 'Variegata', slow growing with pointed leaves edged in cream, and *F. diversifolia*, the mistletoe fig, with rounded leaves on a small twiggy bush, and yellow fruit the size of a pea. These appear apparently without being preceded by flowers, but in fact the flowers were inside the part that turns into fruit—very complicated, but that is the way figs are!

These small-leaved species need more moisture and shade, a winter minimum temperature of 7 °C (45 °F) and more, and humidity to prevent leaf fall, browning of leaf edges, and in-

festation by red spider mite.

You can increase the rubber plant by air-layering. Make a slanting cut halfway through the stem opposite a leaf joint about 30 cm (1 ft) from the top, wedge the cut open with a match and put moist fibrous peat or sphagnum moss round it for the roots to grow into. Enclose it with clear polythene, and stick the ends with adhesive tape. Roots will form in six to twelve weeks, if the layering is done in early mid summer, and the top can then be taken right off and potted. Other ficuses are increased from tip cuttings in warmth.

Fig, fruiting, see **Opuntia**

Finger aralia, see **Dizygotheca**

Fittonia (snakeskin plant)***

Fittonia is a highly attractive small foliage plant, but it needs plenty of constant humidity and a good deal of warmth, steadily supplied—no ups and downs and no draughts.

Fittonias come from the tropical rain forests of Peru, and were named after the Misses Fitton, who published a book in 1850 called *Conversations on Botany*. *Fittonia argyroneura* is a somewhat creeping plant with oval leaves which are covered with a delicate white, net-like pattern outlining the veins. *F. verschaffeltii* has darker green leaves, with a carmine pattern.

Temperature in winter should be no lower than 13 °C (55 °F), when it should be watered only sparingly, higher in summer. Fittonias need shade, and plenty of water and weak feeding while growing.

There is a new form now available called 'Snakeskin', which is rather

easier to grow. It is a miniature of *F. argyroneura*, with small leaves, very heavily and minutely patterned in white, and grows well in most homes, being less particular about humidity and tolerating any light except direct sun, and temperatures down to 7 °C (45 °F).

Increase of fittonias is easy, because the trailing stems will root into peaty compost wherever they touch it at their leaf-joints, and these rooted stems can be removed, cut up and potted individually.

Flaming sword, see **Vriesea splendens**

Flamingo plant, see **Anthurium**

Fly-trap, Venus's, see **Dionaea**

Freckle face, see **Hypoestes**

Fuchsia *

The fuchsias are some of the prettiest of the flowering container plants, as well as being amongst the easiest to grow; in the right conditions they can go on flowering right through the winter, as well as summer, if allowed to.

They were much grown in late Victorian times and in the early part of this century as bedding plants, in the greenhouse and as plants for window sills. They are still very popular and are becoming more so. Interest in the various forms of fuchsia is reviving, as they can easily be trained as standards, pyramids and so on, or grown in hanging baskets, or trained against trellis-work or canes.

Fuchsias were named after Leonhart Fuchs, a German botanist of the sixteenth century, and many come from Central and South America or New Zealand. The large-flowered double hybrids that are so much grown now are mainly derived from *F. magellanica* and *F. fulgens*, although other species are involved. There are so many varieties now that there is a fuchsia society, and whole nurseries are devoted to fuchsia species and hybrids.

The typical flower has a tubular centre of purple petals, with pointed, rosy pink petals surrounding it, and long stamens projecting from the tube. In the cultivated forms the central tube

Above: A standard-trained fuchsia 'Cascade'. Left: The brilliant blooms of fuchsia 'Marinka'. Top right: *Gloxinia* petals look like velvet. Opposite below: *Grevillea robusta*

has become doubled, and the colour is anything from all shades of purple, through rose, red and pink to white flushed with pink and pure white. The outer petals are varied in colour. The flowers dangle from the shoots, either from the tips or all along the stem, depending on variety, and some have a definitely pendulous habit of growth. All are seen best if placed where the flowers can be looked up to; hanging baskets or pots are a good way of displaying them, as well as growing them.

Any specialist fuchsia catalogue will have a list of hundreds of hybrids; a few outstanding ones are: 'Ballet Girl', red and white, double; 'Flying Cloud', creamy white, double; 'Gruss an Bode-

thal', crimson and dark purple, single, small flowered; 'Mme Cornelissen', bright red and white, single; 'Marine Glow', white and deep purple, single; and 'Sea-shells', bright pink and shell-pink, double.

Fuchsias need to be kept on the cool side, with a little shade, and a good deal of humidity in hot weather. In summer they like a spraying with clear water every day, wetting the bark as well as the leaves. Temperature in winter should not drop below about 4 °C (40 °F) for the double-flowered kinds, but the small singles are more or less immune to frost. If kept in a tub on a balcony, however, the tub should be wrapped in straw, polythene or sacking to protect the roots from frost, and a thick mulch put over the crown. In spring, any dead shoots should be cut off.

If grown in containers in the home, fuchsias should be encouraged to rest in winter by putting them in a cool place and giving them little water, only just enough to keep the soil moist. In late winter, the previous year's growth can be cut back by half, or the whole plant may be cut harder, if required. New shoots will appear very quickly once watering is increased and the temperature raised.

Compost can be the standard potting composts, repotting every spring or, if large plants, top-dressing only.

Fuchsias grow rapidly and can be kept bushy by taking out the tips of the new shoots, to leave three pairs of leaves on a shoot. Do not do this later than the end of spring, however, as flowering will be delayed by about ten weeks after the tipping. If all the side-shoots are removed, to leave one central stem, this will grow several metres tall, so that it forms a standard; it will need a cane for support. The leading shoot should be stopped at the height required.

Flowerbuds and flowers drop if the compost becomes dry, if the atmosphere is dry, if there is too much light, or if the plant is moved when it is in flower. Troubles are few, but watch for red spider mite and whitefly, which often infest the plants, producing withered leaves which fall, or curling ones which gradually turn yellow and may develop sooty mould.

Increase is easy from tip cuttings a few centimetres long, taken in summer and put in sandy compost. If taken in late summer, and kept warm, they will root by autumn and can be kept growing slowly through the winter in a temperature of 10 °C (50 °F) so that they will be flowering size by the following spring.

Geranium, see Pelargonium

Gloxinia (*Sinningia*)**

The gloxinias are the most glorious summer and autumn flowering pot plants, with great, big, velvety trumpet flowers, pink, rose, purple, red, blue or white, and equally velvety leaves. Some forms, called the tigrina gloxinias, have flowers heavily spotted or delicately veined in these colours, on a white background, and with frilly edges to the petals, and are then amongst the most sumptuous of blooms. But to grow all this beauty you must be very skilful as they are fastidious plants, needing precise care to grow and thrive.

These tuberous plants, most of which

originally came from the forests of Brazil, can be started in late winter by giving them a temperature of about 16 °C (60 °F) and putting the tubers in a moist peaty compost which must also drain well. Each is put singly in a 10, 12.5 or 15 cm (4, 5 or 6 in) pot, just below the surface, and when growth is well under way the temperature can be lowered a little. A good light, or a little shade, but not direct sun, is preferred. There should be a good deal of humidity. Watering with soft water at room temperature is particularly important, so as not to chill the compost.

To start with, only give a little water, but as growth improves, give more, always watering at the edge of the pot so that water does not lie on the crown. This would encourage crown rotting, and then the stems turn black and the plant is lost. Feed every week with a potash-high fertilizer when the flower buds start appearing. Warmth is necessary in summer. Remove the flowers as they die and, when flowering has finished in autumn, dry the plant off gradually, and leave in the pot quite dry until potting time, with a temperature no lower than 10 °C (50 °F) while it rests. You can remove the dead top growth whenever convenient.

Gloxinias are increased by leaf cuttings, in the same way as *Begonia rex*.

Goosefoot plant, see Syngonium

Grape ivy, see Rhoicissus

Grevillea robusta (silky oak)*

In the western Australian outback, the silky oak will grow into a tree of perhaps 50 m (165 ft); in pots as a house-plant, it grows quite fast to 3 m (10 ft) in a few years in conditions that suit it. It is a graceful, evergreen tree with feathery fern-like leaves up to 30 cm (12 in) long, though when mature and growing in the wild, or in hotter climates, it has curious and attractive golden-yellow flowers.

The silky oak is not a plant needing high temperatures, and in winter likes to be cool, 4–10 °C (40–50 °F), with plenty of light; in summer a little shade and normal temperatures, watering and feeding will suit it. Humidity is not too important, though the occasional summer shower is always good. Repot in standard compost every year in Spring, but not in too large pots. Watch for greenfly and red spider mite in too high a winter temperature.

Gymnocalycium *

This is a fairly ordinary-looking cactus, consisting of a spiny globe generally 5–15 cm (2–6 in) in diameter, which flowers from late spring to mid summer, sometimes longer, depending on species. The blooms are large, often bigger than the plant itself, and mostly in shades of pink or red, but occasion-

ally yellow or white, lasting four or five days.

Gymnocalyciums come from parts of South America, such as Argentina and Bolivia; they are not difficult to grow by the usual cactus cultivation, and are not as demanding for lots of light as cacti usually are. In winter they should not be allowed to dry completely—the compost should be just moist. Seed will germinate easily.

Some gymnocalycium forms have lost all, or most of their chlorophyll, and you may have seen them at shows or in garden shops and wondered what the extraordinary-looking cactus was that consisted of a bright red ball growing on top of a prickly, fleshy, green cylinder. This is the gymnocalycium cultivar 'Red Ball' grafted on to a stock of *Myrtillocactus*; it has to be grafted to continue growing without chlorophyll, and is grown for its red colour. Flowers rarely occur.

There is another which is bright yellow, and a third called 'Hibotan Nishiki', with green and red stripes; all have been introduced from Japan. If the stock begins to rot during the winter, the cultivar should be regrafted on to *Trichocereus*. This is done by slicing the top of the stock to 2.5 or 5 cm (1 or 2 in) high, and fitting the similarly cut gymnocalycium on to it, pressing it closely on to the stock and keeping it in place by tying with string, or a rubber band, put lengthways from the pot base up over the top of the cactus. This is done in spring, and the grafted plant put in a warm shaded place for at least two weeks, keeping it

normally watered. When the graft has taken, the tie can be removed.

Gynura sarmentosa (purple passion vine, velvet nettle)*

You may have seen a pot plant in shop windows, which has intensely purple-furred leaves and stems. This is gynura, also called *G. scandens*, which is a somewhat trailing plant from tropical East Africa, where it grows up in the mountains amongst lightly wooded terrain. It also comes from the warmer parts of

Asia, including India.

Gynura is not too difficult to grow, provided you give it warmth and plenty of light. In winter the temperature should not drop below 10 °C (50 °F), otherwise it will lose its leaves; in summer all the warmth possible is appreciated. Light is essential to maintain the intenseness of its colouring, and to keep the stems short and leafy. Nipping back the growing points in late spring and again in mid summer will keep it reasonably bushy. It looks especially attractive as a hanging plant, or trained up over wires bent into various shapes.

Water and feed normally, supply some humidity, and use the tips of the stems for cuttings, which root easily at almost any time, provided you give them some warmth if you are taking them in autumn or spring. Small

orange-red flowers, a little like daisies —it is one of the daisy (*Compositae*) family—appear later in the summer. They tend to smell unpleasant, but not strongly so; however, as the foliage will be less plentiful if the plant is allowed to flower, they are probably better removed.

As the plant becomes older, it gets less attractive, so it is a good idea to take cuttings in succession every year.

Hearts entangled, see **Ceropegia**

Heath, see **Erica**

Hedera (ivy)*

The small-leaved ivies are some of the most charming and easily grown of foliage houseplants, and even if you think you can't grow any plants in pots, or that your home hasn't a single suitable place for them, you are bound to be able to grow ivies, and find a corner to suit you. There are so many prettily variegated kinds now that if you collect a half dozen different ones, your friends will not only congratulate you on your

Top left: *Gymnocalycium mihanovichii* 'Red Ball'. Left: *Gynura sarmentosa*, or Velvet Nettle. Below. *Hedera helix* 'Chicago'. Right: *Hedera* 'Golden Leaf'. Far right: *Hedera* 'Variegata'. Right below: *Hedera helix* 'Little Eva'

green fingers, but on your artistic sense as well.

Trailing down trellis-work on the wall, twined round wire, hanging from wire or macramé baskets, climbing the banisters or outlined against a white wall, the ivies can do nothing but add to the attractiveness of your home. The

large-leaved Canary Island ivy, with grey-green leaves edged with cream, is different but just as ornamental; each specimen has a different pattern of variegations, sometimes regular, sometimes not.

Some good small-leaved kinds which you will be able to buy from most garden shops or florists are: 'Little Diamond', grey-green leaves with a white margin; *sagittaefolia*, arrow-shaped leaves; 'Lutzii', rather rounded leaves speckled in light green; 'Gold Heart', bright gold centre to dark green leaves; 'Glacier', greyish leaves with cream edges, flushing pink in cold weather; *cristata*, edges of leaves curly like parsley; 'Buttercup', new shoots and leaves yellow, slow-growing; and *minima*, plain green, small leaves.

None of these is really fast-growing,

adding about 12.5–15 cm (5–6 in) a year. *H. canariensis* 'Variegata' ('Gloire de Marengo') is a bigger plant altogether, though. Its leaves are about 7–10 cm (3–4 in) long and new growth may be 30 cm (1 ft) or more in a season. Nipping off the growing tips will help them to bush a little, but some of the little ones are slow to produce side-shoots and may not do so at all.

Give the ivies constantly cool conditions. Put outdoors in summer if possible and bring in in late autumn as most are hardy except to the severest frosts. Humidity is also important. Warmth and dryness will lead to fearsome infestations of red spider mite, which will result in the leaves turning pale brown, withering and falling. Give a good light for the most distinct variegations; the plain green ones will

grow well in shade. Plenty of water in summer, less in winter and occasional feeding while growing, complete their care. Potting, using standard compost, is in spring. Tip cuttings can be rooted easily at any time.

Hemp, African, see Sparmannia

Hibiscus (rose of China)**

Hibiscus rosa-sinensis is in the same family as the hollyhock. It comes from China where it grows into a flowering shrubby plant about 2.4 m (8 ft) tall. As a pot plant it will probably only be about 60–90 cm (2–3 ft) tall, depending on pruning and conditions of growth.

The Chinese rose has the typical hibiscus flower in summer and autumn, usually rose-pink though there are forms with yellow or orange flowers; some are double. There is also a kind with white variegations to the leaf edges. As hibiscus are evergreen, the variegated one is effective in or out of flower.

Hibiscus needs a fairly rich potting compost and warmth all year, with a winter minimum of 10 °C (50 °F), preferably 13 °C (55 °F), and normal summer temperatures. Humidity is also important. Provide plenty of water in summer, less in winter, and feed from early summer to the end of autumn. Remember to use a potash-high feed. A good light is wanted for flowering. After flowering, the plants can be pruned hard at once, removing half or more of the length of stems, or the pruning can be left until late winter. This will encourage the plant to produce plenty of new shoots, on which will be the new season's flowers.

If the flowerbuds drop without opening, dry compost, not enough food, moving, a change in temperature or a dry atmosphere are possible causes.

Watch for red spider mite and scale insect. Increase is only possible with tip cuttings placed in a very warm, humid place such as a propagator.

Himalayan crocus, see Pleione

Hippeastrum (amaryllis)**

The species from which most of today's hybrids have come, *Hippeastrum equestre*, is found in South America and the West Indies, where it flowers in winter or spring, with a bright green and red, trumped-shaped flower. From this have come such hybrids as 'Apple Blossom', white and delicate pink, 'Belinda', dark red, and 'Hecuba', salmon.

The hippeastrum hybrids have large flowers 10–12.5 cm (1–2 ft) tall; a few are fragrant. Colours can be red, white, pink, orange and salmon; some forms have picotee edging. It is possible to treat the plant as an evergreen, and some growers do better with it grown this way than if it is treated conventionally and dried off during the summer.

Hippeastrums have very large bulbs, 10 cm (4 in) across and perhaps 15 cm (6 in) long, and should be potted in 15 cm (6 in) pots of a rather peaty compost, with half the bulb above the surface.

Left: *Hibiscus* hybrid. Above: *Hippeastrum equestre*. Right: *Howea (Kentia)* palm

Time of planting is usually from early mid winter to late winter, but prepared bulbs for early-winter flowering will be available in the shops much earlier than this. Give them a good watering and stand the pots where warmth comes up from underneath and there is an air temperature of at least 21 °C (70 °F). Then water sparingly until leaves and flowerbud begin to appear, when moderate amounts can be given. From this stage a good light will be needed; flowering should begin about eight weeks after potting, though it will be sooner with prepared bulbs.

After flowering, remove the dead flowerhead, and feed with a potash-high feed until the leaves begin to die down; continue to water and keep the plant in a sunny place. If the leaves do not die off, gradually give less water and feed from late summer until the plant is completely dried off, so forcing it to rest from about mid autumn to the beginning of February.

Alternatively, some gardeners keep the plant growing in autumn, but without food after the summer, and repot in fresh compost in winter. Increase is by offsets, though they are slow to reach flowering size.

Holly fern, see **Cyrtomium**

Hot-water plant, see **Achimenes**

Houseleek, see **Sempervivum**

House lime, see **Sparmannia**

Howea (Kentia) */**

Howeas are palms from Lord Howe Island in the Pacific. Kentia is the name of the capital, and the plants have until recently had *Kentia* as botanic name. One species is still called the Kentia palm as a common name.

A howea is one of the palms with feathery leaves, very graceful and eventually growing into a large, imposing plant several metres tall. In natural conditions, when young, the plants grow in considerable shade, so do not worry too much about light. Even when more mature they will be happy in some shade. Temperature in winter should not drop below about 10–13 °C (50–55 °F).

Sparing amounts of water are needed in winter, and only moderate amounts at other times; these palms are not thirsty plants. Use soft water, otherwise the leaf tips turn brown. Feed occasionally while growing, and repot in acid potting compost in spring every two or three years. Be careful with the drainage, giving extra at the bottom, and remember to use deeper pots than usual. Poor drainage can be another cause of brown leaf tips. Watch for scale.

The occasional summer shower bath will help keep the leaves clean, otherwise sponge or spray them with water; the proprietary products sold for cleaning and polishing leaves will damage those of a palm.

Hoya (wax flower)**

The hoyas are climbing evergreen plants, with pink or white, fragrant, star-like flowers in clusters from early summer to autumn. The leaves are rather fleshy, and often slowly turn yellow, though they do not fall. This is because they are either being watered with hard water, grown in an alkaline compost, or being over-watered.

Although they need a good deal of water in summer, do remember that the leaves are fleshy, and can store water; too much will wash the nitrogen out of the compost, and the leaves will lose their green colour. In winter, only just enough should be given to keep the compost moist.

Wax flowers come from east Asia, southern China, India and Australia. In pots the stems of *Hoya carnosa* will grow to 2–3 m (6–10 ft) in length, and need supports around which to twine. They can flower profusely, especially when older. *H. bella* is a much smaller plant, though still very pretty, especially trailing over a hanging basket, and has white flowers with star-shaped red centres. It needs much more warmth than *H. carnosa*.

window and you cannot see them! If any cutting back needs to be done, late winter is the time to do it.

Increase can be by layering the lowest shoots in sandy peat, in summer; with plenty of warmth they will root quite readily.

Hyacinthus (hyacinth)*

The hyacinth is reputedly named after a Greek prince, Hyakinthos, and legend reports that when he was killed by Zephyrus, the god of the west wind, the hyacinth grew from the blood of the dead prince.

The Dutch hyacinths, of which there are many named hybrids, have now reached a standard of beauty which is going to be hard to improve upon. The size of the flowering spikes, the thick clustering of the flowers, their range of colour, and the strong fragrance of most, make an exceptionally beautiful bulbous plant, which can be had in flower from early winter to spring, depending on variety.

There is another kind, the Roman hyacinth, which is altogether more delicate and graceful in appearance. The flowers are not as large, and are more widely spaced on the stem; the bulbs will flower without being prepared from early to mid winter. Colours are more restricted, to pink, white and blue, but all are fragrant.

Hyacinths in containers need the standard potting compost, as much light as possible and cool humid conditions, with plenty of water while flowering, and feeding afterwards until the leaves die down. They are then dried off and left until potting again in autumn.

For early- and mid-winter flowering, prepared bulbs will be needed, and should be potted in late summer or early autumn with their 'noses' just above the compost surface. The larger bulbs will need a 12.5 cm (5 in) pot to accommodate all the roots. Do not firm the compost down too hard especially beneath the bulb, otherwise the roots tend to come up to the surface, which they will also do in a small pot. After watering well, put the pots in a cool, 4 °C (40 °F), dark place,

Give the hoyas a good light, but not shade, steady warmth without draughts, and a winter temperature no lower than 10 °C (50 °F). *H. bella* needs to be warmer, and both need a good deal of humidity. They especially appreciate daily spraying with soft water until the flowers unfold.

Feed carefully, adjusting quantities and intervals between feeds according to the rate of growth. Too much food will easily make the plant leafy rather than flowery, though too little will

mean not only no flowers but also small leaves. Repot about every three years, in acid compost, in late winter, and put plenty of drainage material in the base.

When the flowers have finished, they can be taken off, but very carefully as the new flowerbuds form at the base of the old flower stem and a very small length of this should therefore be left. Once they are beginning to show clearly, do not move the plant, otherwise they fall even if they are facing the

wrapped in black polythene for about ten weeks. Look at them occasionally to see if they need watering. When the shoot is about 2.5–3 cm (1–2 in) tall, bring the pot into a little light and a little warmth, and gradually increase warmth and light after the flowerbud has completely emerged from the neck of the bulb. Too much warmth will produce leaf and no flower. Water as required.

Prepared bulbs can be planted outdoors the following autumn, and will flower at the normal time, but they cannot be forced again. Unprepared bulbs, including the Roman hyacinths, are potted in early or mid autumn, but otherwise treated the same way.

Bulb fibre can be used instead of compost; it consists of 6 parts of fibrous peat, 1 part crushed charcoal and 2 parts oyster-shell. Soak it in water, and then squeeze out the surplus. If you feed the bulbs from flowering time, they should be all right for planting in the garden the following year.

Another method is to use bulb glasses. These are filled with soft water so that when the bulb is put in the top, the base is just above the water surface. The roots will sprout down into this and fill it, and the plant will flower perfectly well, but the bulb will be no use afterwards. Put charcoal in the base to absorb impurities.

Hypocyrta glabra (clog plant)*

The clog plant is a flowering houseplant, and is not difficult to grow in spite of the fact that it comes from the jungles of Brazil, where it is a small evergreen shrub. In early and mid summer it produces quantities of long-lasting, round, orange flowers, gradually turning red, from orange calyces. The shiny dark-green leaves are small and fat, almost succulent, so it will store water, and if you forget to water it occasionally no great harm will be done.

In a pot, hypocyrta will grow to

Opposite: *Hoya carnosa*. Above right: A bowl of colourful hyacinths. Right: *Hypocyrta glabra*

about 24 cm (9 in) tall, with a tendency for its stems to sprawl about. It likes a light position, but not sunlight except for short periods, with normal watering and feeding. Temperatures need not be very high though in winter they should not drop below 10 °C (50 °F) if possible. Humidity and airiness without draughts are important.

Hypocyrta will need pruning. This should be done in late winter, cutting off about a third of the stem length, so that it will produce plenty of new shoots on which it will flower in the coming season. Repotting, if necessary, can be done a little while after this, mixing some extra peat with the compost.

Increase is by tip cuttings taken in late spring and put in a peat/sand mixture. It is not difficult provided a temperature of about 27 °C (80 °F) can be supplied.

Hypoestes sanguinolenta (spotted dog, polka dot plant, freckle face)*

The reason for the common names is obvious if you look at the leaves of this plant: there are spots and blotches on them which are bright pink in a good light, though white in a bad one, making it a very pretty foliage plant. It comes from Madagascar and belongs to the same family as the shrimp plant. Its tiny lilac flowers are insignificant and only appear if the plant has been allowed to become straggly.

Give it plenty of water while growing in spring and summer, but only just enough in winter to keep it ticking over. Feed once a fortnight with a nitrogen-high fertilizer and give some

humidity. Give it as good a light as possible, without burning the rather thin leaves, to intensify the colour of the spots.

Taking out the tips will help to keep it nicely bushy. Repot in Spring, if necessary, in a standard compost, and make sure the temperature does not drop below 10 °C (50 °F) in winter. Normal summer temperatures are suitable.

Tip cuttings will root in a sandy compost in summer provided they are kept warm and humid. Watch for scale insect, which tends to invade this plant in a big way.

Impatiens (busy Lizzie)*

How this plant came to have its common name seems to be lost in the mists of time, but it is certainly busy, as it

Below left: *Hypoestes sanguinolenta.*
Below: *Impatiens wallerana petersiana* (Busy Lizzie). Right: *Impatiens wallerana* 'Variegata'. Far right: *Ipomoea*

never stops flowering all year round, and is constantly extending its shoots or growing new ones. It is exceedingly lively in the right conditions. Place in as good a light as possible but away from direct sunlight.

Impatiens wallerana comes from tropical Africa. The original species can still be found there, but the plants grown in the home as pot plants are hybrids and cultivars whose flowers can be red, orange, magenta, white or pink, salmon or orange-red. There are now also forms whose grey-green leaves are variegated white at the edges —these are usually more compact and bushy and slower to grow than the plain green-leaved types—and *I. wallerana petersiana* is a West African variety whose leaves are crimson and whose flowers are carmine-red.

Impatiens are popular because of their ease of flowering, but their ease of flower dropping also makes some owners despair. This will not happen provided the plant does not become short of moisture in the compost or in the air. The fleshy stems and rapid growth are an indication of the need for a lot of water, which should be soft and at room temperature, and

humidity is also important—central heating is not suitable. One so often sees a busy Lizzie on a window sill above a radiator in bright sunlight, its flowers surrounding it on the window sill, and the leaves festooned with red spider mite and webbing. Keep it moderately warm only, in a reasonably good light, and feed it with a potash-high fertilizer. Allow it some air on really hot days in summer and water as suggested, and you should have a highly satisfactory plant.

Causes of flower and flowerbud drop are draughts, dry atmosphere, dry compost, too much warmth, moving, and bright sunlight in summer.

Repotting in a standard compost will probably be needed in summer as well as spring, and if the plant threatens to become too elongated, take out the tips of the stems, as far back as is necessary. Or you can pinch back the tips when the plant is still small, so as to leave three pairs of leaves only on each stem, and repeat when the side-shoots are the same length.

The plant will be the better for a winter rest, so give it less water from mid to late winter, and drop the temperature a little, to about 7–10 °C (45–50 °F). Increase is so easy that one feels the plant must be invasive in its native habitat; tip cuttings about 7.5 cm (3 in) long will root in water with warmth at almost any time.

Indian crocus, see Pleione

Ipomoea (morning glory)*

It seems hard to believe that the morning glory is a weed in its own country just like bindweed in Britain. Perhaps the big white trumpets of bindweed would be just as popular in the tropics as ipomoea is in Britain. It belongs to the same family as the bindweed, the *Convolvulaceae*, and has exactly the same shaped flowers. In *Ipomoea tricolor* they are coloured the most brilliant blue when they unfold, and change to purple as they fade; the buds are white. Each flower only lasts a day, but one plant produces so many and in such quick succession that there are always plenty in various stages and colours.

Ipomoea climbs by twining, and grows very quickly to about 2.4 m (8 ft) if allowed to. It can be given canes or a trellis to support its vertical growth, or encouraged to hang down, making a most attractive curtain of green. It is a native of tropical America, and is grown in Britain as a half-hardy annual, from seed; the hotter the summer and the more light it has, the better it flowers.

The black-brown seeds are quite large, about 6 mm ($\frac{1}{4}$ in) long, and should be sown with that depth of compost over them in a temperature of at least 18 °C (65 °F). If the seed or seedlings are subjected to cold, the seed leaves and subsequent true leaves turn yellow or white, and the seedling grows very slowly and usually dies. This will also happen if put into bright sunlight while young. Nicking the seed will encourage quicker germination, as also will using warmed compost.

As the roots dislike disturbance, the seeds are best sown in small peat pots, two or three at a time, removing the weaker seedlings carefully and leaving the strongest one when this is evident. Then put pot and young plant bodily in the flowering container, about 20 cm (8 in) diameter, when roots start to show through the peat pot.

A rich and well-drained soil compost is the most suitable, as morning glories are quick growers and heavy feeders. Supply a support when sowing the seed and, after germination, keep the young plants warm. When about 10–13 cm (4–5 in) tall, pinch out the growing tip, to ensure a stronger plant. In late spring they can go out on to a balcony, provided the nights are warm as well as the day, otherwise wait until early summer. Water freely, and feed from mid summer with a potash-high fertilizer once a fortnight.

Iresine herbstii*

The rather pretty generic name of this plant pronounced eye-ree-cee-ny, comes from the Greek word for wool, *eiros*, and is said to refer to the woolly nature of the stems of the plants, though in this species they are completely without hairs, so the connection seems to be rather far-fetched.

Iresines are South American, in fact they come from all the hotter parts of America, and in Britain have been much grown as bedding plants outdoors during the summer. Now they are also being treated as container plants for the home, where their foliage adds a great deal to the décor. *I. herbstii* is wine-coloured all through its leaves and stems, with the leaf veins marked in lighter red. There is a variety whose green leaves are blotched yellow, and veined red, and another dwarf-growing form, with black-purple leaves.

They are usually grown as annuals and discarded at the end of autumn, but you can keep them for the winter and grow on another year. Warmth, humidity and sun will keep the leaves a good colour in summer; regular spraying and plenty of water are essential at this time, though feeding need only be occasional. Taking off the stem tips will keep the plant nicely bushy.

Cuttings taken in spring or autumn will root in warm sandy compost, or even in water at room temperature, and can be potted singly into small pots. The autumn-rooted cuttings will give good plants for the following year. Temperature in winter should not fall below 10 °C (50 °F) and watering should be given in moderate quantities. However, give them as much light as possible. Watch for greenfly at all times.

Iris reticulata*

This is a miniature iris only 15 cm (6 in) or so tall, which grows from small bulbs, planted in late summer. The flowers of the species are deep purple,

with white flecking on the lower petals and orange beards. They are delicately scented and last a long time from when they first open in mid winter. Modern hybrids can be blue-purple or red-purple.

These irises are so easily grown there is really no excuse for not trying them. The main point to remember is the time of planting, in late summer, which can be rather difficult as the winter seems so far away then as to be unlikely

Above left: *Iresine*. Above: *Iris reticulata* 'Harmony'. Right: *Jasminum mesnyi*. Far right: *Kalanchoe blossfeldiana*

to come. Being tiny, they are best put into pans or small troughs so that they are not overwhelmed. Plant the bulbs about 3.5 cm (1$\frac{1}{2}$ in) deep in a standard compost with some coarse sand added, as they like good drainage.

Place them outdoors in a cool shady place until mid autumn and then bring them in, but keep them cool, about 7 °C (45 °F). When the leaves begin to show, give the plants as much light as possible, otherwise the leaves will tower over the flowers, and give a little warmth as the flower stems elongate.

After flowering, take off the flower-heads, but continue to water, and give a potash-high feed until the leaves die down naturally. Then dry the bulbs off and put them in a hot place to ripen, outdoors in the sun if possible, leaving them in the container. In the Caucasus, where these bulbs originate, summers are bakingly hot and dry, apart from the occasional thunderstorm. After flowering, or even before it, each bulb starts to produce a new one, and it is this that will flower the following winter if it has been fed and ripened properly.

Ivy, see **Hedera, Rhoicissus, Scindapsus**

Jasminum (jasmine)*

The jasmines are renowned for the strong fragrance of the flowers of many species, although the winter jasmine, so often grown as a winter-flowering, hardy climber, has yellow flowers which are scentless. *Jasminum officinale* is the most well known and most often grown; its white flowers appear from early summer right through to autumn, on a plant which can climb to 6 m (20 ft) and which is hardy in sheltered gardens. *J. polyanthum* flowers from mid winter onwards, and its pink flowers are deliciously scented; this needs protection all the year.

The jasmines are not truly evergreen, though they may not drop all their leaves when grown in the home. They grow very fast, and need plenty of space and supports; they also need as much light as possible all year. Temperatures need not be high at any time; in winter they can drop to 4 °C (40 °F) or even lower for *J. officinale* and to 7 °C (45 °F) for *J. polyanthum*, raising it a little as flowering begins. Normal summer temperatures will be satisfactory. Use a standard potting compost and feed at regular intervals in summer with a potash-high fertilizer.

The jasmines will be much in need of pruning if they are to be kept under control in the home. The best time to do this is after flowering or when flowering has nearly finished—in late summer for *J. officinale*. Remove the shoots which have flowered and cut some of the others back to keep them within the space available. *J. polyanthum* should be cut back in the same way when flowering has finished, some time in spring, so that it has the rest of the growing season in which to produce new shoots for next season's flowers.

If you are growing a jasmine indoors and it does not flower, but gets very lanky, the cause may be lack of light, too much warmth, or not enough food, through lack of liquid feed or the use of poor or worn-out composts. Watch for red spider mite, especially if the atmosphere is dry; supply humidity and put outdoors occasionally in summer showers.

Jasmine, Madagascar, see **Stephanotis**

Kaffir lily, see **Clivia**

Kalanchoe*

Kalanchoes are succulent plants included in the Crassula family, and the one most commonly seen as an indoor plant is *K. blossfeldiana*. It is sold in flower in winter, and has tiny bright-red blooms in clusters above a bushy mass of shiny green, rounded leaves. The flowers last several weeks at least, and once finished should be removed together with their stems back to a pair of leaves. Since this kalanchoe has been found to be a well-behaved pot plant, other forms have been selected or bred, and there are now yellow- and pink-flowered kinds as well.

It is a 'short-day' plant, so that time of flowering can be manipulated by shortening the day length during spring and summer. After winter flowering

has finished, give the plant less water until it starts to produce new shoots and leaves, then increase it and put the plant in as light a place as possible—in a garden is best of all—in early and mid summer. This will ripen the growth so that it flowers the following winter, but if you want flowers in mid to late autumn then cover the plant with black polythene so that it only receives $8\frac{1}{2}$–10 hours of daylight during early and mid summer, and keep the temperature at about 16 °C (60 °F). Covering it earlier or later will vary the flowering time accordingly.

Since kalanchoe is a succulent, give it the compost suggested on page 56, repotting in spring or autumn, and give a winter minimum of 10 °C (50 °F) with normal summer temperatures. Some humidity is needed and light is important. Feed occasionally in winter, and make sure it does not dry out in summer. Seed sown at a temperature of 21 °C (70 °F) in spring, or cuttings taken in early summer, will increase the plant. The cuttings need a sandy compost and exposure to sun for a few days before insertion.

Kangaroo vine, see Cissus

Kentia palm, see Howea

Ladder fern, see Nephrolepis

Lily, see Clivia, Rhoeo, Spathiphyllum

Lime, house, see Sparmannia

Lithops (living stones)*

These succulents are more like stones than any of the other mimicry succulents and the name is taken from the Greek *lithos*, stone, and *ops*, like. Sometimes also called pebble plants, they come from south and south-west Africa where they grow in desert conditions of sand, gravel and a little soil. There they are almost completely buried and the surface of the succulent leaves is the only part which shows above ground. As the surface is marked with patterns of grey, pink, brown, yellow or dull grey-green, they are effectively camouflaged from browsing animals.

Like the conophytums, the plant consists of a pair of thick swollen, flat-topped, leaves, almost completely joined except for a shallow crack in the top from which the flowers come. The blooms are white or yellow, without a stem, and about 2.5 cm (1 in) wide. Flowering time is late summer to mid autumn, and the new growth comes up from inside the previous season's leaves.

The lithops have a resting period from late autumn until late spring, when they will gradually come to life again. While resting, they should not be watered unless they show signs of shrivelling, and should be kept in a warm place at a temperature of 16 °C (60 °F). The temperature can drop in fact to 10 °C (50 °F), but give them all the light there is.

In summer and autumn, water can be given, but fairly sparingly, with plenty of light and warmth. A very well-drained cactus compost is suitable, and no feeding should be necessary. Growth is slow, and they rarely form clumps, so potting every two or three years is all that may be necessary, in mid to late spring. The plant body should be buried by about a quarter.

Sow seed in spring or autumn and the plants will flower two or three years later. Cuttings can be used as for conophytums.

Above: *Lithops salicola*. Right: *Mammillaria zeilmanniana*. Opposite below: *Maranta leuconeura* 'Kerchoveana'. Top: *Monstera pertusa*

Maidenhair fern, see Adiantum

Mammillaria (pincushion cacti)*

The mammillarias are cacti, mostly natives of the deserts of Mexico and surrounding areas of Central America and the West Indies. Many are completely round, some are cylindrical, and all have spines of some kind and grow to heights from as little as 2.5 cm (1 in) to 15 cm (6 in). They increase quite quickly, so that you will soon have a nest of small round mammillarias scrambling over one another and flowering in great quantities.

The flowers generally appear in a circlet on the top of the plant, pushing through the spines and lasting for several weeks. A plant may be in flower on and off all through summer. Colours are red, white, yellow, magenta, pink or cream, and the flowers may be followed by red fruits, sometimes remaining until the following summer and mixed with the new season's flowers.

Some mammillarias become cristate or 'monstrous', that is, they develop a topknot of much-folded tissue from the growing point, which looks like a crest or cockscomb, densely covered with short bristles or hairs. Such forms will not flower; they are interesting rather than actually beautiful. The shape is thought to be due to a condition known as fasciation, but why this occurs is not definitely known.

The mammillarias need as much sun as possible in order to flower. In summer, they should be watered as other plants are, but after late autumn, if kept cool at 7–10 °C (45–50 °F), they need not be watered at all until early spring, unless they show signs of shrivelling when a little water can be given on a mild day.

Summer warmth is also important. Compost is the special cactus type suggested on page 56. Repotting can be in late spring or during summer. Feed as suggested in the cactus chapter. Increase by seed, which is easily germinated if sown in spring in sandy compost at a temperature of about 21–24 °C (70–75 °F).

Maranta (prayer plant)***

The marantas are handsome foliage houseplants, one form of which has the veins marked rose-pink in a perfect herringbone formation on a background of velvety olive green. They are called prayer plants because as darkness comes their leaves gradually fold together, upright, and stay like this until dawn the following morning.

Most come from Brazil, where they grow in clearings in the forest rather than in the shade. All are evergreen and generally rather low-growing plants, spreading by short runners. *Maranta leuconeura* 'Kerchoveana' has emerald-green leaves, with brown blotches between the veins, and *M. leuconeura* 'Massangeana' has olive-green, slightly smaller leaves, with white outlining the veins. *M. leuconeura* 'Tricolor' or 'Fascinator' is the beautiful form described earlier.

Marantas need a lot of humidity and quite a lot of warmth. Even in winter the temperature should not drop below 16 °C (60 °F). A good light, but not sunlight, is needed. Use soft water, and water sparingly in winter. Feed occasionally when growing—they are not greedy feeders. Use a peaty compost, and pans, repotting in spring and again once or twice during the growing season.

If they get a little straggly, the plants can be tidied up by pruning in summer. The cut-off pieces can be used for increase, by putting in a mixture of sand and peat, with warmth.

Monstera (Swiss cheese plant, Mexican bread plant)*

The 'delicious monster' as this plant is sometimes called—its botanic name is *Monstera deliciosa*—comes from Mexico, and has been grown as a foliage houseplant for more than a hundred years. The very large leaves can be as much as 60 cm (2 ft) and more wide. Although they are rounded, the main characteristic for which the leaves are famous is the deep slashes into the body of the leaf from the margin, which develop as they mature, provided the plant is kept in the right conditions.

A single specimen will easily grow to 1.8 m (6 ft) and with its large leaves on 60 cm (2 ft) stems, is a striking and handsome plant, which needs a lot of space to be properly appreciated. A smaller species is *M. pertusa*, often sold as *M. deliciosa* 'Borsigiana', with leaves only about 30 cm (12 in) long, and this

is much easier to keep under control.

All the monsteras produce aerial roots from the stems, as they are members of the *Araceae* family; if you train these into damp moss sticks or down into water, the plants will be healthier and will not need so much water. You can also encourage them to grow into the compost.

Sometimes *M. deliciosa* will produce a creamy coloured, arum-like flower, which is followed by a long cylindrical fruit, edible and tasting faintly of pineapple. It needs perfect growing conditions to do this, however, and the fruits are usually only seen on plants growing in the greenhouses of botanic gardens or in stove houses where liberal warmth and humidity are a matter of course.

Monsteras need stakes to support them, otherwise they tend to creep rather than climb; it is said that the slashes and holes in the leaves are an indication that the plants come from exposed and windy places; if such large leaves were entire, they would be torn by wind.

It will probably be obvious by now that monsteras need a good deal of water when growing, humidity and steady warmth, though the temperature need not be too high—a winter minimum of 10 °C (50 °F) is acceptable. Give much less water in winter; they are plants whose leaves yellow rapidly with too much or even too little water. Give as good a light as possible, and feed once a week in the growing season from mid summer.

The leaves will need sponging regularly; look for scale insect and red spider mite when doing this. Use a peaty compost when potting, and increase by cutting off the growing tip, with one leaf attached, and put into peat/sand, in early summer, supplying shade, warmth and humidity.

Morning glory, see Ipomoea

Mother-in-law's tongue, see Sansevieria

Mother of thousands, see Saxifraga

Narcissus (daffodil, narcissi)*
The daffodils and narcissi are winter- or early-spring-flowering bulbs, mostly

hardy, which take very well to being grown indoors in containers such as pots or troughs. The miniatures such as *Narcissus bulbocodium*, the hoop petticoat daffodil, and *N. cyclamineus*, whose petals reflex backwards just like those of the cyclamen, can be grown in pans, and are only 10–12 cm (4–5 in) tall.

Plant the bulbs of the normal-sized narcissi so that the 'noses' just show, if in pots, but buried if in troughs (this also applies to the miniatures). Allow a depth of container of at least 12.5 cm (5 in) if you wish them to flower again the following year, though the prepared kinds will not do so without a season to build up. Pans 10 cm (4 in) deep will do for the miniatures.

Use standard potting compost and put the bulbs five to a 12.5 cm (5 in) diameter pot, or at about 3.5 cm (1½ in) apart in a trough or other container. Don't make the compost too firm, especially just beneath the bulbs. Then put the container in a cool, really dark place for about ten weeks; cover it with black polythene to make doubly sure the light is cut off and remember to water if need be.

When the shoots are about 2.5 cm (1 in) above the surface, bring them into a little light and increase the temperature to about 10 °C (50 °F). When the flower buds are well in view, give as much light as possible and a little more warmth.

Prepared bulbs are planted in mid autumn for early-winter flowering, un-

prepared in early autumn for midwinter flowering. The narcissi for early-winter flowering include 'Paper White' and 'Soleil d'Or', and daffodils are 'Golden Harvest' and 'Texas', but there are many more varieties. Specialist bulb catalogues will indicate which are good for forcing and when they will flower.

Nasturtium, see Tropaeolum

Neoregelia **

The shapes and forms of plants are everlastingly different and interesting, and even within the strange family of bromeliads, there are variations of the central funnel and the form of the flowerhead. The neoregelias come from the rain forests of Brazil, and the flowerhead is different from that of the other bromeliads in that it never really comes right out of the funnel. It forms a kind of rosette in the base, barely above the water, and the large, brightly

whose 30 cm (12 in) long leaves are green on the upper side and banded with dark grey on the lower. The inner leaves are purple and the purple to blue flowers are produced in a dense head. *N. spectabilis* has a bright tip to the

Far left: *Narcissus asturiënsis*. Above left: *Neoregelia carolinae* 'Tricolor'. Above: *Nephrolepis exaltata*

hanging basket. The genus is found in all tropical parts of the world so it does need warmth at all times, and in winter a temperature of not less than 10 °C (50 °F).

The fronds are very much cut and

coloured flowers pop out all over the top. Late spring and early summer are the times of flowering.

Probably because the flowers are low down and would be easily missed by pollinating insects, the centre of the funnel of most neoregelias is brightly coloured; if it is not, then the flowers, though small, are plentiful and brilliant.

Whatever the species, all have handsome leaves, plain or variegated, which are their main visual attraction, though the curious flowerhead makes a talking-point. *Neoregelia carolinae* 'Tricolor' is easy to obtain and very showy. It is sometimes called the 'blushing bromeliad'. The dark-green, leathery leaves are centrally striped with yellow, but the funnel is bright rosy red, the colour flushing along the leaves and gradually fading towards the middle of each. The flowerhead deep in the centre is red with violet flowers.

Also well-known is *N. concentrica*,

green leaves like a painted fingernail, grey bands on the undersurface, and pale blue flowers coming from a purplish red flowerhead.

The general care for these plants should follow that advised for bromeliads except that they need a slightly higher temperature in winter, about 13 °C (55 °F), and about 21 °C (70 °F) at least in summer. They also need quite a lot of light to develop their beautiful leaf colouring completely, though they should not receive direct summer sun.

Nephrolepis exaltata (ladder fern)*

This graceful fern is deservedly popular; it is easily grown, elegant and feathery, available in all sorts of decorative forms, and especially pretty in a

divided, and in a well-grown specimen can be up to 1.8 m (6 ft) long; there is another species called *Nephrolepis cordifolia*, whose fronds reach a length of only about 60 cm (2 ft). There are several cultivars of the ladder fern available, each of which has differently shaped fronds, all ornamental, such as 'Bostoniensis', 'Elegantissima' and 'Whitmanii'. If a frond on any of these grows in a different shape to the rest, take it off completely, otherwise the whole plant will revert to its form.

As they are ferns, they will need an acid compost, soft water, humidity (very important), a good light or a little shade, and steady warmth. A liquid feed every two weeks from mid summer with a nitrogen-high fertilizer will give good growth of fronds. Increase by potting runners from the top of the rhizome in late spring or summer; they root quickly in warmth and peaty compost.

Nertera granadensis (bead plant)*

This is a cheerful little plant which smothers itself in bright orange, pea-sized berries. It grows into a low mound about 7.5 cm (3 in) high, formed of thin creeping stems thickly covered with tiny round leaves.

The bead plant comes from the Andes mountains and is nearly hardy. In late spring and early summer it produces white flowers but they are so small and hidden amongst the leaves they are quite often missed completely. The berries develop from them and show to their best from late summer onwards.

Give it normal watering in summer, slightly on the dry side in winter, when it rests. In summer a cool position in a good light is best, with a winter temperature no lower than 7 °C (40 °F). Spray it and feed it occasionally, and repot in late summer in slightly sandy compost, dividing it at this time. Pans are the best containers.

Norfolk Island pine, see **Araucaria**

Oak, silky, see **Grevillea**

Oliveranthus elegans */**

Sometimes sold as *Echeveria harmsii* (syn. *Cotyledon elegans*) oliveranthus is a bushy small plant belonging to the succulent group, though it does not look like a succulent. It is a member of the *Crassulaceae* family, whose leaves are grouped into rosettes; in oliveranthus they do this at the base of the plant and at the top of the main stem, but the long lateral stems have the leaves arranged singly on them rather than in rosettes.

The red, yellow-tipped flowers are tube-shaped, about 2.5 cm (1 in) long, and come singly or in clusters in mid and late summer. They are very pretty and the plant is a most attractive house-plant, not seen as often as it should be.

Oliveranthus comes from Mexico

and, as it ages, drops some leaves from low down on the main stem. You can keep the plant fairly bushy, however, by cutting the stems back after flowering; the cut-off stems can be used for increase, putting them round the edge of a pot in moist coarse sand. Even in warmth, rooting may take some time. Do not disturb them for at least four weeks, except to give water if the sand has dried out, and then only give water by standing the pot in a pot saucer and filling that. After rooting, they will not grow much, and can be left where they are until the spring.

A minimum winter temperature of 7 °C (45 °F) is needed, with normal summer warmth and plenty of light. Water well in summer, but in winter when the plant is dormant, give only a little water occasionally. Humidity is not essential.

Compost is that recommended for cacti and succulents but feeding is not necessary. Cuttings taken in late summer can be moved to individual 7.5 cm (3 in) pots in the spring, and will flower in late summer, but the parent plant will bloom in mid summer.

Opuntia (prickly pear, bunny ears)*

The opuntias come from all the arid parts of North, South and Central America; some are hardy and some can live only where the weather is mostly hot. After being introduced to Europe,

Left: *Nertera granadensis*. Above: The lovely flowers of *Oliveranthus elegans*. Below: Opuntia, one of the most popular cacti. Opposite: *Pachystachys lutea*

South Africa and Australia, they took so well and spread so widely that they are often thought to be native to them.

There are many different species, and the most well-known type is the form whose stems consist of lengths of joined 'pads' sticking out at odd angles, and looking remarkably like ears. In some species these are very heavily spined, others have tufts of hair only, and some are smooth. Other species have a quite different form; they are tree-like and have cylindrical, branching stems.

Opuntia flowers are large and showy, coloured red, purple, yellow, pink, white, yellow-green and so on, but are not often produced in the home, as most species need to grow quite large before they produce them. However, new, smaller strains and cultivars are proving to grow well under home conditions. Flowers are followed by edible fruit and some species of opuntias in America are grown especially for the fruit, which is tinned.

One of the best species for home growing is *Opuntia microdasys albispina*, a smallish, neat plant with pads, and pale-yellow flowers, if you look after it the right way. It is not prickly, but it does have tufts of white hairs, hooked at the ends, on the pads, so be careful handling it. If it gets cold, brown spots appear on the pads. *O. bergeriana* has dark-red flowers, and oval pads; it grows wild in the south of France but may be difficult to flower in the home without sufficient heat and sunlight. *O. ficus-indica* (fruiting fig) grows into a large bushy plant up to 1 m (3 ft) or more tall, and is grown for its fruit as well as its yellow flowers. It needs plenty of room as well as lots of light— a sunny, sheltered balcony would suit it best.

The opuntias are not difficult to grow, given the standard cactus compost, watering and feeding. Plenty of light and heat in summer and a winter minimum of 7 °C (45 °F) will give good plants, which will probably get out of hand so that you will need to give them to an unsuspecting friend!

Orchid cactus, see Epiphyllum

Ornamental pepper, see Capsicum

Pachystachys lutea

This plant is rather like the zebra plant, *Aphelandra,* in form and flower. It is bushy and grows to an average of about 37 cm (15 in) tall in a container, though in tropical South America it grows much taller, to 1.2–1.5 m (4–5 ft) and more, as an evergreen shrub. The flowerheads are long, cone-shaped,

bright yellow. They have small white flowers protruding from between the bracts and they stick upwards like candles. The shrimp plant (*Beloperone*), has the same kind of flowerhead, but drooping, and all three belong to the Acanthaceae plant family.

Pachystachys flowers in summer, and should be watered freely and fed regularly at this time. Give it a good light but protect it from midday summer sun. After flowering, cut it back hard to leave stumps about 2.5 cm (1 in) long, give less water and cease to feed. This will encourage it to rest through the winter when the temperature should not fall below 13 °C (55 °F).

Potting is done whenever necessary, in spring or in summer, using a peaty standard compost. When growth starts again in spring, give more water and increase the temperature, to encourage new shoots for the new season's flowering. Taking out the tips when about three pairs of leaves have formed will make it bushier.

Increase is by cuttings of stem tips, taken in summer, and put into warm compost.

Palm, see Chamaedorea, Howea

Passion vine, purple, see Gynura

Peace lily, see Spathiphyllum

Pear, prickly, see Opuntia

Pebble plant, see Lithops

Pelargonium (Geranium)*

Pelargoniums must have been grown in pots on cottage window sills during the last 150 years at least. They seem to be almost indestructible and will produce a flower cluster or two under the most difficult conditions. They are easy to propagate.

Mostly from South Africa, they grow there in conditions which are hot, dry, brilliantly light and short on plant food; soil is very well drained. In cultivation they can be grown and trained so that a single plant covers the whole of a house wall, flowering all over the wall for most of the summer. In South Africa this can be done outdoors, but here it is only seen in south-facing greenhouses or on the back wall of a lean-to.

There are several different groups; the regals, which have large, single, open-trumpet-shaped flowers; the zonals, whose leaves have a dark band or zone on the surface and whose flowers are small and produced in rounded clusters (geraniums); the miniature zonals, up to about 15 cm (6 in) tall; the scented-leaved; the coloured-leaved, and the ivy-leaved. Flowering is throughout the summer, except for the regals, which bloom for about a month in late spring to early summer. All are easily grown, and there is a tremendous number of varieties and a great range of colours— all except blue, in fact. There are specialist nurseries which sell nothing but pelargoniums and they are so attractive it is very easy to be bitten with the bug of collecting and growing pelargoniums only.

Give them a standard compost but with extra grit added, and plenty of drainage material in the base; clay pots seem to yield better plants than plastic ones. Supply as much heat and light as possible in summer, and forget humidity. Feeding should not be necessary, if they are repotted every spring; if given too much nutrient they become very juicy-stemmed and leafy, grow like mad, and do not flower. Similarly, be careful with the watering; it is better

gold' is flecked and mottled with yellow on the green leaves. *P. griseoargentea* (syn. *P. hederaefolia*) has light grey-green leaves with dark-green veins. The dark-green leaves of *P. caperata* are about 2.5 cm (1 in) long and much

to let them get dryish in summer and then water well. In winter they will probably hardly need watering if kept at about 7 °C (45 °F) so that they rest.

In spring, cut all of them, except the regals, back hard, to leave main stems of about 10 cm (4 in), water well, and repot when they have begun to grow in earnest. The regals are repotted in late summer, after being allowed to rest a little, cut back hard, and kept cool, 7 °C (45 °F), until mid winter. Then they can be given more warmth, watered and brought on so that they flower in spring.

Cuttings of all kinds are taken in late summer, about 7.5–10 cm (3–4 in) long, using the tips of new shoots, without flowerbuds, and putting them into mixtures of sandy compost; sand and peat; vermiculite and so on. Once rooted, they can be potted on to larger pots as required. Stopping the main stem will encourage bushiness and more flowers.

Pests are not usually a trouble, ex-

cept for whitefly on the regals. Reddening of the leaves means too low a temperature.

Peperomia**

The most well known peperomia is probably the *P. caperata*, whose white, spike-like flowers with hooked tips on red stems make the plant attractive and unusual. Peperomias are grown mainly for the decorativeness of their leaves, and this is almost the only species which produces ornamental flowers.

Most peperomias are rather succulent and come from the forests of South America and the West Indies. None are large, and because of this they are convenient for growing in the home. In the last ten years or so, many attractive species have been introduced to cultivation, and quite a few can be quickly collected and grown without much difficulty.

Peperomia magnoliaefolia has rounded, thick leaves, variegated in cream at the edges in the form 'Variegata'; 'Green-

corrugated. Height varies from the 15 cm (6 in) of *P. caperata* to the 30 cm (12 in) or more of *P. magnoliaefolia*, which is more like a small shrub.

Peperomias as a whole like a humid atmosphere in spring and summer, a steady warm temperature, not less than 13 °C (55 °F) in winter, and a good light, but not sunlight. In dry atmospheres or draughts they drop their leaves, especially *P. caperata*, and without warmth or with too much water the thin-leaved ones mysteriously dwindle away until there is nothing left but a few tiny miserable leaves. None of the species should be watered heavily; moderate quantities only are best in summer.

They seem to prefer a soil-less mixture, or standard compost with a good deal of peat in it. Feeding need only be once a fortnight when growing, and water should be applied sparingly in winter. Increase is by stem cuttings, using the tips during summer.

Far left: Pelargoniums are a great favourite for window-boxes. Left: The leaves of *Peperomia griseoargentea* have a quilted effect. Below: *Peperomia caperata* 'Tricolor'. Right: *Philodendron scandens*

Pepper, see **Capsicum**

Philodendron */**

The philodendron group is a large one, consisting mostly of climbing shrubs or small trees. It is one of the Araceae family and has that family's characteristic aerial roots and arum-like flower. The tropical forests of South America are the homes of many species, and the name comes from the Greek *phileo*, to love and *dendron*, tree, indicating that many use trees as support, or grow amongst them.

Some species are easily grown, others need more care with warmth and humidity, but all dislike well-lit places and need some shade so they are very useful plants for the home. They are grown principally for their handsome foliage, very varied in shape from species to species. For instance, *Philodendron scandens*, the sweetheart vine, has heart-shaped leaves, *P. bipinnatifidum* has large leaves 60 cm (2 ft) long, roughly triangular, and much divided within the triangle, and *P. erubescens* has arrow-shaped leaves, about 20 cm (8 in) long. *P. laciniatum* is different again, with leaves 30 cm (12 in) long, cut into broad segments.

The sweetheart vine is an easily grown climber, useful as well as decorative, as it will grow happily in corners away from the light and can be allowed to trail, if preferred. *P. laciniatum* and *P. erubescens* are also climbers but tend to be more upright plants and do particularly well with a damp sphagnum moss stick as a support for their aerial roots. *P. bipinnatifidum* grows into a large plant, not a climber, whose leaves come straight up from the central crown, on 60 cm (2 ft) long stems. When they first unfold, the leaves are entire, and the incisions only develop as they mature.

All philodendrons need humidity, a steady warm temperature, not less than 13–16 °C (55–60 °F) in winter, shade, and normal watering and feeding. They are relatively hardy plants and are less likely to drop their leaves or have them turn yellow than most of the tropical-forest-type houseplants.

They grow fast, and may need re-

potting in the standard composts during the growing season; they take well to hydro-culture. Prune straggling shoots in late winter if necessary.

Increase is by seed of the large kinds, provided it is fresh, or by division of the smaller ones in spring, or by stem cuttings with one leaf attached, put into sandy soil 24 °C (75 °F) in spring and summer.

Pilea (aluminium plant)**

The most well known of the pileas is *Pilea cadierei*, the aluminium plant, whose leaves are splashed with shining white between the veins. It was discovered in the Vietnamese forests and introduced to France in 1938. All the plants that have been grown since have originated from a single plant.

The pileas are foliage plants, small and rounded, not too difficult to grow, and ornamental mainly because of the

leaf colouring. *P. spruceana* 'Norfolk' has leaves almost completely covered with silvery-white markings and has a more compact growth habit. *P. involucrata* (syn. *P. pubescens*) has distinctively arranged brownish-green corrugated leaves in pairs, each pair set crosswise to the pair below it. *P. microphylla* (syn. *P. muscosa*) the artillery plant, is so-called because the seed is shot out of the pods with some force when ripe. Indeed, seedlings can be found growing about 90 cm (3 ft) away from the parent! It is bushy and rather mossy in appearance.

All tropical parts of the world have one pilea species or another in them; they are mostly short-lived perennials, so are best increased every three years or so, from tip cuttings taken in early summer, or by using self-sown plants. The seeds readily germinate from the insignificant nettle-like flowers, and indeed pileas belong to the nettle family, the *Urticaceae*.

Spray the plants daily with soft water, supply humidity in other ways, and do not water too much when growing; in winter give sparing quantities. Pileas are not thirsty plants and are easily drowned. Take out the stem tips once or twice early in the growing season, to get really bushy plants—they rapidly become leggy and leafless in central heating.

Warmth, a good light and a standard compost are all necessary. Temperature in winter should not drop below 10 °C (50 °F). Occasional feeding from mid summer to autumn helps to give well-leafed plants.

Pincushion cactus, see **Mammillaria**

Pineapple, see **Ananas**

Pine, Norfolk Island, see **Araucaria**

Platycerium bifurcatum (stag's-horn fern)**

The stag's-horn ferns are totally unlike one's idea of a normal fern. The frond consists of an entire, rather thick, leaf-like structure, which divides towards the end into a fork-like arrangement that gives it its common name. The fronds are light green, but covered with a grey bloom when young, which gradually disappears as they age.

These showy fronds are the fertile ones. The sterile fronds are the sheath-like ones which form the base of the plant, and which gradually become brown and papery with age, overlapping the edges of the container. The fertile fronds grow from the centre of this mass of folded, fan-like sheaths.

There are many platycerium species, and all grow as true epiphytes, on the branches and in the forks of trees in the tropical and subtropical forests of the world. They are attached by a short stout rhizome and the gradual rotting away of successive sterile fronds provides some of the necessary humus. *P. bifurcatum* (syn. *P. alcicorne*) comes from Australia and the East Indies.

Warmth, shade and humidity are needed; the bathroom is often a good place, or the kitchen, provided there is no gas. Moisture in the atmosphere is vital, but do not spray the plant directly. Temperature should not drop below 10 °C (50 °F) in winter, though the plant will stand 7 °C (45 °F) for brief periods. Plenty of soft water is needed in summer. The stag's-horn likes a peaty or soil-less compost, and takes well to growing on bark, in a hanging basket, or on an artificial tree arrangement. In fact it grows better like this than in a pot.

Pleione (Himalayan or Indian crocus)*

This is an orchid, but although it has exotically shaped flowers as orchids

Opposite: Three modern forms of *Pilea*. Top: *Platycerium bifurcatum*. Below: *Pleioni pricei* is also known as 'Indian Crocus'.

usually have, it is not, unlike many orchids, demanding and difficult to grow. It is a small plant, growing only 10–12 cm (4–5 in) tall at the most. Most of the parts above ground are the flowers, consisting of a central, white, frilly trumpet, dark spotted in the throat, and with a collar of long single petals, in shades of magenta, red, pink, lilac or white, depending on species.

Pleione bulbocodioides (syn. *P. formosana*) is the one commonly grown; there is also a white variety, *P. bulbocodioides alba*, and a deep purple-red one, *P. bulbocodioides limprichtii*. Flowering is from late winter to late spring. The leaves die down in autumn, and then appear again in spring, during flowering.

Pleiones are nearly hardy, but need to be kept dry in their dormant season, from late autumn to mid winter, and it is then that the temperature can be

allowed to drop to 4 °C (40 °F) or even lower. Slight frost for short intervals will be endured, but prolonged hard frost is not advisable.

Compost should consist of a mixture of 2 parts loam and 1 part sphagnum moss (parts by bulk), and the plants will do best in pans. The pseudobulbs are buried to one-third of their depth, potting them just before they start growing again in late winter. Potting in fresh compost will be needed when the pan is full of roots. Old pseudobulbs should be discarded. Feed once a fortnight during the growing season.

Keep shaded from direct sun, supply humidity and water plentifully in summer. Normal summer temperatures will be suitable. Increase by carefully separating the new pseudobulbs at the time of potting.

Poinsettia, see **Euphorbia**

Polka dot plant, see **Hypoestes**

Prickly pear, see **Opuntia**

Primrose, see **Primula**

Primrose, Cape, see **Streptocarpus**

Prayer plant, see **Maranta**

Primula *

The primrose is a species of primula and the primulas grown in pots for flowering in the home have the same kind of flower, but differently coloured and varied in size. All flower in winter rather than spring.

Primula obconica has the largest flowers, pink, white, red, magenta and lilac, and rounded leaves; *P. sinensis*, now *P. praenitens*, has smaller flowers with fringed petals in the same range of colours, and *P. malacoides* is lilac or rose, with small, rather delicate flowers, and frilly-edged leaves. The last is grown as an annual, unlike the other two which can be kept after flowering

to bloom another year.

All come from China where they grow in cool, damp, slightly shaded conditions, often on banks of streams and in light woodland. Those sold in garden shops and florists in mid winter have been grown from seed sown the previous spring or early summer, the young plants being potted on successively to their final 12.5 cm (5 in) pots.

They are very pretty flowering plants, and will continue to flower for several weeks, provided they are kept in a temperature of about 10 °C (50 °F), a little warmer for *P. sinensis*. More warmth than this will give you a drawn-up plant, a short flowering period, and infestation by red spider mite. Feed with a potash-high fertilizer from the time of acquisition unless you have to repot—they are often sold pot-bound and need repotting as soon as bought.

Primulas need watering every day

while in flower but in any case should not go short of water. After flowering, take off the dead flowers, and repot the plants in fresh potting compost if not done when you bought them, continue to water and, in mid spring, put them outside if possible, plunged in a shady border and kept moist.

Bring them in in autumn, and keep them in a cool but well lit place. Keep watered and start to feed as the flowers unfold. Increase is sometimes possible from offsets taken off in spring.

Pteris*

The pteris group of plants are ferns needing warmth or tropical conditions; none of them is hardy but *Pteris cretica* (the ribbon fern) and *P. ensiformis* are the least tender and easiest to grow. *Pteris* was the word used by the Greek physician Dioscorides for a fern, and comes from the Greek *pteron*, a wing, referring to the frond shape.

Left: A group of *Primula obconica*. Above: *Pteris ensiformis* 'Victoriae' bears slender fertile fronds and smaller barren fronds. Top right: *Rebutia* in flower

Two particularly attractive varieties are *P. cretica* 'Albolineata' and *P. ensiformis* 'Victoriae'. Both have clusters of sterile fronds about 15–30 cm (6–12 in) tall, very much divided and with serrated edges—they are variegated with a central white stripe along the main

vein and down each pinna. The fertile fronds grow from the centre of these and are much taller, reaching perhaps 45 cm (1½ ft), and with narrow pinnae curled over at the edges. The main difference between the two cultivars is that the sterile fronds of 'Albolineata' are much broader than those of 'Victoriae'.

Being ferns, they need a peaty acid compost, soft water, and a minimum winter temperature of 10 °C (50 °F), but not much more in summer. As the fronds grow in clusters from a short, rather than a creeping, rhizome, increase is best done by spores, which germinate readily at 24 °C (75 °F); a creeping rhizome can be divided into sections for propagation.

Shade is necessary for the variegated forms, as they lose their white markings in a light place, but the others can be grown in a moderately well-lit place. Potting may well be needed twice in the growing season, and watering should be plentiful in summer but moderate in winter. Humidity is important, particularly when new fronds are unfurling in spring and early summer.

Purple heart, see **Setcreasea**

Purple passion vine, see **Gynura**

Rebutia*

These readily flowering cacti were named after a French cactus grower, P. Rebut, who lived during the nineteenth century. They come from northern Argentina and Bolivia, and can be found growing as high up in the mountains as 3600 m (11,000 ft), almost straight out of the rocks. It is difficult to understand how they obtain any sustenance at all and yet they flower profusely and will even start to do so as one-year-old seedlings. Some flower twice a year.

Though mammillarias are so popular, rebutias are even more so with specialist cactus growers, because of their ease of cultivation and floriferousness, so you can assume they will be a good plant for the home, in a sunny place.

The plant is rounded or slightly cylindrical; offsets will be produced quickly and in large quantities, and it will not be long before you have a pan full of one plant, each offset producing flowers in summer, funnel-shaped and coloured orange, yellow, red, pink, salmon or white. Small red fruits sometimes follow.

Give this low-growing cactus gritty compost, a pan rather than a pot, water in summer while growing, but give virtually none in winter, and supply lots of sun and, surprisingly, some humidity in summer. Keep cool in winter, about 7 °C (45 °F) until early spring. Be careful with the watering when changing over from summer and winter conditions. Increase by removing offsets when repotting in spring or summer.

Rotting is usually caused by wet compost in winter, or too much warmth then. Red spider mite and mealy-bug should be watched for in summer.

Rhipsalidopsis gaertneri (Easter cactus)*

Although this, like the rebutia, is a cactus, it is one of the leaf cacti, an epiphyte which 'perches' on branches of trees and in tree forks, as the epiphyllums do. It is one of the plants which has suffered from the botanists' indecision about which genus it belongs to, and has variously been called *Schlumbergera, Zygocactus* and even *Epiphyllum*; you may find it being sold as either of the first two, as well as *Rhipsalidopsis*.

Apart from the fact that it flowers in spring, the Easter cactus looks different to the Christmas cactus; it has very much more pointed petals to the flowers, the stamens are within the flower rather than protruding prominently from it, and each joint is

notched at intervals, each notch being pointed, rather than blunt, as in the Christmas cactus. So even if you buy it out of flower, the pointed notches should tell you that you can expect it to flower in spring rather than winter—the distinction is important because the treatment for the two cacti is different.

The Easter cactus rests from late autumn to early winter, but from then watering, using soft water, can be increased, feeding started, and the temperature raised gradually to 16–18 °C (60–65 °F). Flowerbuds will start to push out from the tips of the flattened stems in late winter and feeding can then start. After flowering, repot if necessary in a peaty acid compost, and stand the plant outdoors when risk of frost is passed, or put it in a cool sheltered, slightly shaded place. Make sure it does not dry out during this growing period.

Then bring indoors in autumn, keep it cool at about 10 °C (50 °F) and water to keep the compost just moist. Do not subject it to artificial light in the evenings in autumn and early winter, as this can affect the flowering.

Rhoeo (boat lily)**

This genus belongs to the same group of plants as the tradescantias and zebrinas, but *Rhoeo spathacea* (syn. *R. discolor*) is quite unlike them as it grows upright and almost bushy. It was discovered in Central America and needs moderate warmth and a little shade in summer, as well as humidity, to do well. Minimum winter temperature is 10 °C (50 °F).

Grown for its foliage, the boat lily has narrow leaves 23 cm (9 in) long, coming from a central stem in a gracefully arching rosette and coloured olive green on top, purple on the under-

Below left: *Rhipsalidopsis gaertneri*, the Easter Cactus. Above: *Rhoeo spathacea* has impressive foliage. Top right: *Rhoicissus rhomboidea* climbing over a *Philodendron*. Below right: Miniature rose 'Royal Salute'

neath. The variety *vittata* has the green colouring longitudinally striped with white. The small white flowers are enclosed in boat-shaped bracts at the base of the plants, and appear from late spring to mid summer.

Give little water in winter, but plenty of light; feed in summer and repot in spring. Remove the sideshoots when repotting and use these for increase. Too much water in winter will rot the crown at soil level.

Rhoicissus rhomboidea (grape ivy)*

A climbing foliage plant from Natal, South Africa, the grape ivy is nearly as easy to grow as *Cissus antarctica* and it is only slightly less hardy.

Its leaves are diamond-shaped, pro-

duced in threes on long stems which climb by means of tendrils. It can be trained up a single support to grow 1.2 m (4 ft) and more tall, or encouraged quite easily to produce several shoots and turn into a rather more bushy type of plant as wide as it is tall. The grape ivy grows quickly, and will need repotting every spring, sometimes in summer as well, while young, but will eventually settle down in a 23 cm (9 in) pot.

Provided you keep it out of the sun, or in shade, rhoicissus will do very well, and the leaves will be a good deep, shiny green, but if you put it in too much light, they will change to a sickly yellow-green and gradually drop off; new growth will stop and the plant will become thin and weak.

Temperature in winter should not drop below 7 °C (45 °F). Water moderately in summer but give little in winter—it does not need much at all at that season. In a dry atmosphere the leaves curl up at the edges, wither and fall off, so give it humidity and spray it over daily in winter if in central heating.

Feed in summer, and use the standard potting compost. Cut it back to shape or tidy in late winter. Increase from stem cuttings. Use the new shoots

when they are about 7.5 cm (3 in) long with one good leaf and make the cut just below the leaf from whose joint the new shoot has come; put the resultant cutting in a temperature of about 21 °C (70 °F).

Ribbon fern, see Pteris cretica

Rosa (rose)*

Miniature roses are the ideal solution for rose-lovers who have no garden; they are easily grown in troughs, window boxes or other containers. They can be had in flower from early summer until autumn in all the usual colours, depending on cultivar. Some are single, some double, and some are fragrant. The flowers are tiny but perfectly proportioned, and are exact replicas of the garden roses, and the leaves match them in size. Pruning is done with nail scissors! Height is about 15–30 cm (6–12 in).

Most of the truly miniature roses have *Rosa chinensis minima* as one parent; it has tiny pale-pink flowers and grows to about 23 cm (9 in) tall. 'Sweet Fairy' has deeper pink, double flowers and is scented. Other good miniature roses are 'Robin', cherry-red, 'New Penny', copper colour, 'Rosina', yellow and taller at about 45 cm (1½ ft), 'Perla de Monserrat', carmine-red to pink on petal edges, and 'Pour Toi', white. 'Baby Masquerade' is a bicolour, has yellow buds changing to orange-red as they unfold, and is also a little taller, at 45 cm (1½ ft).

The miniature roses are, like their larger relatives, quite hardy, and it is important that they are kept cold in winter during their resting period, so that they become completely dormant. When the leaves have fallen, the plants can be put outdoors or in the coolest part of the home. Provided they do not become completely dry at the roots, they will be quite happy until the spring.

In late winter, cut the oldest shoots off completely, right back to the soil, and also any which are weak, or were infected with disease the previous year. Take off the top 2.5 cm (1 in) of compost, and replace with fresh, and as soon as the new leaves begin to unfold, start watering and bring into a warmer place. Alternatively you can repot in completely fresh compost. Miniature roses have surprisingly large root systems and, in most cases, will need a larger container than you expect.

Dead flowers should be removed, and feeding once a fortnight from early summer with a potash-high fertilizer will give you good flowery plants. These tiny roses are very likely to be infested with greenfly or mildew and, because they are so small, will easily be overcome by quite mild attacks. Keep a close watch on the plants for either of these troubles and stop them as soon as they start, preferably by removing affected parts.

Increase is from cuttings taken in mid summer, or from seed sown in spring, which germinates easily but will not necessarily produce plants exactly like the parent.

Rose of China, see **Hibiscus**

Rubber plant, see **Ficus**

Saintpaulia ionantha (African violet)**

The African violet must be one of the most popular of flowering houseplants, but also one of the most exasperating. They flower like mad for one owner, yet with apparently the same conditions, they will not bloom at all for another, only producing magnificent leaves or fading rapidly away.

From the mountains of Tanzania in East Africa, the original species has been selected and bred to produce pink, purple, magenta and white-flowered forms, as well as blue or blue-violet

with white edges. Some produce single blooms, some double, or frilly petalled, and leaves are either dark or light green. Flowering goes on more or less continuously from mid summer to late winter, longer in some cases.

The saintpaulia has very fine roots and does best in a soil-less compost and a pan, of 8.5–12.5 cm (3½–5 in) diameter. Repot every two or three years in late spring, and feed with a potash-high fertilizer at half strength every week from late summer until late winter if flowering is not good.

Light is important: good light is needed for flowering, though direct summer sun burns the leaves quickly. In winter, putting the plant close to a lamp encourages flowering.

Watering needs to be done carefully.

Above: A vigorous pair of Saintpaulias. Right: *Sansevieria* is easy to grow. Top right: *Saxifraga sarmentosa* syn. *stolonifera*.

Tepid, not cold, water must always be used; water on the leaves causes white marks. Pour it into a pot saucer containing shingle or pebbles so that it can soak up through the compost. Humidity is very important—it is possible that saintpaulias absorb almost more water through their leaves than their roots, so the saucer method has a double advantage and gets over the problem of how to deal with humidity for a hairy-leaved plant.

At all times the plants prefer a steady temperature of 16 °C (60 °F), never lower than 13 °C (55 °F) in winter, perhaps slightly higher in summer.

The plant can be rested from late winter for two months or so, when it will look rather tired and have a bad colour; less water is needed and feeding can stop, until it begins to come to life again of its own accord.

Increase is by leaf cuttings, using a single leaf with the stem attached, put into a peat and sand mixture. Put the stem in to about half its length, and use a 7.5 cm (3 in) pot for three leaves or so. Place a blown-up polythene bag over the pot and put into a warm place to hurry up the rooting. Tiny leaves will push through the compost when the stem roots, and each rooted plantlet can be gently detached and potted separately in 5 cm (2 in) pots or pans.

Sansevieria (mother-in-law's tongue, snake plant)*

The form of sansevieria commonly grown as a houseplant is *Sansevieria trifasciata* 'Laurentii' (mother-in-law's tongue), whose stiff upright leaves are green, edged yellow, about 30–45 cm (1–1½ ft) high and 5 cm (2 in) wide. Other species are also grown; the leaves are similarly transversely banded in grey-green but without the yellow edge. *S.* 'Hahnii' forms a low rosette of leaves, also transversely banded, and *S.* 'Golden Hahnii' has such broadly yellow-edged leaves that it is yellow almost all over.

All the sansevierias have fleshy leaves and, because of this, have a tendency to rot at the base where they are in contact with the compost if they are watered too much in winter, especially if allowed to get cold. Apart from this they are almost foolproof and put up with all kinds of neglect and ill-treatment.

Sansevierias come from tropical Africa and Asia. The species *trifasciata* is still used in West Africa as a source of hemp, made from the fibres in the leaves. Plenty of light all year, and warmth in summer are needed. A dry atmosphere does not affect them; water and feed normally in summer, but water very sparingly in winter. Keep the temperature above 10 °C (50 °F) in winter. Sansevierias will flower in late spring if they have had particularly warm sunny conditions the previous year; the small greenish-white flowers are in the form of a spike, and are surprisingly fragrant.

Repotting need only be done occasionally, when the pot is crowded with roots, using a well-drained potting compost, preferably slightly alkaline.

Increase is by division when repotting, or by leaf cuttings. Chop the leaves up horizontally into sections about 5 cm (2 in) long. Put in warmed compost for reliable rooting. Leaf cuttings will only produce the plain green species without the yellow edge to the leaves.

Saxifraga stolonifera (mother of thousands)*

The saxifrage plant family consists largely of small rock-plants, growing in the form of tightly packed cushions of tiny leaves, which are covered with flowers in spring. *Saxifraga stolonifera*, which is grown as a pot plant, is quite different; it has comparatively large, hairy, kidney-shaped leaves, dark green with veins outlined in white, and with red stems. Airy spikes of small white, gold-centred flowers appear in early summer on 15 cm (6 in) long stems, and there are innumerable plantlets at the ends of metres of runner, or stolon.

These runners can be trained along the compost surface if grown in a trough, or allowed to hang down in a pan or hanging basket, and any number of new plants may be obtained by detaching and planting the babies after they have started to produce roots.

There is a variety called 'Tricolor', the edges of whose leaves are irregularly coloured cream; the stems and young foliage are tinged pink. It is very attractive, though slower growing, and needs more warmth and light.

In general, either form is easily grown, in cool to warm and well-lit conditions; *S. stolonifera* will grow in shade but is unlikely to flower. Keeping it on the dry side in spring and summer also encourages flowering. Temperature in winter can go as low as freezing, though not for long. Humidity is not particularly important. Compost can be any standard variety, and feeding is not essential, an occasional dose is all that is needed. Repot each spring.

Schefflera actinophylla**

Schefflera was named after an eighteenth-century Danish botanist, J. C. Scheffler, who was a friend of Linnaeus, the great botanist who initiated the binominal method of plant nomenclature which is used today. The plant is a native of Australia where it can grow into a tree 40 m (120 ft) tall, covered in scarlet flowers in spring.

However, even in a large container it will not grow more than 1.8 m (6 ft) or so tall, and though it will never flower, the leaves are large, handsome and shining green, palm-shaped and divided into a number of leaflets up to a maximum of sixteen in the largest and most mature; in general there are

Schlumbergera x buckleyi
(Christmas cactus)**

If you see a plant for sale called *Zygocactus truncatus*, that is another name sometimes still used for the Christmas cactus. Sometimes you will see one called *Schlumbergera gaertneri*, but this is not the same; it is another name for the Easter cactus (see *Rhipsalidopsis*), which flowers much later.

Like the Easter cactus, the Christmas cactus is one of the leafy cacti, an epiphyte from the rain forests of Brazil, where it grows on the trees. Hence it prefers a humus compost with peat and/or sphagnum moss.

The magenta to rosy-red, fuchsia-

three to seven to each leaf.

Temperature must not drop below 10 °C (50 °F) in winter, and should be prevented from going above 16 °C (60 °F) at that time, otherwise the plant tries to grow when it should be resting and gets weak and leggy; then it gets infested with scale insect.

In summer normal temperatures are suitable, some humidity is preferred, and the leaves will enjoy an occasional sponging. Draughts and direct sunlight will produce leaf drop and sun scorch; leaf drop will also occur with cold in winter. Feed occasionally in summer and repot in spring as required. Increase is from fresh seed sown in late winter in warmth, or from cuttings trimmed of leaves and put in a temperature of 18–21 °C (65–70 °F).

like flowers start to unfold in late autumn and continue until mid winter; the buds push out from the end of the terminal pad in the chain of pads that make up a single stem. The more stems there are the better, as only one flower comes from each stem. A well grown plant can be 45 cm (1½ ft) wide, with masses of stems, though maximum height will only be about 23 cm (9 in).

While the plant is in flower, water it as you would an ordinary indoor plant, give it a good light and a temperature of about 13–18 °C (55–65 °F),

Opposite: Keep the leaves of *Schefflera actinophylla* free of dust. Below: *Schlumbergera x buckleyi.* Bottom right: *Scilla mischtschenkoana* is easy to grow and not often seen

and a humid atmosphere. Bud drop will occur if you move the plant, change the temperature or the light, keep the plant short of water or in a draught, or expose it to gas or a dry atmosphere. They are rather temperamental at this time!

When flowering has finished, decrease the watering considerably so as to keep the compost barely moist, but leave the plant in the same conditions otherwise. In late spring, it can go outdoors in a sheltered, slightly shaded place to be rained on. Raise it on bricks to help drainage. Too much light in summer makes the stems go red. During this time it will grow new stems or lengthen the old ones. In late summer and early autumn, keep it slightly on the dry side to help ripening.

As the weather turns colder bring it in, water it thoroughly and a few weeks later start to liquid feed with a potash-high fertilizer every two weeks. Flowerbuds will form during short days and in cool conditions; you can delay the onset of bud formation if you want to by keeping the plant artificially lit in the evenings during autumn.

Repotting is not required annually; once every third year or less often is sufficient, using a standard compost, with plenty of extra humus, and a sprinkling of bonemeal.

Increase and pests and diseases are as for the Easter cactus.

Scilla (squill)*

The squills are early-spring-flowering small bulbs, sometimes blooming even in late winter. They are the first of the spring-flowering bulbs to push up leaves above the soil, in the autumn before, but then they have a kind of prolonged pause in their growth until early winter.

Squills come from southern Europe, China and the Near East; like all bulbs from these areas they have a dormancy

period during summer when they ripen during the hot dry conditions which prevail. The flowers are an open bell-shape, clustered in a short but open spike about 10 cm (4 in) tall. *Scilla siberica* is brilliant blue, *S. mischtschenkoana* (syn. *S. tubergeniana*) has a deep-blue stripe down the centre of the otherwise pale-blue petals, and *S. bifolia* is turquoise blue, or pink or white in the varieties.

Scillas are easily grown. Plant the bulbs 2.5 cm (1 in) deep and the same distance apart, in well drained compost, using pans, troughs or window-boxes. Pot in late summer or early autumn, leave the pots in the dark and the cool, 4 °C (40 °F), for six to eight weeks or until shoots begin to appear, then bring them into moderate light and a cool, 7–10 °C (45–50 °F), temperature, and gradually increase the temperature a little as the flowers start to appear.

At no time do they need or want high temperatures. Water normally and feed occasionally during and after flowering. Once the leaves have died down, keep the bulbs quite dry and put the container in a sunny place, and repot in fresh compost when the time comes. Use offsets for increase; they will flower in two or three years.

Scindapsus aureus (devil's ivy)**

The devil's ivy is a climbing plant grown for its attractive foliage which is strikingly handsome and unusual. It belongs to the aroids, and has aerial roots, but tiny ones, though it will still be grateful for a sphagnum-moss or bark-covered support into which these roots can penetrate. Much larger leaves will be produced as a result.

Introduced from the Solomon Islands, warmth and lots of humidity are required, no less than 10 °C (50 °F) in winter and normal temperatures in summer. A little shade is preferred for the species, which has asymmetrical heart-shaped leaves, flecked with yellow, but too much shade will turn it into a plain, green-leaved plant. Stopping the leading shoots late each winter will prevent it getting straggly, without checking its climbing habit unduly.

There are two strikingly coloured varieties: 'Marble Queen' and 'Golden Queen'. The first is variegated white to such an extent that you could describe the plant as being white, flecked with green; the same can be said of 'Golden Queen', substituting yellow for white. Both are very slow growing, and need more warmth than the species, together with a good light, particularly in winter. Too much light or summer sunshine will scorch the leaves.

Give plenty of water while growing, less in winter. Feed during the growing season. Pot in a soil-less compost, or a very peaty standard compost, using a pan rather than a pot. Increase by detaching low growing stems which have rooted into the compost and potting them separately.

Sempervivum (houseleek)*

The houseleeks are succulents, living in poor soils on the hot, stony hillsides and lower slopes of the mountains of central and southern Europe. They apparently grow straight out of the rock. They are subjected to baking heat in summer and have extremely good drainage all the time. Their fleshy, triangular, pointed leaves can

store a lot of water, and they are virtually plants of desert-like conditions, growing close against the ground in tightly packed rosettes of leaves.

The name comes from the Latin, *semper*, always, and *vivo*, to live; they certainly seem to survive a very long time, and produce baby offsets very freely; large clumps will form in a few years. Once a rosette has flowered, it dies.

The ordinary houseleek, *Sempervivum tectorum*, also called St. Patrick's cabbage, forms rosettes about 7.5 cm (3 in) wide, but sometimes very much wider, with purple tips to light-green leaves. The flowers are purplish-red, in a cluster at the end of a 25 cm (10 in) long stem in mid summer. It is often seen growing on house roofs in the warmer parts of Britain. *S. arachnoideum* is the little cobweb houseleek, whose tiny rosettes may be only 1.3 cm ($\frac{1}{2}$ in) wide, covered with white webbing stretched from leaf tip to leaf tip. Each rosette sends up a single flowering stem about 10 cm (4 in) high with a cluster of pink flowers on top, also in mid summer. This species multiplies at a prodigious rate, virtually without any care.

The houseleeks like the hottest, sunniest places of all, very gritty, stony compost, pans rather than pots, and only an occasional deluge in summer. No feeding is necessary, and in winter, watering need only be once a month, if that, depending on whether they are kept in central heating. If they are kept

dry, winter temperature can drop to freezing for short periods. Increase is by detaching the offsets in early spring.

Setcreasea (purple heart)*

The tradescantias and zebrinas have a relative in this plant, as it is part of the same family, the Commelinaceae, and has the same habit of growth. *Setcreasea purpurea* was cultivated long before it was named in 1955; it comes from Mexico and is a creeping or trailing plant grown for its foliage, which is deep purple, as are its fleshy, jointed stems. The upper surface of the leaves may have a dark-green tinge if grown in a poor light; it will have its best colour in plenty of light, though not direct sunlight.

Setcreasea looks particularly attractive grown in a hanging basket, but any pot or pan placed where the stems can hang downwards will show it off.

The leaves get much larger than those of the tradescantias, and will grow to 15–17 cm (6–7 in) long, with furry edges. Flowers are small, purplish-rose and white, and of no great interest.

Besides needing a good light for a good colour, setcreasea also needs to be warm, with winter temperatures preferably not less than 13 °C (55 °F) and normal summer warmth, otherwise it goes almost completely green. A peaty compost is best; repotting can be done in spring, but older plants get rather straggly and it is best to take cuttings every other summer so as to have a constant supply of new plants coming on, to maintain colour and a good habit of growth. Humidity and

Far left: Golden leaves give Scindapsus aureus *its name. Left: A parsley pot displays varieties of* Sempervivum. *Below:* Setcreasea purpurea. *Top right: Fruit and flowers of* Solanum capsicastrum

watering as for tradescantias will suit it well.

Shrimp plant, see **Beloperone**

Silky oak, see **Grevillea**

Snake plant, see **Sansevieria**

Snakeskin plant, see **Fittonia**

Solanum capsicastrum (Christmas cherry)*/**

The Christmas cherry belongs to the family which contains the potato, tomato and deadly nightshade. It is a native of Brazil where it grows as a small evergreen shrub about 30–60 cm (1–2 ft) tall. You will see it being sold in early winter, a cheerful little bush of about 23 cm (9 in) festooned with red, marble-shaped fruit.

To ensure that it keeps these fruits for the normal length of time, put it in as good a light as possible, and a really humid atmosphere, otherwise it will drop them and the leaves fairly rapidly. Spray it every day, put it with other plants if possible and supply trays of water or dishes with shingle and water. The dryness and stuffiness of central heating are not good for these plants.

Temperature should be not less than 10 °C (50 °F). Water very moderately

until the berries fall, then keep slightly drier until spring. At this time pot into fresh compost, with a pot only slightly larger, cut the shoots back by about a third, and put outdoors in a warm sunny place in late spring. Feed from then until the autumn, and do not let it get dry. White flowers will come in early summer, and spraying the plant every day will help fruit setting. The berries will be green, turning to yellow, orange and red, and the plant should be brought in during the autumn. From then until spring is its resting period, so watering should only be enough to keep the soil moist. Increase is easy, from seed sown at a temperature of 21 °C (70 °F) in early spring.

Sparmannia africana (African hemp, house lime)*

The house lime is an evergreen, tall-growing plant with large, pale-green, hairy leaves and clusters of white fragrant flowers each centred with a powder-puff of red and yellow stamens, in late winter and spring. It comes from South Africa, where it grows into a tall shrub 3–6 m (10–20 ft) tall—in a pot it grows fast to 90–120 cm (3–4 ft) tall.

The lower leaves turn yellow and drop, often because of a shortage of

nitrogen, due in turn to the fact that it has grown faster than expected and used up the available nutrient in the compost. Draughts can also produce leaf drop, as can a dry atmosphere or dryness at the roots.

Water freely in summer, moderately in winter. Feed weekly during the growing season, and supply some humidity, including overhead in hot weather. Watch for greenfly at this time.

Light should be good, and temperature no lower than 7 °C (45 °F) in winter, not too hot in summer. The standard potting composts can be used, and the plants repotted in spring and sometimes also in early summer, depending on the rate of growth. Pruning can be done after flowering, as required to keep the plant under control. Tip cuttings will root rapidly in summer, even in water.

Spathiphyllum (peace lily)**

The spathiphyllums come from Central and South America; as aroids they will need warmth, humidity and well-lit conditions in the home, though a little shade will not hurt. Direct sun is not suitable.

They are grown both for their foliage and for their flowers, so are a good plant for the house; being evergreen they will be ornamental all year and doubly so when flowering. The leaves are shiny green, oval in shape ending in a point, and come in an upright cluster from the base of the plant.

The flowers consist of a large white spathe with a cream-coloured spadix, carried on long stems above the leaves.

The species *Spathiphyllum wallisii* flowers in spring and again in autumn; it may even flower on and off during the summer, and *S.* 'Mauna Loa' flowers in spring only but is very fragrant. The spathes gradually turn green in due course but then remain healthy for some time.

Flowering is more likely to occur if you keep the plants in reasonably high temperatures. Although the winter temperature can drop to 10 °C (50 °F), flowers will only be produced if the

Top left: *Sparmannia africana* is a vigorous grower. Above: *Spathiphyllum wallisii*. Right: *Stephanotis floribunda*. Opposite top: A blush-pink hybrid form of *Streptocarpus*. Opposite right: *Syngonium podophyllum*

temperature is maintained at 13 °C (55 °F), preferably higher.

Height of the species will be about 30–40 cm (12–16 in) and twice that for 'Mauna Loa'. Both are long-lasting plants and should grow for many years without much trouble.

A good deal of atmospheric moisture is important, otherwise the leaves dry at the edges, and become infested with red spider mite; overhead spraying and sponging of the leaves are both welcome. In summer while growing, water freely, and also feed occasionally. Repot every spring using a peaty compost, and a pot slightly on the small side.

Increase is easy, by division at any time when the plants are not in flower, though summer is probably better than winter.

Spotted dog, see Hypoestes

Squill, see Scilla

Stag's-horn fern, see Platycerium

Stephanotis floribunda (Madagascar jasmine)**

Stephanotis must be familiar to many as the heavily fragrant, white waxy flowers used in wedding bouquets, corsages and button-holes. The tubular flowers are produced in clusters from spring, on and off through the summer, on an evergreen shrub which climbs by twining to perhaps 4.5 m (15 ft). It has been grown as a very popular pot plant for more than 150 years and although the stems can get very long, it can be kept under control and encouraged to flower by careful pruning and training along wires and canes.

As a native of Madagascar, it needs a good deal of warmth in summer, 21–27 °C (70–80 °F), and a temperature round about 13 °C (55 °F) in winter. If too high at this time, the plant tends to get straggly and weak and then becomes infested with mealy-bug and scale insect.

It also needs humidity, and daily

spraying with clear water in summer, together with plenty of light (but not sun). Use soft water freely in summer, sparingly in winter so as to keep the compost just moist. Feed once a fortnight when growing.

The leaves have a tendency to turn yellow rather easily; this may be due to using alkaline water, an alkaline compost, letting the roots get dry or waterlogged, or allowing the temperature to drop too low in winter. If flowers and flowerbuds drop, it will be because the plant was moved, the temperature went up and down, there were draughts, the compost became dry, or the atmosphere was not moist enough.

Potting is done in late winter, but only every few years, once the plant is mature, depending on the condition of the roots. Pot size should be about 23 cm (9 in). Prune just before repotting, to take off weak shoots, cut long ones back by about half if necessary, and cut the side shoots back to spurs of 7.5 cm (3 in) or so.

Increase is from cuttings of the previous year's shoots, a few centimetres long, put singly into 5 cm (2 in) pots in spring with a temperature of about 18 °C (65 °F); use a peaty compost. Rooting will take several weeks, and plastic bags will help to keep the close atmosphere needed.

Stones, living, see **Conophytum, Lithops**

Streptocarpus (Cape primrose)*

The Cape primroses are very pretty flowering pot plants which are not grown anything like as much as their appearance and ease of cultivation warrants. Although commonly called a primrose, they are members of the *Gesneriaceae* family, which provides several ornamental flowering pot plants for home and greenhouse, such as the African violet, the columnea, and the gloxinia.

The flower is trumpet-shaped, about 3.5 cm (1½ in) long, in ones or twos on slender stems 10 cm (4 in) or so high; the leaves are in a rosette like those of a primrose, with the flowers growing from the middle. Colours in modern hybrids are blue, violet, pink, red, white and lilac—sometimes striped. 'Constant Nymph' is a beautiful blue-violet, but there are many others. They flower for a long time, from late spring until autumn and, being perennial, are well worth growing in the home.

During the spring and summer, cool well-lit conditions are preferred, with moderate watering and occasional feed-

ing with a potash-high fertilizer. Remember that strong sun will produce brown spots on the leaves. Humidity is important; in winter the temperature can drop to 7 °C (45 °F). Keep the plants just moist while they are resting, otherwise the base of the leaf rosette will rot. A covering of gravel on the compost surface will help avoid this.

Standard potting compost, with a little extra peat, can be used, repotting every spring. The oldest leaves will turn yellow every season, and should be removed. Increase is by leaf cuttings in the same way that begonia leaves are used (see page 23), or by seed (which needs great care as it is very fine) sown in spring in a temperature of about 16 °C (60 °F), or by careful removal of new rosettes in spring.

Syngonium (Nephthytis) podophyllum (goosefoot plant)**

The goosefoot plant comes from Central America and is an evergreen climbing plant, but rather slow to climb; it has a tendency to form a long stalked cluster of leaves to start with, from which a central stem gradually elongates. Like the philodendrons and the monsteras, it is an aroid, but aerial roots are rarely seen.

Its leaves are its main attraction and show to their best in the cultivar 'Emerald Gem'. The youngest plants have leaves which are not divided in any way, but which have a silvery-

green colouring. As they mature the leaves divide into three, to form the so-called goosefoot shape, with veins outlined in white, and eventually they may have seven, eight or more leaflets in the shape of a fan, but by then are plain green.

If it produces a flower, which it seldom does in home-grown conditions, it will be greenish, and shaped like an arum lily with a reddish-purple spathe; spring or summer is the flowering time.

The goosefoot plant is not difficult to grow, but it does need a high minimum winter temperature of 16 °C (60 °F), and proportionately higher in summer. A moist atmosphere, a good light but not sun, and very moderate watering during summer will give a good plant; occasional feeding in summer is advisable. In winter as in summer, little water is needed.

Pot in spring, if needed, in standard compost, and increase from 10 cm (4 in) stem cuttings in summer, in heat.

Thunbergia alata (black-eyed Susan)*

Black-eyed Susan is a good example of the difficulties which can occur from calling plants by common names only; there is a herbaceous perennial plant, *Rudbeckia hirta*, which is also called black-eyed Susan and which is a hardy plant with daisy-type flowers.

Thunbergia alata, in contrast, is a tender climber from tropical Africa whose tubular orange flowers open out into a flat disc with several lobes, centred with such a dark brown as to appear black at first glance. It flowers profusely all summer until mid autumn.

Thunbergia is not a woody climber like stephanotis; the twining stems are thin, as are the leaves, and it appears to be rather a fragile plant, growing at most to about 3 m (10 ft). But, grown well, with plenty of light and a good compost, it is very pretty and flowery. You can grow it up a tripod of canes, or in a circle, or let it trail and hang down, from window-boxes, troughs, or hanging baskets.

Young plants can be bought in late spring, or you can grow your own from seed without much difficulty. Sow the seed thinly in seed compost and a temperature of 18–21 °C (65–70 °F) in late winter or early spring. When the seedlings have grown three leaves they can be moved into individual pots and then potted once or twice more until they are in their final 12.5 cm (5 in) pots, using standard potting compost.

Normal summer warmth, plenty of water and feeding from about mid summer will give good plants; light is very important so that they don't get

straggly and poorly flowered. Spraying at intervals, or standing out in summer showers will help to keep red spider mite at bay; watch also for whitefly, which are very partial to them.

They are usually discarded at the end of the season, as they are easily grown from seed, but can be kept over winter when they should be given a temperature of about 10 °C (50 °F), and cut back hard in late winter, followed by repotting.

Tradescantia (wandering Jew)*

This is the long trailing plant with white-striped pale-green leaves, so often seen in greenhouses hanging down from the staging or growing underneath it. It is very good grown in a hanging basket; several cuttings put into one such container can completely fill and cover it on the outside in a season, making it look like one tremendous ball of green and white foliage. The best one to use to get this effect is the larger of the two, *T. albiflora* '*Albovittata*', whose leaves are larger, and the stems thicker and fleshier.

Tradescantia was named for John Tradescant, a plant collector, and gardener to Charles I. It comes from South America and was introduced to Europe during the seventeenth century.

Tradescantia fluminensis is a generally less robust plant, with slender stems, and smaller, rather thin leaves, with a tendency to pink flushing if kept slightly short of water. There is a cultivar of this with yellow-striped instead of white leaves which is very attractive. *T. blossfeldiana* is a hairy species, with leaves coloured red-purple on the underside, and dark green on top. Clusters

of white and pink-purple flowers are produced on upright stems, and the plant's habit of growth is rather stiff.

Care is simple; plenty of water, a good light, and moderate warmth with humidity will suit them in summer. In winter, minimum temperatures of 7 °C (45 °F), and less water will suit. Root from stem cuttings a few centimetres long, broken off at any time in spring or summer, and put into water or moist peat (put several in a container to get the best effect). Standard potting compost is suitable; regular feeding will be necessary from mid summer. Plants are likely to be worn out after about three years and should be replaced.

Tropaeolum majus (nasturtium)*

The secret of growing good, flowery nasturtiums is to give them terrible soil or compost and as much sun as possible. A lot of warmth, and a stony, quick-draining, starved compost will give a quickly climbing plant festooned with orange, red or yellow flowers. Shade, water and normal potting compost will result in juicy stems, and large leaves, fit only for caterpillar fodder.

Nasturtiums are easily grown from seed sown 2.5 cm (1 in) deep in spring, with a little heat if sown in early spring. Put two or three in a 12 cm (5 in) pot, and train them up canes, or let them trail down the sides of the pot. Use them in hanging baskets, or in troughs or tubs on a balcony. Put them in a porch, or anywhere in the home that they can get plenty of light.

There are now a good many hybrids and cultivars of the dwarf form of *T. majus*, which does not climb but forms clumps increasing in size slowly through the season and flowering profusely. Colours include deep red, cream, salmon, brown-red and cerise as well as the usual shades of red, yellow and orange. In some strains, such as the Dwarf Jewel Mixture, the flowers grow above the leaves, instead of partly tucked under them; they may be double or semi-double, and some are fragrant. Some of the bushy kinds produce short runners and there is a variety with cream-variegated leaves

called 'Alaska', and another sort called 'Whirlybirds', which do not have the spur behind the flower—this simply sits on top of the leaves with the trumpet facing upwards.

Watch for blackfly, which infest the stems and the underside of the leaves.

Umbrella plant, see Cyperus

Urn plant, see Aechmea

Venus's fly-trap, see Dionaea

Vine, see Cissus, Cobaea, Gynura, Philodendron scandens Rhoicissus

Vriesea**

The vrieseas are bromeliads, named after a Dutch botanist, W. H. de Vriese who lived during the last century. The Central and South American rain forests are the home of these striking and dramatic-looking plants whose flowerheads are coloured red, yellow, or red and yellow together. They are most handsome but, unlike the majority of bromeliads, they need more warmth and a good deal of humidity to do well.

One of the most commonly grown and attractive is *Vriesea splendens* (flaming sword), a bromeliad whose 50 cm (20 in) long leaves are cross-banded in dark brown-purple. The sword-shaped flowerhead is red with yellow flowers, and appears in mid to late summer; it will take about four years for a flower

to appear from a detached offset, and this accounts for the high price of these plants. The flowerhead may last two months and the leaves will be attractive for long after that.

Another good species is *V. gigantea* (syn. *V. tessellata*) whose 45 cm (1½ ft) long leaves have a kind of snakeskin marking of yellow on the upper surface and red-purple beneath; the flower rarely appears in home cultivation. *V. psittacina* has shiny light-green leaves, and a red flowerhead in mid summer from which green-tipped flowers protrude.

Give these plants the normal bromeliad treatment as regards light, com-

Opposite: top, *Thunbergia alata;* below, *Tradescantia fluminensis* 'Quicksilver'. Above left: *Tropaeolum majus* 'Whirlybird Gold'. Above: *Vriesea splendens.* Right: *Zebrina pendula*

post, food and potting, but do not let the winter temperature fall below 18 °C (65 °F). Keep them in a very humid atmosphere, and water moderately in summer with tepid soft water, but in winter, empty most of the water from the 'vase' and thereafter give very little. The humidity will supply the moisture needed. Watch for rotting of the base, which will indicate too much water.

Wandering Jew, see Tradescantia

Waterlily cactus, see Epiphyllum

Wax flower, see Hoya

Zebra plant, see Aphelandra

Zebrina pendula*

This is closely related to tradescantia. It is easily grown and is a highly coloured foliage plant, with leaves the same shape as tradescantia but larger, striped silvery; green, dark green and purple, with purple flushing on the underneath. The cultivar 'Quadricolor' has white added to the other three colours, though the purple tone predominates, and the underneath is more purple than green. The species *Z. purpusii* has leaves in varying shades of purple only, and small purple-pink flowers.

Zebrina trails as does tradescantia, though less readily; it tends to grow erect while young. All keep their colours best in a good light. They also look best if kept slightly on the dry side, so do not water too much in summer and keep only just moist in winter.

Temperature should not drop below 10 °C (50 °F) in winter. Use a sandy compost and water with soft water, otherwise treat as for tradescantia (see page 132), but only feed occasionally, otherwise the colouring will change to mostly green.

SPECIALITY PLANTS
& ARRANGEMENTS

Balconies, hanging baskets and window-boxes

If you are not strictly confined to growing plants indoors, but have an outside window sill or balcony, then you can have even more fun with plants. You can grow some of the indoor plants in these outside situations. You can also grow plants that can't be grown indoors, either because they dislike hot close conditions and must have a time when they are really cold in winter, or because they are what are often known as 'bedding plants', lasting only for a season when the light and warmth suit them.

Window-boxes and troughs provide bigger and more natural-looking displays than single pots, and the plants seem to be happier when they are grown in a group. Boxes provide more space for the roots to grow in. The choice of flowering plants for balconies is larger and brighter than for indoor plants, and the view through your window can be improved out of all recognition.

Not only that, there is no reason why you shouldn't try a little cropping—there are dwarf tomatoes for window-boxes, such as the cultivar 'Pixie', there are herbs, lettuce, Alpine and ordinary strawberries, peppers, beans, shallots and so on. You can try many of these on sunny window ledges indoors, especially the herbs, but they will do even better in the open air.

Wind and extreme sun are two of the main problems. The wind can be very strong, especially high up on a tower block, and can whistle round corners, or funnel through gaps in buildings. Plants subjected to air under pressure like this will lose a great deal of moisture quickly, as well as possibly being torn or actually blown over.

Sometimes protection can be put up in the form of

Previous page: Front row – *Peperomia griseoargentea, Hedera helix* variety, *Echeveria setosa, Euonymus fortunei radicans*; Back row – *Codiaeum variegatum pictum* hybrid, *Pilea cadierei, Pteris, Peperomia magnoliaefolia* 'Variegata', *Chlorophytum comosum variegatum.* Left: Bushy pelargoniums and petunias. Left below: Alyssum and lobelia in front of petunias, pelargoniums and nasturtium

Opposite right: Use less showy blooms when the container itself is the focal point. Left: A balcony garden looks colourful from inside and cheers up passers-by. Below: *Asparagus densiflorus* grows best in a hanging basket out of direct sunlight.

glass panels at either end of the balcony, or wrought iron, which will support quickly growing, tough, climbing plants, or even simply polythene sheet. If the wind blows directly onto the balcony or window sill, it will be best to grow smallish plants, to present as little surface area as possible to the wind.

Plants in containers rely heavily on water being artificially applied, and when the summer sun beats down on them—whether they face east, south or west—they dry out fast, and can need watering twice or even three times a day.

Shade is sometimes another difficulty. It may be that plants are in shadow, or simply in a position facing north or one which is low down. There may appear to be a reasonable amount of light but when plants start to grow very tall very fast, with not much leaf, it is a sign that they are not receiving enough light and they should be replaced with plants that positively need shade.

Birds, especially pigeons and sparrows, can be great nuisances, walking all over the plants, tweaking them out of the soil and pulling the flowers off, but conversely you will find that butterflies and bees are attracted, even right in the centre of a town where there are no gardens or parks nearby.

Before you start to plant up containers, do consider their weight. Clay pots, tubs, troughs and barrels are very heavy when filled with a compost containing soil, and even more so when the plants are added and watered regularly. A window sill often slopes slightly downwards, and it doesn't take much to knock a box or pot

off it. Wedges underneath the outside corners or edges of boxes or pots will make them steadier, and hooks on the boxes can be attached to rings on the wall.

Balconies will have room for a number of containers, and there will be your own weight to consider, and possibly the weight of other people as well. The weight can be diminished somewhat by using soil-less composts of peat and sand and by using lightweight containers. Expanded polystyrene pots and troughs are excellent—they are not only very light but retain heat and nearly always feel warm to the touch. There are fibreglass containers as well, moulded and coloured so beautifully that it is not possible to tell the difference between them and the lead originals they are modelled on—until you try to lift them. Plastic pots are now replacing clay ones, in many shapes and designs, and there are also tower pots, which slot into one another to form a mini-tower.

The composts to use for plants on balcony or window sill are the standard potting composts containing soil, used for the indoor plants, or the peat and sand mixes. As with houseplants, some balcony plants will do best in one kind of compost, some in another, but it is worth remembering that outdoors the soil-less composts can become dry and powdery on the surface and blow away. Putting a layer of gravel on top will prevent this, without adding too much weight. Remember also that by concentrating on lightweight compost and containers, you may find the plant is top-heavy, and may blow over with disastrous results.

The drainage of surplus water from containers is im-

Above: *Tradescantia* 'Quicksilver' softens a bleak wall. Above right: *F. pumila* is one of the most attractive and versatile members of the *Ficus* family
Far right: A colourful hanging basket is a novel idea to brighten up a stairway

portant. Heavy rain can quickly make plants water-logged unless pieces of broken clay pot, shingle, gravel, broken brick, or even pieces of the polystyrene used for packing, are put at the base at least 1.5 cm ($\frac{1}{2}$ in) thick in pots. 2.5 cm (1 in) is better in troughs and boxes and medium-sized pots, and more in barrels and tubs. Containers will also be better drained if lifted off the ground slightly by wedges, brick, tin lids or anything which allows about 1.5 cm ($\frac{1}{2}$ in) gap underneath so that water can escape.

Having organized this good dispersal of extra water on the plants' behalf, try to ensure it disperses well on your neighbours' behalf also, especially those below you. Unsuspecting passers-by are not going to be happy about a sudden shower of moisture from above.

If you are planning to have plants all the year round, there are plenty which are certainly hardy, but in containers their roots are more vulnerable to frost than they would be in open ground. Many roots will touch the container wall, and frost does not have to penetrate far or be very severe before it affects them. The compost in pots or boxes can easily be frozen solid. As the liquid in the cells of the roots freezes, it expands, then when the thaw comes, the walls of the cells will have been ruptured, and many of the roots will have been killed. The top growth of plants may be killed by frost but the plants will still recover and grow new shoots if the roots have not been frosted. Lagging containers with sacking, straw, bracken, polythene sheets or whatever during the winter may not look attractive, but it is worth doing to save your plants.

Choosing your plants for balconies and window sills is not so much a matter of gathering together sufficient to make a good show, but more a question of deciding which to grow out of the many, many different species available. The habits of growth suited to these positions are bushy or trailing, or climbing if strong supports can be supplied. Compact or low-growing plants are less likely to suffer wind trouble, will obscure the light less if on a window sill, and will give a generally stronger visual impact than vertical plants. Trailers can be used to cover the sides of containers, hang down from baskets or over the edges of balconies; climbers will cover bare walls, hide windproof trellises, or twine round balcony railings.

You will find, too, that in small spaces like these colours must be sharply defined and bright if you are not to end up with a vaguely greenish, woolly mass of vegetation without any particular shape or attractive coloration. Blue, violet, lilac, cream, white and pink, in particular, will easily be lost unless you put three or four plants of one of these colours together and next to a contrasting hue, such as blue next to white. You might even clash colours a bit with, say, pink next to orange, but be careful! Too much of that produces a very restless picture, tiring to the eyes and by no means tranquillizing.

Red, yellow or orange flowers always stand out, and are often the ones which grow best in sunny places, where they are more brilliant than ever. In a small space, these will be the kinds to grow, as you will only need one or two of each to make an impression.

You can have plants in flower all year round, or you can go in for a brilliant display through the summer, followed by plants with evergreen leaves for the winter, so that you can have a rest from watering, feeding, protecting, tidying and spraying. The following list of plants is divided into seasons of flowering; C means climbing, T = trailing, E = evergreen.

Spring wallflowers, pansies, crocus, daffodil, hyacinth, scilla, grape hyacinth, primrose, polyanthus, forget-me-nots, cultivated daisies, auricula, violets, saxifrages, clematis (C).

Summer Campanula isophylla (T), *Campanula* 'Pouffe', *C. portenschlagiana* (T), nemesia, ageratum, petunia, pelargonium (some T), nasturtium (C, T), marigolds, lobelia (T or bushy), periwinkle (*Vinca*) (E, T), *Lysimachia nummularia* (creeping Jenny) (C, T), mesembryanthemum, dwarf antirrhinums, pinks, *Senecio maritima* (grey-leaved), *Cobaea scandens* (C), jasmine (C), fuchsia, begonia, London pride (E), clematis (C), miniature roses, *Thunbergia alata* (black-eyed Susan) (C).

Autumn bedding dahlias, autumn crocus, nerine, pompom chrysanthemums, dwarf Michaelmas daisies, autumn-flowering heaths (E); many of the summer-flowering plants continue until the first frosts in mid autumn.

Winter snowdrops, bergenia, Christmas rose (*Helleborus niger*), winter-flowering heathers such as cultivars of *Erica carnea* (E) which will grow in an alkaline soil, winter aconites (*Eranthis hyemalis*), *Mahonia aquifolium* (E), *Iris reticulata*, dwarf conifers (E), variegated ivies (E, T, C), *Senecia laxifolius* (ever-grey), *Euonymus japonicus* (E), *Stachys lanata* (lamb's ears (ever-grey)), *Saxifraga stolonifera* (mother of thousands, E, T), *Hebe* × *andersonii* 'Variegata' (E).

In order to have a continuous display, you may have to remove troughs or boxes bodily and replace them with new ones already planted for the next season. If you grow plants in pots, then the boxes can be left in place and refilled with suitable potted plants, packing the spaces between the pots with moist peat. Sometimes the boxes have metal linings which can be lifted out; these are particularly useful for bulbs because they need to continue growing after the flowers are over if they are to flower the next year. Permanent plants can be mixed up with the seasonal displays, or they can go into their own boxes or tubs, and stay there without disturbance.

Throughout the growing season, these balcony and window-box plants will need the same kind of care as the indoor plants: watering frequently, especially in sunny weather—be prepared to water in the morning and again at night; overhead spraying in hot weather; feeding on average every week from about six weeks after planting, so that you have a lavish display of flowers and foliage; and regular tidying.

Plants in these positions are almost under a microscope, so closely and frequently are they discussed and observed. Poorly leafed, straggling stems, dying flowers, yellowing leaves, diseased parts and broken shoots should all be removed, therefore, as soon as seen. Cutting back the trailers and climbers occasionally will prevent legginess; breaking up the compost surface with a small fork also improves the general look of the display, and keeps the compost aerated and drained. Keeping an eye open for debris on the floor of a balcony, in the tops of drainpipes and so on is important as well —the wind can make an awful mess of somebody else's tidy balcony with leaves and flowers from your plants.

Watch for pests, greenfly and whitefly in particular, which have no natural predators to keep them under control on the majority of balcony and window-ledge plants. They increase unbelievably quickly, and it really

Hanging baskets, window boxes and tubs enhance the quaintness of this London town house does pay to destroy the first one or two as soon as seen, and to use a systemic insecticide, such as dimethoate or menazon, which are effective for more than a day or two. Bioresmethrin is good for whitefly in particular, and for ants, which are often troublesome. Slugs, too, will enjoy these lush and moist conditions; they feed at night and hide in the bottom of pots, as well as under boxes, stones and so on. Hand picking is usually enough of a control.

Compost can be re-used, but will be better if some thoroughly rotted organic matter of some kind can be mixed into it first. Treated and dried products made of this can now be bought in garden shops and by mail order, if you cannot obtain garden compost or farm manure. Plants which are perennials will not necessarily have to be completely repotted every year but can be top-dressed instead, in spring.

A very pretty feature of balconies or window sills can be the hanging basket. You can grow much the same plants in these, but those particularly suitable are the

A perfect setting for window-boxes: at a level where all can enjoy their fragrance and colour, seen against the simple white frontage and soft brick paving

trailing and hanging kinds, which ensure that the basket is festooned all over with vegetation, as well as hanging down below it. The pendulous fuchsias, ivy-leaved pelargoniums, trailing lobelia, hanging begonias, creeping Jenny, ivies, nasturtiums, *Campanula isophylla* and mother of thousands are all suited to hanging baskets. You can hide the mechanics of the basket by putting the plants in the sides as the basket is filled with compost.

Hanging baskets are made of galvanized or green plastic-coated wire, proofed against rust; they may also be of polythene in various colours. Special wooden, slatted kinds are used for orchids, but these are intended for greenhouses, not the situations being discussed here. Some of the plastic ones have a kind of saucer in the bottom which collects water; this prevents some of the drips and lessens the frequency of watering.

When you plant up a hanging basket, use damp sphagnum moss or hay to line it; for the average-sized basket about 2¼ litres (½ UK gallon; 4 US dry pints) of moss will be needed. Some people use black or green polythene sheet with holes pierced in it instead, or this can be used as interlining on top of the sphagnum moss. You will find that the easiest way to prepare the basket is to balance it on the rim of a bucket or large pot.

Take the moss or hay lining right up to the top of the basket, and then fill in with moist compost to about halfway. Place small plants so that they will grow out of the sides of the basket through the wires. Spread their roots out so that they are firmly anchored. Put larger plants in the centre. Fill in with compost and firm it round and over the plants until the basket is nearly full. You can add more of the smaller plants if there is any space, and finally cover those with compost. Then firm and level the surface which should slope slightly inwards towards the centre to prevent water overflowing.

Water the plants in thoroughly, and then hang in position; chains are usually supplied with the baskets and you should make sure that the hooks or other supports are really solid. A full hanging basket weighs a great deal and could be very harmful if it fell. Also make sure your basket is high enough to be out of the way of heads, and remember that it will drip after watering, unless lined with polythene.

Watering can be a bit of a problem, as the baskets are heavy but awkward to reach without taking down. Steps are one answer; a small pulley in place of the hook is another. Wire or really strong cord is attached to the ring on the basket, put through the pulley and then the other end is secured to a cleat on the nearest convenient wall. The basket can then be easily lowered and is much more likely to be watered when it needs it.

Growing plants from fruit pips and stones

There are a good many exotic, subtropical or tropical fruits to be bought from greengrocer or supermarket, which contain seeds of one kind or another. Because of modern methods of storage and transport, the fruit is fresh enough for the seed to be still viable and, indeed, some oranges when peeled have pips already beginning to germinate inside them.

Pips and stones from citruses, avocado, date, peaches and apricots are mostly quite easy to germinate, and the resulting plants will, at least, provide a pleasantly evergreen foliage plant. With luck, you may grow one which also flowers and fruits; it is by no means impossible to grow seedling peaches, apricots, oranges and so on which carry the chromosomes in them for flowering within three or four years. However, one or two species will only fruit when they are fully grown large trees, and even then they need greater warmth than occurs in temperate climates.

The fruits which can just be grown out of doors in temperate climates, in sheltered warm gardens, include peaches and apricots, the stones from which will germinate if stratified and then sown in suitable compost. Stratifying helps the hard shell to soften and ensures that the seed is subjected to cold, which is essential for germination.

Put peach and apricot stones into a pan containing a mixture of half sand and half peat so that they are well buried, and then put the pan outdoors—plunged in a border if possible, otherwise on a window sill or balcony—from autumn to late winter. If they are frosted, so much the better.

In early spring take the stones out, put them into a good 2.5 cm (1 in) of seed compost so that they have a good covering of compost, cover them further with black plastic sheet, and keep in a temperature of 18–21 °C (65–70 °F) until they germinate. Then remove the black plastic and allow the seedlings to grow. When they are large enough to handle move them into a larger container. Eventually the plants can be in a small tub. Use good standard potting composts at all stages.

In general, the trees resulting from these seeds will not flower but occasionally one will, and set fruit. They can be put outside for most of the year, but should be brought in while frost is likely, and great care must be taken with temperature when trees are flowering.

Dates come from the date palm, *Phoenix dactylifera*, and in their native habitat reach 30 m (100 ft) but must have extreme heat to do so—only then will they fruit. However, the stone will germinate in a sandy compost, if it is put in 2.5 cm (1 in) deep and given a temperature of 24 °C (75 °F). A date stone will take about six weeks to germinate after a late-winter sowing, producing small, palm-like leaves. It will grow into a neat little palm tree in about two years or so (see general care of palms).

An avocado pear (*Persea americana*) contains a single enormous stone, 5 cm (2 in) and more long, and at least 2.5 cm (1 in) wide, conical in shape. To germinate such a seed seems impossible under ordinary household conditions, but they do sprout, though sometimes they may take five or six months. A single seed is put into a 9 cm (3½ in) pot, half buried in a good seed compost with the lower, larger half in the compost. A temperature of 16 °C (60 °F) will result in germination, the first signs of which will be the splitting of the stone into two halves from the top downwards. The cotyledon stem will come up from between the two halves and a strong taproot will develop at the same time. It is advisable to move the seedling into a larger container within a few days as it grows fast. Leaves will not appear until the stem is at least 20 cm (8 in) tall. Taking out the growing tip will not make a bushy plant, and it is best to keep it in as much light as possible to prevent it becoming tall at the

With a little care, attractive foliage plants can be raised from grapefruit and orange pips

expense of leaves. The leaves are large and evergreen; if they fall, the atmosphere is too dry, there is a lack of water in the compost, or the temperature has fluctuated or fallen too low.

Avocados will not survive outdoors in winter in temperate climates, and they will not fruit until about 9 m (30 ft) tall, at the age of seven years. They are native to tropical America and are not in any way related to the sweet dessert pears.

Oranges, lemons, grapefruit and other citrus fruits can be grown from their pips, though, like the peaches, it is a matter of luck if the resultant plant flowers. They grow into bushy little evergreen pot plants, whose leaves are aromatic when rubbed or bruised, smelling of the fruit peculiar to the tree. Flowers, which are white and heavily fragrant, may appear in spring when the tree is between three and eight years old. Commercial orchard trees are increased by budding or grafting cultivars onto suitable stocks.

Sow the pips 1.5 cm ($\frac{1}{2}$ in) deep in sandy or soil-less compost, in spring or summer, and provide a temperature of about 16–21 °C (60–70 °F). Germination should occur after about a month, sometimes sooner, and the seedlings should be moved as soon as large enough to handle, into individual 7.5 cm (3 in) pots. Their main root lengthens quickly, and will coil round the bottom of the pot if you do not act quickly.

In the foreground, an avocado plant grown from a stone. A well-established orange tree sits behind

Sometimes two or even three seedlings sprout although only one pip has been sown. This is because some citrus species produce a normal seedling as the result of a fertilized egg, and also others which are formed vegetatively from the pip. These will be virtually identical with the parent plant, so are likely to fruit. The sexually produced seedling will vary as much as any which is formed as a result of random pollination; you can often recognize it by its shorter and less strong growth.

Citrus plants will grow in a good standard potting compost. If possible, put them outdoors in summer, otherwise in a sunny place indoors. Water and feed normally while growing, but cease to feed in winter, and give little water then. Temperature can drop to 4 °C (40 °F) in winter. An occasional spraying in summer is acceptable, and pinching out the shoot tips once or twice while growing, especially when the plants are young, will make them nicely bushy. Potting-on in spring will be needed for the first few years, but as growth slows down can be less frequent and can be replaced by topdressing. Watch for scale insect and red spider mite.

Finally, a tropical fruit which you can propagate yourself, using a part of the fruit: the pineapple. You will need a fruit which is as fresh as possible, and you can get an idea of how recently it was harvested by the state of the 'topknot'. The brighter green it is, and the lusher-looking the leaves, the fresher the fruit, and the better chance you will have of getting roots to appear from the part used for increase. Pineapples whose crown of leaves has turned brownish and withered-looking should not be used; those which have had the crown removed before sale cannot be used.

The pineapple fruit is produced midway up the flowering stem, and the original flower will have had leaves above it. After pollination the seed receptacle turns into the fruit, still with its leafy crown, and this crown can be sliced off horizontally with one or two rows of 'pips' attached. Then put the crown into a 9 cm ($3\frac{1}{2}$ in) pot of sandy compost so that the flesh and pips are firmly covered with compost up to the leaf bases. Cover with a blown-up clear plastic bag, secured round the pot with a rubber band. One of the hormone rooting compounds can be used on the base of the cutting. If put into a shaded place and a temperature of about 21 °C (70 °F), roots should appear during the next four to eight weeks, and you can move the newly rooted plant into an 11 cm ($4\frac{1}{2}$ in) pot of standard potting compost. From then on give the plant plenty of warmth, humidity and light. See also *Ananas*, in the A–Z section.

Right: Various stages of propagation from stones

There is a tropical fruit which you can propagate yourself, using a part of the fruit: the pineapple. You will need a fruit which is as fresh as possible, and you can get an idea of how recently it was harvested by the state of the 'topknot'. The brighter green it is, and the lusher-looking the leaves, the fresher the fruit, and the better chance you will have of getting roots to appear from the part used for increase. Pineapples whose crown of leaves has turned brownish and withered-looking should not be used; those which have had the crown removed before sale cannot be used.

Two other tropical fruits you might like to try, which are grown from their central stones, are the litchee and the mango, and another, which is grown from the crisply fleshy pips inside a leathery rind, is the pomegranate. *Punica granatum*, to give it its botanic name, comes from the sub-tropical regions of the Mediterranean and North Africa, so does not need a great deal of warmth. In fact it can grow out of doors in mild districts, close to a wall, and forms an attractive shrub with many bright orange-red flowers, 3 or 4 cm long, in summer.

The best time to sow its pips (seeds) is March, but you can try it any time in summer, provided the temperature is about 21 °C (70 °F). Cover the seeds with 6 mm ($\frac{1}{4}$ in) of moist seed compost, keep it moist and they should

Below: Plants can easily be grown from lemon pips

germinate easily within two or three weeks. Then treat them like ordinary seedlings and move them on to larger pots as necessary. Because they are seedlings, they are unlikely to be exactly like their parent, but you should get one or two which would be satisfactorily ornamental at any rate.

Litchees are those round brown balls about the size of a small golf-ball sold in greengrocers in the winter. The skin or rind is tough and warty, but the white flesh inside (the aril) is sweet, juicy and slightly scented. Within this is the brown stone, to use for propagation.

Bitchi sinensis comes from China, where it is a small evergreen tree having greenish white flowers in May, and does not need high temperatures; about 18 °C (65 °F) should be sufficient to germinate the seed within two weeks. However, you should sow the stone as soon as it is removed from the flesh, and if the fruit is more than 21 days old, the stone is unlikely to germinate. Viability is rapidly lost from these seeds. Put the stone 15 mm ($\frac{1}{2}$ in) deep, use acid compost and keep it moist and shaded. If you are lucky, you will eventually have a pleasantly attractive small leafy bush, but it is slow-growing and unlikely to flower for about ten years.

The delicious tropical mangoes have enormous stones at least 7 cm (3 in) long, and have been grown in the tropics for thousands of years as cultivated crops. They need high temperatures for germination, 24–27 °C (75–80 °F), and may produce several seedlings from one stone, instead of only one. If the fruit has had to withstand temperatures of lower than 10 °C (50 °F), as may be the case when being transported to Britain, it is unlikely to germinate, otherwise you can expect it to sprout about three weeks after sowing. Put the stone 25 mm (1 in) deep. Mangoes grow on evergreen trees at least 15 m tall (50 ft), and do not appear until the tree is well grown.

The peanut (*Arachis hypogaea*) is the ground-nut or monkey nut, and you can grow your own supply of 'nibbles', provided you start with unroasted, unsalted peanuts. They should be in their shells and not treated in any way. Remove the shell and sow one or two 2 cm (1 in) deep and in a 15 cm (6 in) pot of moist peaty compost, preferably in spring, and put them in a temperature of 24 °C (75 °F). Keep them moist and warm and expect to see yellow flowers in summer.

The plants will grow to about 30 cm (12 in) tall.

Being a legume, arachis will produce pea-type pods, and the stems carrying them will hang down towards the compost until the pods penetrate the compost. They then mature there and produce the shells and nuts you started with, after which the plants die. Temperature throughout needs to be fairly high, about 24 °C (75 °F).

Herbs in the home

The herbs commonly used in cooking are easily grown in containers on sunny window sills, in the kitchen for example. But there is no reason why herbs should not be grown in living rooms as well—many have decorative leaves, though flowers are often insignificant. Some herbs, such as angelica and fennel, grow very tall, to 1.5 m (5 ft) and more, but these are not often needed in the kitchen. Parsley, chives, sage, mint and thyme—the big five—do well in pots and boxes.

The history of herbs stretches back so far that it is more than likely that Neolithic man used such plants, first for medical purposes, and then, after experimental chewing which probably had fatal results sometimes, mixed with food as they were gradually found to have agreeable flavours. Fascinating stories and legends have grown up round herbs over the course of the centuries. For instance, bay was thought to 'resist witchcraft very potently' and sage was considered a veritable cure-all by the Romans—there is even an Arabic proverb which says: How can a man die who has sage in his garden?

Parts of plants were originally used for curing illness and injury, and although cooking, decoration and cosmetics claim most of the herbs now used, some still have a considerable part to play in medicine. There are signs that this use is extending as it is realized that side-effects of herbs, if used correctly, are virtually non-existent. For cooking, the leaves, stems or roots often help in digesting food, as well as enhancing the flavour by contrasting or blending with it.

One great advantage of home-growing is that herbs can be kept growing for longer, right into winter, started earlier in spring, or retained through the whole year.

Herbs will grow in boxes or pots; some are better in

Below: With a little care and attention, herbs can easily be grown indoors

boxes and most need a pot no less than 12.5 cm (5 in) in diameter. Herbs often do badly in containers because their roots do not have enough room. Thought to be tough and undemanding, they are forced into, or left, in tiny pots in which even they quickly become starved, and a prey to greenfly and red spider mite.

Use a standard potting compost—some herbs like some gritty sand added for extra good drainage, especially the Mediterranean natives of which there are many. Too good a compost, one which is too rich and watered too often, will produce a soft and less aromatic plant, but remember to combine the well-drained compost with adequate light and pot size.

Herbs are not fussy about temperature; normal summer warmth will be suitable, and winter temperatures about 5–9 °C (40–48 °F) will prevent complete die-back. If you can keep them above this, so much the better—some are like houseplants from tropical countries and rest in winter even though there is some warmth. Humidity is not too important, but the occasional overhead spraying for evergreens in winter will prevent leaves from withering at the edges or falling.

Water moderately in summer and sparingly in winter, especially in the lower temperatures. You will find that the compost takes a long time to dry out, and watering it while it is still wet will kill the plants, sooner or later. Feeding is not usually necessary, provided good compost was used, though one or two need it, as noted in the individual descriptions.

Increase can be by seed, division or cuttings, in spring or early summer, again without difficulty, and pests and diseases are very few and far between. It is said that herbs have their own built-in resistance to troubles, and

A tray of mixed herbs ready for planting out

that is one reason why they are good to eat. They may occasionally be infested with greenfly or red spider mite, but this is nearly always an indication that they are really short of water, or growing in an inadequate container.

All the herbs described in the following paragraphs are easily grown into good plants, apart from basil, tarragon and garlic, which will need a little more care and experience, but are still not difficult to grow.

Basil

Basil is a half-hardy annual. Grow it from seed sown in early to mid spring. It needs a warmer temperature than most herb seeds to germinate, 16 °C (60 °F), and even then is rather slow. Growth after germination is also rather slow, and careful watering is needed to get the seedlings going. It is best to sow the seed really thinly, and move the seedlings into their own container or trough only when several leaves have been formed. The roots dislike disturbance, which should be kept to a minimum. Give plenty of light, and take out the grow-

The sweet bay, *Laurus nobilis*, an aristocrat amongst herbs

ing tips when a few centimetres high, to make them bushier and leafier. Use the bush basil, *Ocimum minimum*, 15–23 cm (6–9 in) tall, for container growing.

Sweet Bay

Sweet bay, *Laurus nobilis*, grows naturally as a large evergreen shrub or a small to medium-sized shrubby tree, but is perfectly happy in a pot or tub in a sunny place indoors, or on a balcony sheltered from draughts. It is usual to buy a small plant, though cuttings are possible but slow and difficult to root.

Give it standard potting compost, don't water too much and, if you repot it every year, don't feed. Protect from frost. Watch for scale insect which likes it, and clip it in summer to shape it or keep it under control. It is slow-growing. In late spring it will flower—small fluffy creamy white balls in clusters.

Chives

Chives, *Allium schoenoprasum*, are indispensable, and can be snipped into all sorts of salads, soups, sandwiches and cold dishes. They start to grow in late winter, and will be flowering by late spring, with round heads of purple flowers on stems 15 cm (6 in) tall. You can leave the flowers on as they are very decorative, and do not really take up so much of the plant's energy that the grass-like leaves stop growing. Chives will continue to grow until late autumn, when they normally die down, but if kept in warmth will grow, more or less, through the winter. Any standard potting compost and normal watering and feeding will suit them; ordinary summer temperatures and light will give good plants. They can be divided in spring, or grown from seed sown in spring. Watch for greenfly on the base of the stems.

Garlic

Garlic, also an allium, *A. sativum* can be grown in containers but give each clove either a 12.5 cm (5 in) pot, or put four in a 60 cm (2 ft) long trough; the leaves can be 60 cm (2 ft) or more tall, and the plants need more root room than might be thought. Use the garlic sold by the greengrocer, and take off the very largest cloves from the outside of the biggest bulb you find. Put them just below the surface of good potting compost, in late winter or, better still, in mid autumn so that they

have plenty of growing time. Give all the light and warmth you can in spring and summer, but water moderately, and feed from late spring with a potash-high fertilizer. The bulbs should be ready in late summer, or whenever the leaf tips start to yellow.

Marjoram

Pot marjoram, *Origanum onites*, is a good plant for containers, with a strong aromatic scent. It will die down completely in winter, unless kept warm, but it is a perennial and will sprout again in spring. Give it a pot at least 12.5 cm (5 in) wide and a gritty compost, plenty of light and warmth, and not too much water. It can be pruned, so that it is almost like groundcover, by taking off any vertical shoots. There is no need to feed, but provide fresh compost if you keep a plant from year to year.

Wild marjoram, *O. vulgare*, is oregano, which grows wild throughout Europe, including Britain. It is also perennial, but stronger flavoured and taller, to 90 cm (3 ft) and not so suitable for container cultivation. Pot marjoram can be grown from seed sown in spring in a temperature of 13–16 °C (55–60 °F) and, like basil, is slow to germinate. Pot when large enough to handle.

Marjoram in flower

Mint

The main trouble with mint is to stop it growing, rather than to encourage it. In its enthusiasm it will take over a whole box of other plants so it is best grown alone, in a large, 15 cm (6 in), pot. Use standard potting compost, water freely, grow in sun or a little shade, and feed from mid summer with a nitrogen-high feed. Take off flowers when they appear. It will die down in autumn, but sprout again from mid winter onwards. Being hardy, temperatures can go down to freezing without harming it.

The commonly grown garden mint is spearmint, *Mentha* × *spicata*. *M. pipenita* is peppermint, a variety of which is used for tea in North Africa. Eau de Cologne mint, a variety of peppermint also, really does smell of that perfume, and has round, purplish-edged leaves and stems. Woolly French or Bowles mint is a form of *M.* × *villosa* with round furry leaves and a particularly good flavour. It is less liable to pests and diseases than spearmint. Pineapple mint, *M. suaveolens* 'Variegata', has a strong aroma of pineapples, and cream-variegated leaves; it does not like heavy composts which hold the water, and must have good drainage. It is also slightly tender.

Parsley

Parsley, *Petroselinum crispum*, can be grown for use all year round if sown in spring and again in mid summer. Provided it is sown in warm compost, that is at a room

A parsley pot is useful on the kitchen windowsill

Mentha × *spicata* (spearmint) in flower.

temperature of about 16–20 °C (61–68 °F), the seed will germinate in 7–10 days in spring, and even more quickly in summer when there is more warmth. In cold conditions, it is very slow to sprout, taking four or five weeks. Sow it thinly in a 45 cm (1½ ft) long trough whose depth should be at least 15 cm (6 in). Thin out once or twice to leave about five plants. Parsley often does badly because the container size is inadequate. Give a good potting compost and sun or shade, though deep shade is not suitable, and water freely in summer. Feed from early summer onwards. The mid summer sowing will provide plenty of leaf through the winter. Watch for greenfly in hot weather and dry conditions.

Rosemary

Rosemary, *Rosmarinus officinalis*, has perhaps the most strongly and satisfyingly aromatic leaves of all; it has a sweet piercing scent which seems to trickle right up into the forehead. Another easy-to-grow herb, it will survive all sorts of neglect, and grows as an evergreen shrub to whatever size you wish. Ideally, it should have plenty of sun and a frostproof place, gritty compost and moderate watering, but in practice it will grow in shade, it will live through frost, it will overcome water-logging and still put out new growth. Cuttings of new growth root at any time in spring or summer. The small blue flowers in spikes during mid to late spring are pretty, and popular with bees if you grow it by an open window or on a balcony.

Sage

Sage, *Salvia officinalis*, can be grown easily from seed sown in spring with a little warmth, or bought as a small plant. It is a Mediterranean plant and so well-drained compost and moderate watering combined with a sunny position will give plenty of leaves for flavouring. Besides seed, it can also be increased by division in spring, or by layering, pulling the lowest shoots down onto the compost and covering them with it. There are several ornamental varieties such as purple sage, 'Dunpurascens', with purplish-tinted grey leaves, 'Tricolor', whose foliage is variously coloured pink, purple, white and grey-green, and 'Icterina', which has yellow-edged leaves. All can be used for cooking as well as ornament.

Savory

The savories are herbs unfortunately not much used in this country, though they are popular on the Continent. They are a very spicy herb, strongly aromatic and especially good with beans, and pork.

Summer savory (*Satureia hortensis*) is a tender annual (perennial in its native countries of the eastern Mediterranean); winter savory (*S. montana*) is a tiny evergreen shrub, so leaves can be obtained in winter as well as summer. Summer savory has the best flower. Good drainage of the compost and a sunny window are important; use a 12–15 cm (5–6 in) diameter pot, and clip winter savory back to a few centimeters in early autumn; summer savory in spring.

Sorrel

There are two commonly grown sorrels, English (*Rumex acetosa*) and French or Buckler-leaved (*R. scutatus*). The French kind has the best flavour, and has thickish leaves, rounded, but with lobes, unlike English sorrel, whose leaves are long and narrow. French sorrel soup is delicious, made with cream and lettuce, and the leaves add a piquant spiciness to salads.

It is easily grown in any standard potting compost, with sun or a little shade. It likes plenty of water but without waterlogging, and increases rapidly in size. Any container, from a 12 cm (5 in) pot to a whole window box depending on how much you want, is suitable.

Sweet or Knotted Marjoram

Marjoram is one of the great culinary herbs and this kind (*Origanum marjorana*), a half-hardy annual, has a strong, sweet aroma, the best of the three commonly

Left: *Salvia officinalis*, sage, is one of the most popular herbs

grown. It is used in sausages and, in fact, has preserving qualities. Marjoram-flavoured potatoes are excellent, and the herb goes well with mushrooms and the legume family of peas and beans. The minute white flowers appear from round green buds like peas, hence the term 'knotted'.

Sow the seed in mid-winter indoors, harden the seedlings off and transplant them to window boxes or larger pots when the weather is warmer. The leaves dry well and become even more aromatic; they should be harvested just as flowering starts, and a second batch can be gathered in September.

Tarragon

Tarragon, *Artemisia dracunculus*, hates a heavy soil, so make sure the compost is a sandy one and that there is a good layer of drainage material in the base of the container. Give it plenty of light and warmth while growing. You can keep it growing through the winter, but it tends to become rather pale and leggy unless you can provide a good deal of light, and it is probably better to make it rest by giving low, but not freezing, temperatures and only a little water, at room temperature. Increase is by division,

Thyme

The thymes are particularly good for pots, in well-drained compost and a sunny place. Very easily grown from cuttings, garden thyme, *Thymus vulgaris*, is a little bushy evergreen plant with tiny, very aromatic leaves. *T. × citriodorus*, lemon thyme, has lemon-scented leaves and *T. herba-barona* is the caraway thyme, with a strong aroma of caraway seed. Water moderately, do not feed, and keep free from frost in winter. Its tiny mauve flowers appear in mid summer, and plants should be gently clipped after flowering to maintain their shape.

These popular herbs can all be successfully grown indoors and will prove very useful in the kitchen. Remember that most herbs are from sunny, warm countries and therefore must be kept in a very light position, such as a window ledge

Carnivorous Plants

The dividing line between animals and plants is so thin as to be near invisible, but one would think that their methods of nutrition and degree of mobility would separate them fairly definitely. However, plants do move about, for instance strawberries extend runners, climbers go up trees, and there are some curious and rather repellent, jelly-like fungi which move slowly about on rotting wood. Some tropical plants grow so fast that they can almost be seen to elongate and unfold.

Nutrition, too, is not just a case of animals absorbing flesh as well as vegetable matter, whereas plants only take in minerals and gases – plants can also absorb animal material, usually in the form of insects.

Such plants are, again, often tropical, but they do all have one thing in common; they grow in situations where there is an acute shortage of nitrogen in the soil and which are often permanently wet, such as bogs and swamps. In such places, it is difficult for the roots to function in the normal way, and nitrogen has to be obtained from another source; in this case decaying animal tissue.

There is an astounding variety of adaptation amongst this group of plants to ensure that they can obtain their food. All the alterations are geared towards trapping, and many plants put out some kind of bait to entice their unfortunate prey. In general, it is the leaves which are, literally, re-formed, for example into 'pitchers', long cylindrical containers or into bristle-edged leaves, which close instantly the prey has landed on the leaf or into leaves with sticky glands on the surface, and so on. The bladderworts have developed tiny stalked bags on their roots with a one-way trapdoor through which their prey, often daphnia, swim, never to return.

Apart from their interest as carnivorous plants, this group are mostly highly ornamental, and very rewarding to grow. The most familiar of them in Britain are the Venus' Flytrap, *Dionaea muscipula* (see p. 89), and the Sundew (Drosera rotundifolia). Butterwort (*Pinguicula grandiflora*) is another native, now becoming rare, and is one of the sticky gland variety.

Besides these, there are the Trumpet Pitcher-plants (Sarracenia species) from North America and Australia which, although they look exotic and tropical, are easily grown in cool temperatures. Even the Nepenthes, from tropical Malaysia, will grow in warm conditions (minimum 10 °C (50 °F) and 24 °C (75 °F) in the daytime), though fairly slowly. The Cobra Pitcher plants (Darlingtonia) are handsome in a sinister way,

and the Butterworts have gaudy flowers with a long spur at the back.

The sundews have what looks like hairs on their leaves, each topped by a small round ball. These are the sticky glands which trap mainly the flying insects. In *D. rotundifolia* the leaves are round and form a rosette at ground-level, from which the white flowers appear in July on stems up to 15 cm (6 in) tall.

These plants need moist compost at all times, and when actively growing in summer, should have their pans contained in a saucer or on a tray of water with a depth of about 6–15 mm ($\frac{1}{4}$–$\frac{1}{2}$in). The water should be soft and the compost neutral to acid. Permanent humidity is vital, but too moist an atmosphere will encourage diseases such as grey mould. Keep shaded from the midday sun, use a compost of living sphagnum moss and supply plenty of ventilation and protect from severe frost.

Sarracenias are not found in Britain—they come from the southern part of North America. They are known as the Trumpet pitchers, and are an adaptation of the leaf to a long narrow, upright container, flaring at the mouth, and topped by a rear, petal-shaped structure. Insects are attracted to the pitchers by the scent of nectar, but get trapped inside them by hairs

Below: *Drosera capensis*. Right: Sarracenia purpurea

154

near the base, and will often drown in the fluid at the bottom. The flowers are beautiful shades of reds, yellows and purples on stems 30 cm and more high, appearing in June and July. The pitchers themselves are colourfully veined.

Sarracenias like cool conditions, e.g. 7°C (45°F), minimum shade from hot sun, watering as for the sundews, and a compost mainly of peat and sphagnum moss, with a little sand.

Nepenthes are plants with hanging pitchers, descending from a tendril at the end of a leaf and having a lid. This latter is for attraction only—it does not close once the insect is inside. Bladderworts such as *Utricularia*

minor, being floating plants, can be grown in clear glass bowls filled with water, provided there is some peat and shingle in the base.

Growing carnivorous plants is not difficult if you give them the right compost and moisture, and they do a really useful job of fly-catching. If you would like to know more about them and their cultivation, the Carnivorous Plant Society is well worth joining and can be contacted through the Secretary, 13 Grange Farm Rd., Ash, Aldershot, Hants. GU12 6SJ. A nursery specialising in these plants is Marston Exotics, Spring Gardens, Frome, Somerset BA11 2NZ.

Below: The beautiful Sarracenia comes from America

Bottle gardens, terrariums and Wardian cases

When plants from hot countries were being discovered and sent back to Europe for cultivation, they had to be grown with protection, and greenhouses were found to be more or less perfect for the purpose.

It was subsequently found possible to grow many of these tropical plants in the home with a good deal of success. However, during the last few years, it has been recognized that central heating produces very dry air which is bad for us, for furniture and also for plants.

Various ways of solving the problem of supplying moisture to the air are suggested elsewhere in this book, but one which needs no continuing effort on your part is to grow plants in a bottle. The plants give off water vapour while growing; the stopper in the opening of the bottle prevents this escaping; some goes back into the compost and the air remains as humid as the plants need it.

A bottle garden is a highly attractive arrangement for growing plants; the glass makes the plants look larger than life and the whole scene within the bottle takes on a slightly mysterious and jungly appearance. A bottle garden is portable, it doesn't need bright light,

the plants look after themselves, more or less, and, once planted, will keep going for years. Pest and disease troubles are eliminated.

You can use any sort of large bottle which has clear or pale-green glass; carboys with narrow necks and balloon-shaped bodies, of 22.5 to 45 litres (5 to 10 UK gallons; 6 to 12 US gallons) capacity, are the most frequently used, but sweet-jars, hanging plastic or glass bubbles, champagne magnums or chemist's jars can all be pressed into service. In fact, any glass container which can be stoppered can be used for a bottle garden.

The one disadvantage of bottle gardens is the reduction of the available light, so only the leafy plants can be grown—practically all the flowering plants need more light to bloom. However, there are plenty of low-growing and slow-growing foliage plants and many of them have leaves which are not coloured green.

You should choose plants which will not be cramped by the size of the container. It is no good putting a palm

Below: Plants that like moist growing conditions and a humid atmosphere will thrive in a bottle garden

otherwise it will be too big to get out without damage, especially if the container is a narrow-necked carboy. Groundcover-type plants are good, too, and add to the jungly effect.

Some plants which can be used in bottle gardens are: the small-leaved ivies, the creeping fig (*Ficus pumila*), the smaller of the starfish bromeliads (*Cryptanthus* spp.), dwarf dracaenas, *Pilea cadierei* and *P. spruceana*, ferns such as *Pteris cretica* 'Albolineata' or the maidenhair, tradescantias, the smaller palms such as *Chamaedorea elegans*, fittonia, marantas, *Peperomia caperata*, and any other small bushy plants with ornamental leaves.

When you are about to start planting, don't try to cram the container full straightaway; remember that the plants will grow and gradually fill in spaces between them, and watching the scene change as they do this is half the fun of a bottle garden. Use quite small plants, from 5 cm (2 in) pots; you will find that between five and nine of these will be enough for a carboy, depending on its size. Sweet-jars and wine or champagne bottles will take perhaps four, five or six.

Planting a bottle garden is a fiddly job and you will find it a help, before you start planting, to put the plants on a piece of paper the same size and shape as the base of the container and arrange them in the pattern you prefer. You can see what goes with what, you can contrast or blend colours, and you can fit the creepers in among the bushy plants, with one or two upright kinds to break up the horizontal line. This will also help you to see how many you can grow in your size of container. Remember to choose plants which like the same conditions of warmth, light and moisture. Remember also that glass will make this miniature garden look larger and more beautiful than life, but it will also magnify mistakes in the arrangement.

For the planting you will need: a household fork and spoon, and an empty cotton reel, each bound on to the ends of canes (or the cane can be forced into the hole of the cotton reel), a piece of stout wire with a hook on the end or a pair of long-handled sugar-tongs, a funnel of rolled-up stiff paper, long enough to reach to the bottom of the container, a small piece of sponge also attached to a cane, a child's paintbrush, a length of narrow tubing or an indoor watering-can with a narrow spout, potting compost, gravel or other drainage material, charcoal—which is not essential but good for absorbing impurities—and, of course, the plants.

The compost should be moist, and extra peat mixed into it will make it even more like that found on the forest floor. It must be sterilized to prevent the introduction of fungus disease or weed seeds.

Put in the drainage material first, with charcoal if used, through the funnel, in a layer between 2.5 and 5 cm (1 and 2 in) thick, then gently add the moist compost in the same way, and spread it about with the fork so that it is evenly thick, to a depth of 5–10 cm (2–4 in), depending on the container size. Firm it down with the cotton reel. Use the spoon to make the hole for the first plant.

Start with a plant which will be nearest to the wall of the bottle in your design, or at the furthest end, and remove all the compost from its roots. Holding it with the tongs or the wire hook (lightly, otherwise you won't be able to detach it), lower it into the hole in the compost. Pull the compost over the roots with the spoon or fork, and firm it with the cotton reel again, making sure that the plant is upright and the roots spread out as much as you can manage.

Do the same with the other plants, working towards the centre or near-end of the bottle until all are planted.

Then run water at room temperature gently into the bottle, down the sides with the help of the tube or watering-can, until the compost is moist but not saturated. Any extra water cannot drain out as with an ordinary container, though it can collect in the gravel, so if in doubt it is better to put slightly too little, than too much.

Watering like this will help to clean the sides of the container, and if any dirt is still left, it can be wiped off with the sponge. The leaves of the plants can be cleaned, if necessary, with the paintbrush. Finally, put the stopper in and put the bottle in a shaded, warm place.

If there is condensation all over the inside of the bottle within the next few days, there is too much water in it, and the stopper should be removed and replaced, if necessary several times during the next few days until the plants settle down. If there is only a little near the top of the container, you can leave the stopper in; it will clear and even if it does re-form, not to worry, it may do this at intervals. No condensation at all indicates the need to add water.

When you have got the water balance right, the stopper can be left in and the garden left to itself for weeks and even months. Feeding should not be necessary, and watering only occasional if some moisture escapes through the stopper. After about three years, the plants will have outgrown their space, or come to the end of their life, and the garden can be re-made.

Left: Wide-necked terrariums are easier to plant

In principle a terrarium is no different to a bottle-garden, since it also involves growing plants in a glass container. But a terrarium container is usually square or rectangular, and one of the best containers is an old aquarium tank, perhaps one which sprang an un-mendable leak. Another difference is that it is possible to design a definite landscape in them, with miniature valleys, plains and hills and even a lake, or to make a garden with lawn, paths, pool and planted beds.

Like bottle-gardens, terrariums must be closed, and a sheet of plate glass or plastic glazing make good lids. Similarly, there should be a layer of drainage material in the base such as gravel or shingle, about 3 cm deep, with potting compost on top, at least 5 cm deep. It can be deeper, depending on your landscape or garden

Above: This orchid case ensures the plants are kept at the correct temperature. Right: A successful plant arrangement in a terrarium

design. Planting is obviously much easier; the compost should be moist, but not soaking, and you should be particularly careful to use plants completely free from disease. If leaves are yellowing or browning at the time of planting and flowers fading, remove them.

The terrarium should be in good light, but preferably not sunlight, as it can get extremely hot inside, and even cacti would find things difficult. Once the lid is on, leave it in place with only occasional removal every few weeks for ventilation and a little watering in the form of leaf spraying.

It can be assembled any time in spring or summer,

and should not need feeding until the following spring. In time, it will have to be completely replanted, as the plants will be too large, and no amount of applied feeding will be enough to replace the exhausted compost.

Plants suitable for use can be any of the bottle-garden plants, together with African violets, chlorophytum, the Rex begonias, the peperomias, kalanchoë, miniature bulbs, Mother-of-thousands, and so on. Choice is mostly a case of what you like, and what fits into your design, provided the plants are not too large and do not grow too quickly.

A desert garden is an interesting exercise in plant arrangement, in which the plants will need very little water, but plenty of sun and plenty of warmth in summer. The winter temperature can be quite low, even near to freezing. Drainage material should be about 5 cm (2 in) of coarse sand, with only 2.5 cm (1 in) of top compost.

Alternatively you could try a collection of woodland plants for which the temperature should mainly be about 16–20 °C (60–68 °F) in summer, and normal seasonal temperatures in winter. Seedlings of trees— holly, pine, juniper, yew, larch, beech and so on—and mosses, ferns, violets, anemones, polyanthus and primroses are some of the plants that could be mixed with them.

Wardian cases are the prototype of terrariums. They were invented in response to the need for a container which would transport newly discovered plants from the tropics back to Britain alive and well. Nathaniel Ward, after whom they were named, publicized their additional usefulness for plants grown in Victorian homes which needed protection from the polluted atmosphere resulting from coal fires and open gas jets.

Great variety of design of these cases followed; the size could be anything from 30 to 180 cm long (1–6 ft) and 150 cm (5 ft) high, and they were square, rectangular, round, domed, barn-roofed and so on. Fern cultivation was a major Victorian passion, and the Wardian cases were ideal for miniature ferneries and gardens.

Bonsai

The miniature trees which are generally known as bonsai have been grown for centuries, first by the Chinese, and then by the Japanese, who took up the art with such enthusiasm that the little trees are now treated with reverence and regarded in much the same way as Japanese floral art is, as part of their religion and philosophy.

The word 'bonsai' is made up from two Japanese words, *bon* and *sai*, meaning a shallow pan and a plant, respectively. Originally the word meant a plant growing in a shallow tray or other shallow container, but the modern equivalent has come to be 'artificially dwarfed tree'—that is what is implied when bonsai is discussed.

The first trees grown by this method were tiny specimens dug out of rocky mountainsides, or from cliff edges, which looked exactly like the forest trees, but in miniature, as though looked at through the wrong end of the telescope. Gradually the art of artificially forming the trees like this evolved, by using suitable containers and by training, root pruning, and shoot and leaf removal. The results are some really fascinating tiny replicas, with perfectly good trunks and branches, leaves in proportion, and flowers and fruits.

Growing bonsai is a slow process; the Japanese consider that a tree does not reach its full beauty until half a century old, and there are specimens in existence which are four to five hundred years old, seedlings when Queen Elizabeth I was on the throne. However, if you start with seedlings, the form will begin to show in only a few years, and you will have the fun of training them exactly as you wish; neither training nor cultivation is difficult.

A surprising number of trees can be grown by bonsai; the deciduous ones include weeping willow, *Ginkgo biloba*, oak, beech, sycamore, the purple-leaved barberry (*Berberis thunbergii atropurpurea*), the swamp cypress (*Taxodium distichum*) and larch. The conifers make good evergreen specimens such as *Juniperus sargentiana*, *Picea pungens kosteriana*, *Chamaecyparis obtusa*, yew (*Taxus baccata*) and *Pinus sylvestris* (the Scots pine). For flowering, you could try japonica, *Chaenomeles speciosa*, forsythia, the winter-flowering jasmine, peach or cherry, ornamental apples, tamarisk, and wisteria, the last-named being very attractive as it can be trained so that the clusters of flowers hang downwards.

Although there are many gardeners and growers who think that growing plants by bonsai should result in the formation of an R.S.P.C.P., Royal Society for the Prevention of Cruelty to Plants, in fact, if bonsai were starved and injured by their training they would die quickly. These trees are fed and watered, supplied with good compost, and the right light, air, temperature and humidity, just as ordinary indoor plants are.

The only differences in their care are that the roots are cut back when repotted, which makes them produce more of the feeding roots, and fewer of the anchor roots which they no longer need, and the shoots are stopped when the trees are very young and throughout their lives. This has, however, to be done with as little bruising as possible, otherwise the injured stem could die back. So the health and well-being of the plants is

Left: A particularly graceful bonsai juniper in a simple setting.
Right: A perfectly proportioned bonsai pyracantha, one pale stone receiving its shadow

the main concern; any wiring for shaping must be done gently, with padding if necessary, otherwise the bark cracks or the flow of sap is interrupted.

If you are lucky enough to be given a bonsai already formed, its care through the growing season will be much the same as for an indoor plant, except for watering and temperature. Provided you do not treat them like hothouse plants, they will do well.

Watering needs are very different; they absorb a great deal of water, and in spring, on average, will need a daily watering, in summer twice a day, sometimes three times, and in autumn and winter about once a week, perhaps less for the deciduous trees. Liquid feeding will be needed once a week from about mid spring to the end of summer; be careful not to give too much otherwise the plant will become sick, or grow very soft.

Light should be good; sunlight is needed for the flowering specimens, though strong summer sun will burn delicate young leaves. Reasonable humidity is required with daily spraying in hot weather.

As for temperature, bonsai need only moderate warmth in summer and coolness in winter. Although hardy, moderate or severe frost will damage the roots as containers do not give much protection, so if outdoors plunge the containers in a border, or if on a balcony, lag them with sacking, straw or polythene sheet.

To grow bonsai successfully, they must have a period of low temperatures while resting in winter and so in Japan and China they are kept outdoors for most of the year, only being brought into the home occasionally to be enjoyed for one or two months. But if you have several plants, they can be 'house-bound' in succession, to give a constant display without coming to any harm. If you have no garden or balcony, keep the plants in the coolest room in the house in winter so that they become dormant, and at other times give them a position which is light, cool and airy without being draughty.

Repotting is done in late winter to very early spring, just before growth starts again and, with established plants, need only be done every two to three years unless they are strong and vigorous species. Young plants, up to about five years old, need annual repotting. The compost can be a standard potting compost, or a balanced mixture of fibrous loam, coarse sand and leafmould.

You can repot into the same container, or use one only slightly larger. Young plants need potting-on until a few years old. Containers are always shallow, perhaps only 5 cm (2 in) deep, usually square or rectangular, and preferably not glazed at all, or at least not on the inside. There should always be at least one drainage hole. The colours of a container should blend with the tree and not overwhelm it; they should be dull rather than bright. Choose greens, browns, blues, or black.

Established plants are carefully removed from the container, and about a third of the compost removed, mostly from round the underside and sides of the root-ball, and a little from the surface. The roots laid bare by this and any long roots are cut back so that about 2.5 cm (1 in) space will be left between the root ends and the sides of the container. Use a very sharp knife or secateurs. Put some fresh compost over the drainage material, pieces of broken clay pot, single or small brick, in the base of the container, sit the root-ball on top so that the plant is at the same height as it was before, and crumble moist compost round and over the roots, so that the tree is once more firmly planted. Leave a space at the top for watering, about 1.5 cm ($\frac{1}{2}$ in) deep.

Plants which are growing rather slowly will need a complete change of compost, and all of it should be removed from the roots. A pointed stick will get into the centre of the most tightly packed roots. After repotting, water the plant and put it in a cool, shady place while it settles down.

Training the plant is partly a matter of actually removing growth, and partly of using raffia or copper wire round the shoots and branches. Starting in spring, remove the tips of new shoots when they are about 2.5 cm (1 in) long; continue this process as long as new growth appears. Scissors can be used. You will find that secondary growth will form, on which leaves will be much smaller, and the tips of this should also be cut off.

For exceptionally strong and vigorous trees, leaves can be taken off completely, with only a tiny piece of the leaf stem allowed to remain. For still strong but less vigorously growing trees, the leaves can be either cut in half or alternate leaves can be removed. The time to do this is early to mid summer.

Wiring is also needed if you want to shape the tree. Branches and trunk may be wound round with copper wire into the required positions, pulled down with raffia, which is tied to strong wire pushed into the compost or bound round the outside of the container, or twisted round canes, but this is rather complicated and to be undertaken only if you are experienced. There are various styles into which the trees can be formed: cascade, upright, winding, gnarled and forest are some; the training is done in early summer for the deciduous tree, in winter for the evergreens. Aim for as natural looking a tree as possible, giving the impression of great age and, possibly, subjection to prevailing winds; the head should balance the size and shape of the bowl.

Right: A beautiful *Malus baccata mandshurica*

Training of bonsai is best started when the trees are still young, about three or four years of age. You can manipulate the shape of the tree and direction of growth by pruning, by weighting shoots and by wiring. If you are trying to decide on a style to use, suit it to the natural habit of the tree.

The variety of styles that can be used for training bonsai is immense, but there are several which are quite simple and easy, if you are in the early stages. The most obvious is the upright or diagonal. For this the tree need only be tied with raffia to a cane, fixed firmly in the compost, and angled in the direction in which you want the main stem to grow. Beech or sycamore are good subjects.

The cascading style has a good and interesting line, is not difficult and is satisfying to do. Japonica (*Chaenomeles spectiosa*) looks very pretty, and weeping willow is well suited. Start with a young plant and put a stiff wire bent in half at right angles into the container, so that one half is buried in the compost, and the other half projects down obliquely over the container rim. Then pull the main stem gently over towards the wire, tying it with raffia to the wire in several places, and putting a pad beneath each raffia tie to protect the bark. The side branches will probably need wiring later to coax them into positions in keeping with the new position of their parent.

Incidentally, any pruning that has to be done to the japonica should be left until July, and the plant should have a sunny place or flowering will be poor.

Another interesting style is the one which imitates a forest. You can try this with Scots pine. The young tree, while dormant, is planted so that the main trunk and lowest branches are partly buried, and partly lying on the surface of the compost. The trunk is anchored with ties over it and round the container. Those branches on the lower side which would extend into the compost are cut off flush with their parent stem, the top shoot of the trunk is also removed completely, and the uppermost branches are left to grow and be trained if required, to form the 'forest'. Alternatively, they can be cut off completely to leave the dormant buds in the axil, which then sprout and become the forest.

The art of bonsai is highly absorbing and fascinating. If you get a really good collection going, trying to remember all the different treatments that need to be done and the times to do them during the growing season becomes bewildering with a large and varied collection. However, you can simplify your bonsai gardening if you start a diary, first marking in when and what treatments are needed, and then noting what you actually do, when it is done, and the state of the tree at the time. It will be instructive and revealing to look back over it in succeeding years, and it will help you to deal with new subjects and more complicated techniques.

Below left: This pretty landscape is made up of bonsai spruce and elm. To achieve the best effect, always plant trees in odd numbers

Below right: Bonsai Pyracantha can easily be grown with the correct training. Never allow the roots to become dry and keep it in a sunny position

Conservatories

Plants grown in your home usually have to be chosen carefully to fit the place where they are to stand, if they are to be healthy and ornamental. This is mainly because, in most rooms, light will only be available to the plant on one side.

But if you are lucky enough to own a conservatory—a greenhouse attached to the home—light for the plants will be available from three sides and the top, almost as much as they would receive naturally. They will still be protected from bad weather, and will be warmer, even without artificial heat, than they would be outdoors.

Conservatories can be any size, provided they will fit on to one of the house walls. You can have a lean-to with one sloping roof, three-quarter span, or flat, though a slight slope is preferable. It can be glazed with glass or one of the new rigid plastic materials such as shatterproof polycarbonate, or corrugated plastic, and the structure may be wooden or aluminium, just as free-standing greenhouses are.

The smaller the conservatory the more difficult is it to regulate the temperature, but the cheaper it is to

Below: As well as being an ideal place to grow plants, the conservatory can be an attractive extension to the house

provide heat for in winter. Conservatories which face south do not necessarily have the best aspect; they can get very hot in summer, well over 40 °C (100 °F), and cacti are the only plants that really enjoy such temperatures, unless you are prepared to supply the kind of humidity found in tropical rain forests. East, west, south-west or south-east make for a much more manageable conservatory though even a south-west aspect can become oppressive during sunny summer afternoons. North has surprising potential, although the light is not so good, and artificial heat will be needed. Of course, you can fit your plants to your conservatory, and one of the factors determining your selection will be whether you are prepared to go to the expense of heating, and the trouble of keeping it going through cold weather.

When you really get down to choosing plants, remember that they can be a tie, almost as much as a pet. They could need some attention in winter—watering and heating are two jobs—and they will need considerable attention from spring to autumn. Without any heat at all, you will need to stick to only slightly tender plants to ensure that they will survive the winter, but you can widen the choice if you insulate the conservatory.

There are half a dozen different substances to use for insulation, all of which are plastic, such as bubble-sheet, polythene sheet, Correx, or 3 mm ($\frac{1}{8}$ in) mesh netting. The last-named will improve the temperature by about 4–5 °C (8–10 °F) in winter, an excellent saving in fuel costs. It will also provide some shade from sun in summer, too, so can be left in place all year, without noticeably cutting down on the light.

You may want to regard the conservatory as another room, a kind of outdoor or garden room with all the pleasures of being in the garden, but without the aggravations of chilliness and dampness characteristic of British weather.

Hence the plants will be purely for decoration as accessories, and the furniture will take precedence. This being the case, you simply decorate it between April and October, and retire some of the plants to the house in winter, leaving the hardy ones behind, whether evergreen or not.

Regarded as a home for plants, you can either grow the ornamental kinds in profusion, or crop plants, or some of each. Look for decorative plants of Australian or New Zealand origin; they are more likely to flower in autumn or winter, and will be hardy with conservatory

The conservatory can also be used as an indoor garden without the drawbacks of the English weather

protection. House-plants will be particularly happy and, again, you can grow the whole range, the limit only being decided by the supply of warmth.

Crop plants can include tomatoes, cucumbers, aubergines, peppers, okra; herbs such as basil (a tender annual), marjoram, sweet bay—which is highly ornamental when clipped to shape and grown in a tub—thyme, tarragon; forced strawberries, melons, grapes and citrus fruits, and of course you can use a corner of it as a propagating unit for early seed sowing, and taking cuttings.

If you are concentrating on ornamentals, you can go in for a mixture of types of plant; the half-hardy annuals for summer, or the hardy annuals sown in late spring to get them to flower in winter (cinerarias, primulas, salpiglossis, schizanthus); bulbs and corms including freesias, gloxinias, achimenes, begias, lachenalias, spring-flowering bulbs, and winter-flowering *Iris reticulata*; foliage house-plants; shrubs such as camellia, azalea, dwarf rhododendron and climbers, of which morning glory (Ipomoea) campsis, passion-flower, *Cobaea scandens*, ivies and bougainvillea are a few.

Alternatively, you can specialise in growing a particular genus, such as pelargoniums in all their variety of zonals, regals, coloured-leaved, miniatures, scented and aromatic-leaved and ivy-leaved; cacti, many of which are easily grown and flower profusely every year, and succulents with colourful and handsome leaves; begonias, the large-flowered doubles, singles, winter-flowering, and the tremendous range of ornamental foliage varieties including the Rex forms; chrysanthemums, early and late-flowering, singles, double incurves and reflexes, Koreans and pompoms.

As you can see, the problem is not what to grow, but what not to grow; they are all highly desirable. But before you get carried away and rush to the order page of the catalogues, consider what is involved in their management.

You will need containers. Pots, troughs, tubs, pans—any of these may be needed, together with pot saucers and trays in many cases, or decorative outers, to prevent the floor or display shelving being stained and possibly rotted by water.

You will need compost. A new supply every spring, and drainage materials, and you will need an easily accessible supply of water, preferably at the conservatory temperature, and preferably soft. You will also need time. Time to water, feed, re-pot, prune and groom, and treat for pests and diseases, to say nothing of increasing.

If you have holidays in summer, some arrangement for watering and temperature regulation is essential, whether you have helpful neighbours, a local plant-sitting service, or can organise drip-watering, and permanent ventilation. Winter holidays will bring the problem of warmth—you can get round this by taking all the plants into the home, if all else fails, and growing the less heat-demanding species.

In hot weather the plants will probably need watering every day, otherwise every two or three days in spring and autumn, dwindling to once a week or less in winter. Feeding (liquid or dry) depends on the type of compost used, the frequency of potting and the size and species of plant, but see the general advice given on pages 17–22 for house-plants, much of which applies to conservatory plants.

Watering the plants will be your main job, so get a good watering-can. A galvanized metal one will not go rusty, nor will it grow a green covering of algae internally, as do the plastic kind. One with a long spout and a coarse and a fine rose (spray attachment) is the easiest to handle and the most versatile for water application. Another necessity is a thermometer which shows the lowest temperature at night, and the highest during the day, known as a maximum and minimum thermometer.

Both will be a great deal of help in the management of conservatory and plants. Knowledge of the night temperature, combined with listening to the weather forecasts, will help save many plants from damage, if not death. To heat the conservatory, you can run electric heating tubes or fan heaters off the domestic circuit, or you can use the special greenhouse paraffin heaters, or the portable gas heaters, connected to a cylinder.

In winter, the ventilators need only be opened a fraction; but in summer should be used to regulate the temperature in combination with any overhead spraying that is done to increase the humidity. If the conservatory atmosphere feels comfortable to you, it will be so for the plants as well—fresh and pleasantly warm, but not stuffy or invigoratingly cold. Shade the roof with a proprietary greenhouse wash, or use blinds or netting.

As well as the satisfaction obtained from the actual care of the plants, there is considerable pleasure to be found in their presentation. The possibilities are endless, as everyone has different ideas, and display is very much a personal creation. Shelves on the walls, of varying lengths and widths, are an obvious container

This wooden conservatory greatly enhances the attractiveness of this home

support. Metal or wooden staging supporting metal trays can be built up in tiers and varying lengths as required.

There are wrought iron wall supports or decorated clay wall containers for plants hung on walls. Hanging baskets and macramé hangers can descend from pillars or roof. Plant stands of bamboo, metal or wood will fill corners or act as focal points. Bookcases painted in a suitable colour make good display units and dividers, with plants on top as well as on the shelves. Small tables (old television tables are useful), tanks, beds of compost made up on the floor, boxes and tubs, will all help to give the impression of a luxuriously tropical garden.

A conservatory can be simple or elaborate to suit every type of home

For unavoidably sunny sites, a display centred round water will help the plants, and provide the illusion of coolness, particularly if you can put in one of the small electrically-operated fountains. Tubs, old cisterns, and aquariums will hold water, and make a miniature pool. Alternatively a pool formed from premoulded fibreglass, either sunk in the conservatory floor, or suitably supported and edged by marble, paving or stone, and surrounded with plants, is no trouble, provided it is connected to drains for easy emptying and cleaning.

Plants to grow can be dwarf water-lilies, marsh marigolds, the Japanese iris (*I. laevigata*), surface floaters such as salvinias and Hydrocharis, and underwater plants to oxygenate the water, e.g. myriophyllum or *Anacharis canadensis*.

AT A GLANCE
SUITABILITY CHARTS

Bush Plants

Foliage house plants	Easy to grow	For average rooms in which the lighting is reasonable, there is some sunshine and which are heated for some hours daily during the winter	Unheated areas (halls, landings and staircases)	Especially suitable for centrally-heated rooms and continuously warm rooms. (Care must be taken to see the air that surrounding the plants is humid.)*	Rooms without sun
Adiantum		●		●	●
Aglaonemas				●	●
Aralia (see *Dizygotheca*)					
Araucaria excelsa			●		
Aspidistra elatior	●	●	●	●	●
Asplenium nidus				●	●
Begonia semper florens	●	●			●
B. masoniana				●	●
B. rex				●	●
Bromeliads (Cryptanthus and Nidulariums)	●	●		●	
Calathea mackoyana				●	●
Cordyline terminalis		●		●	●
Cyperus diffusus (Grass)	●	●	●		●
Dieffenbachias				●	●
Dizygotheca (Aralia) elegantissima				●	
Dracaenas				●	●
D. sanderi				●	●
D. godseffiana		●		●	●
D. fragrans				●	●
Fatshedera lizei	●	●	●		
Fatsia japonica	●	●	●		●
Ficus		●		●	
Fittonias				●	
Grevillea robusta	●	●	●		
Howea		●			●
Marantas				●	●
Monstera deliciosa		●		●	●
Nephrolapis	●	●			●
Peperomias		●		●	●
Philodendrons	● *(P. scandens)*	●		●	●
Pileas		●		●	
Sansevieria trifasciata 'Laurentii'	●	●		●	●
Saxifraga (stolonifera) sarmentosa	●	●	●		●
Schefflera actinophylla		●	●		●
sempervivum	●	●		●	
Setcreasea purpurea	●	●		●	

* This is best done by placing them on wet pebble trays or packing them in wet peat.

Plants that flourish in full sun	Suitable for dark rooms and full shade	Small plants suitable for limited areas	Plants suitable for offices where winter heating is switched off for short periods	Plants for flower arrangers	Plants that withstand dry atmospheres
		●		●	
	●		●		
	●		●	●	●
		●	●	●	
				●	
		● (cryptanthus)	● (cryptanthus)	●	●
			●	●	
			●		
		●			
				●	
			●		
			●		
	● (F. elastica 'Decora')				●
	●	●			
			●		● (occasional spray)
			●		●
		●			
			●		●
			●		
		●		●	
			● P. scandens		● P. scandens
		●			
●			●		●
	●	●	●	●	
			●		
				●	
●		●	●		●

Climbers and Trailers

Foliage Plants	Easy to grow	For average rooms in which the lighting is reasonable, there is some sunshine and which are heated for some hours daily during the winter	Unheated areas (halls, landings and staircases)	Especially suitable for centrally-heated rooms and continuously warm rooms. (Care must be taken to see the air that surrounding the plants is humid.)*	Rooms without sun
Chlorophytum elatum variegatum	●	●	●		
Cissus antarctica	●	●	●		●
C. discolor				●	
Ficus pumila	●	●		●	●
Hederas	●	●	●		●
Philodendron erubescens				●	●
P. scandens	●	●	●	●	●
Rhoïcissus rhomboidea	●	●		●	●
Scindapsus aureus	●	●		●	●
Syngonium podophyllum (Nephthytis)				●	●
Satcreasea purpurea	●	●		●	
Tradescantias	●	●	●		
Zebrina pendula	●	●		●	

Flowering Plants	Easy to grow		Unheated areas		Rooms without sun
Campanula isophylla	●	●	●		
Cobaea scandens	●	●			
Dipladenia				●	●
Hoya bella		●		●	
Jasminum polyanthum	●	●	●		

	Easy to grow		Unheated areas		Rooms without sun
Aechmeas	●	●			●
Anthurium scherzerianum				●	
Aphelandras				●	●
Beloperone guttata	●	●	●		
Billbergia nutans	●	●	●		●
Chrysanthemum	●	●	●		
Clivia miniata	●	●	●		
Euphorbia (Poinsettia)				●	
Hoya carnosa				●	●
Impatiens petersiana	●	●			●
Saintpaulia ionantha		●		●	●
Spathiphyllum wallisii				●	●
Vriesea splendens		●			

* This is best done by placing them on wet pebble trays or packing them in wet peat.

Plants that flourish in full sun	Suitable for dark rooms and full shade	Small plants suitable for limited areas	Plants suitable for offices where winter heating is switched off for short periods	Plants for flower arrangers	Plants that withstand dry atmospheres
			●	●	
			●		●
					●
	●	●		●	
	● (plain leaved)	● (small leaved)	●	●	
			●		
	●		●		
	●		●	●	
	●			●	
				●	
		●	●	●	
				●	
			●	●	●
●			●	●	
				●	
				●	
			●	●	
			●		●
				●	
●			●	●	
			●		●
●			●	●	
					●
					●
					●
		●			
				●	
					●

GLOSSARY

GLOSSARY

A

Aerial roots Roots produced from above-ground parts of a plant, usually from the stem above the soil. The plant uses them mainly to enable it to cling to a support, though moisture may also be absorbed through them.

Alga (pl. algae) The simplest plant known, often containing chlorophyll, and ranging in complexity from single-celled plants to the seaweeds. Algae form the green covering found on moist paving, damp rocks, etc.

Alpine A plant native to the alpine zone (the top of tree growth to the permanent snow line).

Annual A plant whose life cycle, the time from which the seed germinates to the time when it flowers and sets seed, is completed in one year or less.

Aril A protective coating for the seed, often fleshy; the spice called Mace is also an aril, being the covering for a seed which is another spice: nutmeg.

Aroid A plant which is a member of the family Araceae.

Axil The angle formed between a stem and the organ which arises from it, usually a leaf-stem.

B

Biennial A plant whose life cycle is completed in two years and which then dies.

Blind (non-flowering) Failure to produce flowers or fruit; usually from disease, improper nourishment, or too deep or too early planting.

Bract A cluster of modified leaves at the base of a flower, usually green and leaf-like, but sometimes coloured and petal-like, as in poinsettia.

'Break' Shoots which sprout from dormant buds on a stem are said to break, and breaking can be induced by removing the growing tip of a stem. It is a shortened way of saying 'breaking dormancy'.

Bubble-sheet Consists of 3 layers of clear polythene sheet fused together with the central one containing pockets of air, in bubbles 6 or 25 mm ($\frac{1}{4}$ or 1 in) in diameter, depending on brand.

Bulb A modified bud whose leaf bases have become fleshy due to food in the form of carbohydrates being stored while it is dormant. Daffodil is a common plant which produces bulbs.

Bulbils Small miniature bulbs often formed at the base of mature bulbs or on stems above ground.

C

Cactus A plant which always has an areole on the stems, a small bump from which come the flowers, leaves and spines.

Calyx The outermost ring of the floral parts; its constituents are called sepals and are either small and green or coloured and very much like the petals which make up the inner ring or corolla.

Capillary action By capillary action moisture is held between and around particles of soil.

Carnivorous Applied to plants, implies that they obtain food, chiefly nitrogen, from insects and related creatures, instead of absorbing the minerals they need from the soil.

Cell All living things are made up of millions of individual cells, microscopic in size. The wall of the cell is cellulose, and a cell is in effect a bag of salts in solution; each contains a nucleus and all the genetic instructions which go towards making the organism what it is.

Chlorophyll The green colouring matter in plants without which they cannot carry on photosynthesis.

Compost The medium in which plants in containers are grown, which can consist of—or be composed of— loam, peat, sand, chalk and fertilizers, in varying proportions or, if one of the soil-less composts, of peat and sand, with or without nutrients.

Corm The modified base of the stem of a plant, such as crocus, which becomes fleshy and stores food. Like a bulb, it is a storage organ.

Cotyledon A seed leaf; the first one or two leaves produced when a seed germinates are cotyledons. In the subclass of flowering plants called dicotyledons, two seed-leaves appear together, but in the monocotyledons, one grass-like one is produced. The monocotyledons include the grasses and many bulbs, such as daffodil, lily and hippeastrum.

Cristate With a comb-like tuft of hairs or soft bristles, found on petals, in particular some iris species.

Crown Usually refers to the part of the rootstock just below or at soil level from which shoots grow, and to which they die back in autumn.

Cultivar A plant variety which has arisen in cultivation, as in a garden, nursery, park or similar situation; it is a subdivision of a species. (See Variety.)

Cutting A part of a plant, generally the seem which is cut off and induced to produce roots at the cut end, by potting into compost or water, with warmth. Stem cuttings for pot plants are generally of the 7.5 cm (3 in) tip of a new season's shoot, and will root best if the cut is made immediately below a leaf or pair of leaves. Leaf cuttings (saintpaulias) and root cuttings (dracaenas) are also possible.

D

Dead-head To remove a faded head of flowers.
Deciduous A plant which sheds its leaves every year in autumn is said to be deciduous; applied to trees and shrubs.
Dioecious Plants that have single-sexed flowers on separate plants.
Division Method of propagation used for all types of plants that increase in size by suckers, rhizomes or underground growths.

E

Epiphyte A plant which lives literally on other plants, but which does not absorb food or water from them (epi=upon, phyton=plant).

F

Family Plants are classified into families, the botanic name being denoted by the ending 'ae', as Compositae. All the plants within a family will have some common characters which are not found in other families.
Fern Plant without flowers.
Fimbriated Petals which are fimbriated have the edges more or less fringed, as some begonias.
Florigen A hormone in plants which is thought to be responsible for the formation of flowers, and which needs certain conditions in order to be produced, such as warmth, nutrient and/or light.

G

Genus A group of plants whose flowers, fruit and/or seed are botanically alike; some of these parts will be different from those of other genera within the same plant family. Flowering plants are classified according to the characteristics of the floral parts, and leaves and habit of growth within one genus may vary considerably.
Germination First stage in development of plant from seed.
Glabrous Smooth, not hairy or rough.
Glacous Covered with a white powder that rubs off.

H

Half-hardy Of plants, those which will not withstand frost without being severely damaged; in some cases temperatures which are merely in the range 1–4°C (32–40°F) will be harmful.
Harden-off To accustom plants to lower temperatures than the one in which they have been growing.
Hardy Referring to plants which survive frost in the open year by year.

Heel The basal end of a cutting, tuber or of propagative material.
Herb Technically a plant with soft, rather than woody, tissues, but generally applied to plants used for cooking, medicine, cosmetics, perfumery and dyes.
Humidity Moisture in the atmosphere, essential for good plant growth.
Hybrid Obtained by cross-pollination between two dissimilar parents.

I

Imbricated Closely overlapping; usually referring to scale, bract or leaf arrangements.
Inflorescence The arrangement of flowers in a cluster; inclorescences are classified according to the floral arrangement, as spikes (lavender), racemes (hyacinth), panicles (gypsophila), or umbels (allium).
Internodal The length of the stem between the nodes (joints).

L

Lanceolate leaves Leaves that are more or less lace-shaped.
Lateral From the side.
Lobe Any projection of leaf, rounded or pointed.

M

Midrib Large central vein of a leaf.
Monocarpic A term applied to a plant which dies after flowering and seeding.
Monoecious Stamens and pistils in separate flowers on same plant.

N

Node A joint in a stalk where leaves form.

'Nose' The upper point of a bulb from which the shoots, leaves and flowers come.

O

Oasis A type of expanded polystyrene, coloured green, which absorbs a great deal of moisture, yet still retains its shape and firmness when dried out.

Offset A miniature edition of a plant, generally produced at its base, which can be detached to grow into a new plant, exactly the same as the parent. Bulbs are plants which produce in this way.

Osmosis The process by which a weaker solution percolates through a permeable membrane into a stronger solution until the concentration of each solution is equal and no further flow takes place. This is how water enters roots, but if too much fertilizer is added to a compost so that the moisture in it becomes more concentrated than that in the root cells, water will leave the roots until equalization is obtained. Thus they become dry, and the whole plant suffers.

P

Pendant Hanging down from its support.

Perennial A plant which lives three or more years, producing flowers and seeds in its second season and thereafter. The top growth dies down completely in most cases after flowering, but the rootstock sprouts again the following year.

Petal Flower-leaf.

Petiole A leafstalk.

Photosynthesis The process by which green plants manufacture oxygen and sugars from the carbon dioxide of the air, and water, with the help of energy supplied by sunlight.

Pinch out To remove the growing point of a stem, to promote a branching habit or to induce formation of flower buds.

Pinna (pl pinnae) A lobe or leaflet, on which there are more leaflets, forming part of a feather-shaped and divided leaf. Pinna is the Latin word for feather or wing; pinnate means feathery, or feathers, and the terms are mostly applied to ferns.

Pip The raised crown or individual rootstock of a plant; pips are sometimes valuable for propagation purposes; also colloquial for small seed.

Pistil Female organ of a flower.

Plunge Of potted plants, when they are buried up to the rim of the pot in soil or peat in an outdoor border or indoors, to keep them cool and moist, or while they are resting or ripening, to prevent them becoming too hot and drying out.

Pollen Fertilizing powder at top of stamen.

Potting-on The moving of a plant into a larger container.

Propagation Increase of plants.

Prostrate Lying flat.

Pseudobulbs False bulbs; swollen, bulb-like structured between two stem joints which in some cases resemble bulbs.

R

Racemes Unbranched flower arrangements; the individual flowers are stalked and spirally arranged, e.g. hyacinth.

Rachis The main stalk of a flower cluster or the main leafstalk of a compound leaf.

Repotting Moving a plant into a similarly sized container to the one it was in.

Rhizome An underground stem, usually creeping, often mistaken for a root. It will have buds on it, however, which differentiate, and these will sprout to produce shoots and flowers.

Rootbound Pot-bound; plants growing in pots or ruts, where the roots are so closely packed that there seems little room for further growth (some plants bloom best in these conditions).

Rosette Cluster of leaves radiating in a circle from a centre usually near the ground.

S

Sepal One of the separate parts of the calyx; the sepal is usually green and protects the petals and sex organs.

Sori The collection of spore sacks under or in which are the spores; the sori usually occur on the underside of fern fronds, and resemble small, fruiting bodies.

Spadix The flower of plants of the Araceae family, which consists of a narrow fleshy spike, in which the minute flowers are more or less buried.

Spathe A showy bract found on flowers of the Araceae family, which is large, leaf-like and coloured green or other colours. It encloses and later protects the spadix. The brown papery covering to a daffodil bud which gradually peels back as the bud unfolds is, technically, a spathe also.

Species A member of a genus which, when grown from seed, will always be the same as its parents—it is said to breed true. The specific name of a plant is the second name, the first the generic name. Varieties of a species do not always breed true; they differ from the species in small details, such as flower colouring, height, .size and flower and so on.

Sporangia Sacks containing the spores.

Spore The name given to the seed of a fern; it is minute and dust-like.

Stoma (pl. *Stomata*) The pores of a plant, mostly on the underside of leaves, but some also on the upper side, and occasionally on the stem, through which water vapour is given off. They close in very hot conditions.

Stratify Seeds are said to be stratified when sown in layers in moist sand or peat in order to break down a hard or fleshy seed coat, and so hasten germination. Some seeds need to be frozen as well to break dormancy but in any case, once stratified, the containers should be put outside for the winter.

Succulent Usually applied to plants with fleshy or swollen leaves or stems, often highly ornamental. Practically all cacti are succulents, but many succulent plants are not cacti.

T

Tender Applied to plants which may be frost damaged.

Terminal Topmost Referring to the uppermost shoot, branches or flowers.

Terrestrial Growing in the ground.

Three-quarter span A lean-to greenhouse in which one side of the roof is full width, the other only three-quarters of the width as its side edge is against the back supporting wall. It is more economical of heat than the ordinary lean-to.

Topdressing For plants grown in containers, this means the removal of the top 2.5–5 cm (1–2 in) of compost, and its replacement by fresh compost, as an alternative to complete repotting. It may be done to plants which grow slowly or

which have completed their extension of growth.

Transpiration The giving off of water vapour from the leaves by plants, which goes on continually.

Tuber A thickened, fleshy root (dahlia) or all underground stem (potato) which serves as a storage organ and means of surviving periods of cold or drought.

Tuberous Having a swollen root, usually known as a tuberous root.

U

Umbels Flower clusters where all the individual flower stalks arise at one point.

V

Variegated Applied to leaves or petals that are patterned in a contrasting colour.

Variety A division of a species, in which the plants are botanically similar, but differ in perhaps size of plant, colour of leaves or flowers, or have doubled petals. These characteristics will always be reproduced if the plant is propagated vegetatively, and sometimes appear in its seedlings. Variety always arises in the wild. See *Cultivar*.

Viable Applied to a seed which is capable of germination.

Season equivalents

January	mid winter
February	late winter
March	early spring
April	mid spring
May	late spring
June	early summer
July	mid summer
August	late summer
September	early autumn
October	mid autumn
November	late autumn
December	early winter

Index

The publishers would like to thank the following individuals and organisations for their kind permission to reproduce the photographs in this book:

A–Z Botanical Collection Ltd. 40 below, 43, 64–65 below, 74, 76 below, 84 above, 85 above, 88, 96 above left, 97 right, 99 below, 106 below left, 114 left.

Bernard Alfieri 36 right, 46, 114 above right, 119 below, 126 left, 127.

Bryce Attwell 2–3, 4–5, 6–7, 8–9, 30–31, 134–135.

Pat Brindley 81 above, 84 below, 86, 98 above and below, 102 above, 108 right, 116 left, 125 above, 133 above.

P. R. Chapman 89 above, 90.

Bruce Coleman/Eric Crichton 146, 154, 160, 166.

W. F. Davidson 34 above left and above right, 66, 92 below, 106–107, 108 left.

Dobies of Chester 120.

Tony Evans 123 below.

Melvin Grey 15 above right, 16 right, 124, 144, 162 left.

Susan Griggs (Michael Boys) 68.

Anthony Huxley 116–117, 118, 128–129.

George Hyde 40 above, 55, 70, 82, 94, 109 right, 129, 130 below.

Paul Kemp 58–50.

Jackson and Perkins 12, 14, 67, 96 below, 111 left, 158, 163.

Leslie Johns 86–87, 143, 144.

Marshall Cavendish 15 left.

Bill Mason 77 left, 91 centre left, 122–123.

Giuseppe Mazza 32, 34 below left, 48 inset, 83 right, 85 below, 110 above, 121 left.

John Moss 33 left, 35 right, 37, 38 below, 39 right, 44, 47, 62 left, 68–69, 69, 78 below, 80, 87, 91 above, 99 above, 100 centre and below, 101 below, 115, 123 above, 128 above left, 132 below, 133 centre and below, 137 right, 138 left.

Bill McLaughlin 15 below right, 45, 48, 136 below left, 137 left.

Octopus (Heather Angel) 149, 152–153, 155, 156, (Bryce Atwell) 161, (Peter Rauter) 147, 165, (George Wright) 139, 140.

E. A. Over 54 above left, above right, below left and below right.

Frances Perry 62 right, 64.

Dieter Schact 104.

John Sims 26 left, centre and right, 27 left and right, 33 right, 36 left, 42, 49, 61, 65, 72, 78 above, 89 below, 91 below centre, 92 above, 97 left, 100 above, 105 below, 113, 119 above, 125 below, 126, 131 below, 138 right, 145 right, 157.

H. Smith Horticultural Photographic Collection 38 above, 41, 51 below left, 52, 53 above left and above right, 57, 60, 63, 73, 74–75, 77 right, 79, 81 below, 93, 96 above right, 102 below, 105 above, 106 above, 107, 111 right, 112 below, 112–113, 128 above right, 131 above, 132 above, 136 right, 143.

Spectrum Colour Library 51 above and below right, 53 below, 56, 57 inset, 71, 76 above, 83 left, 95 left, 101 above left and above right, 110 below, 114 below right, 116 above right, 117, 121 right, 122 below, 130 centre, 136 above left, 142.

Suttons Seeds 39 left, 75, 95 right.

Michael Warren 109 left.

Elizabeth Whiting 13, 16 left, (G. Henderson) 103, (Tim Street-Porter) 11, 145, 167, 168–9, 171, 172, 173.

PDO 83-048

Houseplant notes